A History of
CHINESE LITERATURE

A History of
CHINESE
LITERATURE

by

HERBERT A. GILES, M.A., LL.D. (ABERD.)

with an introduction to the new edition by
TERENCE BARROW, Ph.D.

---◆---

CHARLES E. TUTTLE COMPANY
Rutland, Vermont & Tokyo, Japan

Representatives
Continental Europe: BOXERBOOKS, INC., *Zurich*
British Isles: PRENTICE-HALL INTERNATIONAL, INC., *London*
Australasia: PAUL FLESCH & CO., PTY. LTD., *Melbourne*
Canada: M. G. HURTIG LTD., *Edmonton*

Published by the Charles E. Tuttle Company, Inc.
of Rutland, Vermont & Tokyo, Japan
with editorial offices at
Suido 1-chome, 2-6, Bunkyo-ku, Tokyo, Japan

Copyright in Japan, 1973, by Charles E. Tuttle Co., Inc.

Library of Congress Catalog Card No. 73-77576

International Standard Book No. 0-8048-1097-4

First edition, 1901 by
D. Appleton and Company, New York
First Tuttle edition, 1973

0298-000335-4615
PRINTED IN JAPAN

TABLE OF CONTENTS

v

INTRODUCTION TO THE
NEW EDITION

Every field of scholarly knowledge has an inspired pioneer classic that can never be rendered obsolete. *A History of Chinese Literature*, by Professor Herbert Allen Giles, is such a book. First published in 1901, it remains to this time the only formal history of Chinese literature in the English language. Rich in critical wisdom and facts, it is composed as a systematic compendium of eight books, one for each major period of Chinese literature.

The hopelessness of doing justice to a survey of their voluminous literature, and of accomplishing such a task to the satisfaction of their countrymen, either daunted the Chinese literati, or they never felt the need of a panoramic view. Whatever the fact, it is generally true that foreign scholars can venture into studies of cultures not their own with a confidence rarely found in native scholars, who tend to be too tied to their traditions to take the broad view. Giles successfully surveys the enormous range of Chinese literature in one small book, just as his contemporary W. G. Aston had done just two years previously in 1899 in writing *A History of Japanese Literature*.

Chinese scholarship, after its foundation 2,500 years ago, followed the path of Confucian stability, and until the advent of twentieth-century communism, based its social order on family ties. Puritanical morality was always strong, as it is in modern China, yet eroticism in Chinese literature and art has a long tradition, with eras of efflorescence like the Ming dynasty (as described and illustrated in *Chinese Erotic Art* by Beurdeley and others).

By tradition, candidates in state examinations were first tested for character, then given grueling written papers in which calligraphy and style were of primary importance. Degrees were awarded at three levels of attainment, much in the manner of the bachelor's, master's, and doctor's degrees in a modern university. In old China, however, literary achievement assured the scholar of a government post, the most talented individuals getting the highest offices. In Chinese eyes no dignity compared with that of the scholar and literary man, and the true administrator was always a man of learning. The effect of this tradition was to draw the talented to administration from all levels of society, regardless of their wealth or poverty. The Chinese people, being the most practical on earth, recognized that talent breaks through at all levels of society and that it should be given opportunity. Here was founded a democracy of intellect that yielded the most diverse and longest-lived of any world literature. (For a good selection of Chinese writing see William McNaughton's *Chinese Literature: An Anthology from the Earliest Times to the Present Day.*)

Not all writing had official sanction, indeed only that which was approved had importance, namely the formal essay (*ch'uan chi*), or philosophical discourse (*p'ing hua*). Narratives or fiction were not considered literature and were regarded by the literati as mere diversions at the level of folk tales. The composition of novels or short stories never aided a man to state office. Professor Herbert Giles was among the first few to discern literary worth in Chinese fiction, notably as it appeared in the *Liao Chi* of P'u Sung-ling (that gentleman of the Manchu dynasty who was in his time an academic failure because of his "neglect of the beaten track of academic study").

Herbert Giles was born at Oxford, England, in 1845, just eight years after Queen Victoria ascended the throne to reign until her death in 1901. Giles was a true-blood Victorian who expressed the expansive scholarship of an era that was confident, industrious, and interested in all corners of the British Empire. The foundations of modern Oriental scholarship were laid by great Victorians, including Sir Edwin Arnold, Sir Richard F. Burton, Powys Mathers, W. G. Aston, H. A. Giles, and a host of men who combined diplomatic work with scholarly pursuits.

In 1867, while still a young man, Giles went to Peking to join the British consular service. Thereafter he was appointed vice-consul at Pagoda Island (1880) and Shanghai (1883), then as consul at Tamsui (1885) and Ningpo (1891). He left China for England in 1892. The years of his stay in China were relatively quiet, for the Opium War and the T'ai P'ing Rebellion were over, while the Boxer Rebellion was yet to come. Communism was half a century in the future. Giles experienced on intimate terms the old China where traditional manners and codes of behavior were much as they had been for two thousand years. It is little realized today how technologically backward China remained throughout the nineteenth century. The late decades of the century in which Giles lived enjoyed an uneasy quiet in a country whose history is marked by turbulence rather than peace.

The unique quality of *A History of Chinese Literature* and its fine translations may be attributed to the close practical experience of Giles with China and the Chinese, plus his rare skill with the Chinese language. This experience, with his fluency in Chinese and his direct literary style in English, allowed him to achieve verbal accuracy while conveying the spirit of the original. When Giles died at the age of ninety, at Cambridge in 1935, he had for fifty years written on Chinese subjects. Books on how to teach or learn Chinese, catalogues of Chinese books, works on Chinese traditional religions, folklore, and the wisdom of Chunag Tze all appeared from his fertile pen. He is also well known for the standard Wade-Giles romanization system for Chinese.

Fate had indeed provided Giles with unusual opportunities to pursue Sinology. He experienced China in favorable times, and when he returned to England he received a chair in Chinese studies at Cambridge University—an appointment that allowed him to concentrate and to write. The situation paid no cash at the outset and thereafter only a modest honorarium, for in those days scholarship was unrelated to money. Those who could not afford it could not become professors of obscure subjects. There were positive advantages in being at Cambridge. Students were few—no one attached any importance to Chinese studies— so leisure was abundant for reading and writing in the academic peace of a charming university town. Giles's predecessor, Sir T. F. Wade, had left to the university a large collection of Chinese books that proved to be a great asset to Giles. Indeed, at the time no place in the world, including China, was more likely to satisfy an experienced scholar wishing to write on things Chinese. By the banks of the River Cam he could contemplate undisturbed the grandeurs of China and its arts. A tradition of Chinese studies has grown up at Cambridge that has produced Joseph Needham's *Science and Civilization in China*, those volumes of enormous authority, and other valuable works.

The fascination of China dawned on the West after Marco Polo, in the thirteenth century, described the wealth of the court of Kublai Khan. The Western world had known of China long before Marco Polo from the silks, spices, and porcelains that reached the Middle East via the tortuous camel routes over Asia's hinterland. China's cultural riches are of permanent benefit to mankind, yet they are of recent appearance in the West. It was not until the nineteenth century that substantial translations were made from Chinese, and Professor Giles was among the pioneers who opened the way to understanding this great literature. He was followed by a distinguished band of colleagues, including Arthur Waley, James Legge, T. L. Cranmer-Byng, Lawrence Binyon, Burton Watson, and others who worked also on broader fronts of Chinese art. Scholars, art historians, and archaeologists have now laid before the Western world a fascinating picture of artistic China as an enduring civilization of over 4,000 years, if we take into account its beginnings before the Shang dynasty. Archaeology reveals that there is much more to come.

The arts of China are many, yet it is its literature that is traditionally most esteemed. The literati of China, through most of its history, enjoyed the patronage of emperors and nobles who commissioned them to compile books on poetry, painting, geography, and other enterprises, often to help secure their names in history as patrons of culture. There are of course high points and low points in Chinese literary history, although there is general agreement that the Sung dynasty (960–1279) represents the great age of Chinese literature, which compares in its brilliance with Hellenic Greece, Elizabethan England, and the great eras of Indian literature. India contributed much to Chinese civilization in a direct way, particularly by sending the philosophy of Buddhism, which in turn was passed on to Japan. Buddhism reached China two thousand years ago, but it was the arrival of the Indian monk Bodhidharma in A.D. 520, that laid the foundation for the Ch'an or Zen school in China, which, via Japan, has had such an impact on Western thought in the twentieth century. China also contributed to the world many inventions that made civilization possible, notably paper, movable printing type, and gunpowder.

Until the years following World War II the average Westerner thought of the Chinese as a nation of coolies—yellow men

and inscrutable—who were best suited to serve as a race of rick-
shaw boys and cooks. It is said that some of Shanghai's exclusive
colonial clubs and restaurants hung out notices: DOGS AND CHI-
NESE NOT ADMITTED. But times have changed in recent decades.
The supremacy of Western man in both East and West is no
longer a fact of life in the Middle or the Far East. Indeed, it
now seems likely that whereas the last five centuries have belonged to Western man, the twenty-first century will see Oriental man in the ascendancy through the rise of China and Japan.
Such a transition of power can be peaceful, if there is mutual
understanding, and this is an area in which books have a unique
role. The general shift of economic and military power from
the Old World nations of Europe to the New World nations of
the Pacific has taken place before the eyes of anyone over forty
years of age and has shaken the former confidence of many
Westerners in the future of their respective cultures.

China especially poses a problem to the Western democracies,
which are surprised that a country with such a wealth of literature, art, and philosophy should turn to the communist solu-
tion. But the actual changes that have taken place in China are
not so radical. The communist way of life is but one of the three
great traditional modes of Chinese thought, namely Confucian
conformity with benevolent regard for ancestral spirits, Taoist
mysticism with absolute individual freedom of choice, and the
realist school of law based on "the actual facts of the world as
it now exists" (to quote Han Fei-tzu). This last mode is the
ancient communist formula for social order in which the individual citizen surrenders his private interests to the welfare
of the state. In this respect communism in China is not new.
For example The Book of Lord Shang describes "a society in
which people are mutually responsible for each other and . . .
obliged to denounce each other's crimes." Chinese communism
has adapted the teachings of Karl Marx and Russian applica-

tions to its remodeled society, but the original pattern is in the literature of dynasties long past. The old realist ideals are merely put into a modern frame, with of course the additions of a twentieth-century world. Foreign domination, economic chaos, and their own tradition of oppressive landlordism caused this turning to an ancient mode. The quality of realism is at the root of Chinese character. In any Pacific community from the remote island in the South Seas to the modern port town or city of Asia, one sees industrious Chinese working while others sleep, and disregarding the ordinary distractions of life.

Professor Giles sees clearly the relative achievements of the various dynasties. He describes the Sung dynasty as the golden age of Chinese literature, with the reservation that T'ang poetry surpasses even the best of Sung poetry. The Manchu dynasty, during which Giles lived, he denounces in his *Gems of Chinese Literature* (Shanghai, 1922) as "hardly past beyond the limits of essayism and artificial verse," which suggests that he was somewhat intolerant of his own times. His critical judgment, although often severe, is generally reliable to this day. His dynastic chronology, however, is quite out of date because of the advances in archaeology over the past seventy years. On the authority of the *Encyclopaedia Britannica* (1970 ed.) and historical research, the following dates will better serve the reader of this book:

Shang, or Yin: c. 1776–c. 1123 B.C.

Chou: c. 1122–256 B.C.

Ch'in: 221–207 B.C.

Han: 202 B.C.–A.D. 221

Six Dynasties: 221–589

Sui: 589–618

T'ang: 618–906

Five Dynasties and Ten States: 907–960

Sung: 960–1279
Yüan: 1280–1368
Ming: 1368–1644
Ch'ing: 1644–1912

Biographical Note

Herbert Allen Giles was born at Oxford, England, in 1845. After a long life of ninety years he died at Cambridge in 1935. For fifty years he wrote books on Chinese subjects which he based on his sound knowledge of the Chinese language and a quarter century of personal experience living in China. As a young man Giles joined the British consular service in Peking in 1867 and thereafter served on various posts until 1892, when he returned to England.

Chinese studies had a very low priority in British universities in the late nineteenth century, but professorships were in existence, and of these Giles took up a chair of Chinese at Cambridge University in 1897. Students were few there, but Chinese books many. Also the leisurely life of a Cambridge professor gave Giles an unlimited opportunity to write. Books flowed from his pen. His command of the Chinese language coupled with great fluency in English yielded some of the clearest and most graceful translations of Chinese literature yet made. In 1922, the Royal Asiatic Society awarded Giles its triennial gold medal with the compliment that he had "beyond all other living scholars humanized Chinese studies."

Professor Giles truly did much to reveal to the English-speaking peoples of the world the depth and the beauty of Chinese culture. In an age that regarded the Chinese as exotic curiosities, by turns inscrutable or ridiculous, Giles brought about a better understanding of the greatness of China and the talents of the Chinese over the ages. *A History of Chinese Literature* is one of the most enduring literary achievements of his endeavors and is certainly a unique contribution to Chinese studies. The work of Professor Giles will no doubt be given renewed attention as the role of China in the modern world assumes an ever increasing prominence.

TERENCE BARROW Ph.D.

PREFACE

THIS is the first attempt made in any language, including
Chinese, to produce a history of Chinese literature.

Native scholars, with their endless critiques and
appreciations of individual works, do not seem ever to
have contemplated anything of the kind, realising, no
doubt, the utter hopelessness, from a Chinese point
of view, of achieving even comparative success in a
general historical survey of the subject. The voluminous character of a literature which was already in
existence some six centuries before the Christian era,
and has run on uninterruptedly until the present date,
may well have given pause to writers aiming at completeness. The foreign student, however, is on a totally
different footing. It may be said without offence that
a work which would be inadequate to the requirements
of a native public, may properly be submitted to English readers as an introduction into the great field which
lies beyond.

Acting upon the suggestion of Mr. Gosse, to whom I
am otherwise indebted for many valuable hints, I have
devoted a large portion of this book to translation, thus
enabling the Chinese author, so far as translation will
allow, to speak for himself. I have also added, here and
there, remarks by native critics, that the reader may be

able to form an idea of the point of view from which the Chinese judge their own productions.

It only remains to be stated that the translations, with the exception of a few passages from Legge's "Chinese Classics," in each case duly acknowledged, are my own.

HERBERT A. GILES.

CAMBRIDGE, *October* 1900.

BOOK THE FIRST

THE FEUDAL PERIOD (B.C. 600–200)

BOOK THE FIRST

THE FEUDAL PERIOD (B.C. 600–200)

CHAPTER I

LEGENDARY AGES—EARLY CHINESE CIVILISATION—ORIGIN OF WRITING

THE date of the beginning of all things has been nicely calculated by Chinese chronologers. There was first of all a period when Nothing existed, though some enthusiasts have attempted to deal with a period antecedent even to that. Gradually Nothing took upon itself the form and limitations of Unity, represented by a point at the centre of a circle. Thus there was a Great Monad, a First Cause, an Aura, a Zeitgeist, or whatever one may please to call it.

After countless ages, spent apparently in doing nothing, this Monad split into Two Principles, one active, the other passive; one positive, the other negative; light and darkness; male and female. The interaction of these Two Principles resulted in the production of all things, as we see them in the universe around us, 2,269,381 years ago. Such is the cosmogony of the Chinese in a nutshell.

3

The more sober Chinese historians, however, are content to begin with a sufficiently mythical emperor, who reigned only 2800 years before the Christian era. The practice of agriculture, the invention of wheeled vehicles, and the simpler arts of early civilisation are generally referred to this period; but to the dispassionate European student it is a period of myth and legend: in fact, we know very little about it. Neither do we know much, in the historical sense, of the numerous rulers whose names and dates appear in the chronology of the succeeding two thousand years. It is not indeed until we reach the eighth century B.C. that anything like history can be said to begin.

For reasons which will presently be made plain, the sixth century B.C. is a convenient starting-point for the student of Chinese literature.

China was then confined to a comparatively small area, lying for the most part between the Yellow River on the north and the river Yang-tsze on the south. No one knows where the Chinese came from. Some hold the fascinating theory that they were emigrants from Accadia in the ancient kingdom of Babylonia; others have identified them with the lost tribes of Israel. No one seems to think they can possibly have originated in the fertile plains where they are now found. It appears indeed to be an ethnological axiom that every race must have come from somewhere outside its own territory. However that may be, the China of the eighth century B.C. consisted of a number of Feudal States, ruled by nobles owning allegiance to a Central State, at the head of which was a king. The outward tokens of subjection were homage and tribute; but after all, the allegiance must have been more nominal than real, each State being practically an independent kingdom. This condition of things was the cause of much mutual jealousy, and often of bloody warfare, several of the States hating one another quite as cordially as Athens and Sparta at their best.

There was, notwithstanding, considerable physical civilisation in the ancient States of those early days. Their citizens, when not employed in cutting each other's throats, enjoyed a reasonable security of life and property. They lived in well-built houses ; they dressed in silk or homespun ; they wore shoes of leather ; they carried umbrellas ; they sat on chairs and used tables ; they rode in carts and chariots ; they travelled by boat ; and they ate their food off plates and dishes of pottery, coarse perhaps, yet still superior to the wooden trencher common not so very long ago in Europe. They measured time by the sundial, and in the Golden Age they had the two famous calendar trees, representations of which have come down to us in sculpture, dating from about A.D. 150. One of these trees put forth a leaf every day for fifteen days, after which a leaf fell off daily for fifteen more days. The other put forth a leaf once a month for half a year, after which a leaf fell off monthly for a similar period. With these trees growing in the courtyard, it was possible to say at a glance what was the day of the month, and what was the month of the year. But civilisation proved unfavourable to their growth, and the species became extinct.

In the sixth century B.C. the Chinese were also in possession of a written language, fully adequate to the most varied expression of human thought, and indeed almost identical with their present script, allowing, among other things, for certain modifications of form brought about by the substitution of paper and a camel's-hair brush for the bamboo tablet and stylus of old. The actual stages by which that point was reached are so far unknown to us. China has her Cadmus in the person of a prehistoric individual named Ts'ang Chieh, who is said to have had four eyes, and to have taken the idea of a written language from the markings of birds' claws upon the sand. Upon the achievement of his task the sky rained grain and evil spirits mourned by night. Previous to this mankind had no other system than rude methods of knotting cords and notching sticks for noting events or communicating with one another at a distance.

As to the origin of the written language of China, invention is altogether out of the question. It seems probable that in prehistoric ages, the Chinese, like other peoples, began to make rude pictures of the sun, moon, and stars, of man himself, of trees, of fire, of rain, and they appear to have followed these up by ideograms of various kinds. How far they went in this direction we can only surmise. There are comparatively few obviously pictorial characters and ideograms to be found even in the script of two thousand years ago; but investigations carried on for many years by Mr. L. C. Hopkins, H.M. Consul, Chefoo, and now approaching completion, point more and more to the fact that the written language will some day be recognised as systematically developed from pictorial symbols. It is, at any rate, certain that at a very early date subsequent to the legendary period of "knotted cords" and "notches," while the picture-symbols were still comparatively few, some master-mind reached at a bound the phonetic principle, from which point the rapid development of a written language such as we now find would be an easy matter.

CHAPTER II

CONFUCIUS—THE FIVE CLASSICS

IN B.C. 551 CONFUCIUS was born. He may be regarded as the founder of Chinese literature. During his years of office as a Government servant and his years of teaching and wandering as an exile, he found time to rescue for posterity certain valuable literary fragments of great antiquity, and to produce at least one original work of his own. It is impossible to assert that before his time there was anything in the sense of what we understand by the term general literature. The written language appears to have been used chiefly for purposes of administration. Many utterances, however, of early, not to say legendary, rulers had been committed to writing at one time or another, and such of these as were still extant were diligently collected and edited by Confucius, forming what is now known as the *Shu Ching* or Book of History. The documents of which this work is composed are said to have been originally one hundred in all, and they cover a period extending from the twenty-fourth to the eighth century B.C. They give us glimpses of an age earlier than that of Confucius, if not actually so early as is claimed. The first two, for instance, refer to the Emperors Yao and Shun, whose reigns, extending from B.C. 2357 to 2205, are regarded as the Golden Age of China. We read how the former monarch "united the various parts of his domain in bonds of peace, so that concord reigned among the black-haired people." He abdicated in favour of Shun, who is described as being profoundly wise, intelligent, and sincere. We are further told that Shun was chosen because of his great filial piety, which enabled him to live in harmony with an unprincipled father, a shifty stepmother, and an arrogant half-brother, and, moreover, to effect by his example a comparative reformation of their several characters.

We next come to a very famous personage, who founded the Hsia dynasty in B.C. 2205, and is known as the Great Yü. It was he who, during the reign of the Emperor Shun, successfully coped with a devastating flood, which has been loosely identified with the Noachic Deluge, and in reference to which it was said in the *Tso Chuan*, " How grand was the achievement of Yü, how far-reaching his glorious energy! But for Yü we should all have been fishes." The following is his own account (Legge's translation) :—

" The inundating waters seemed to assail the heavens, and in their vast extent embraced the mountains and overtopped the hills, so that people were bewildered and overwhelmed. I mounted my four conveyances (carts, boats, sledges, and spiked shoes), and all along the hills hewed down the woods, at the same time, along with Yi, showing the multitudes how to get flesh to eat. I opened passages for the streams throughout the nine provinces, and conducted them to the sea. I deepened the channels and canals, and conducted them to the streams, at the same time, along with Chi, sowing grain, and showing the multitudes how to procure the food of toil in addition to flesh meat. I urged them further

to exchange what they had for what they had not, and
to dispose of their accumulated stores.   In this way all
the people got grain to eat, and all the States began to
come under good rule."

A small portion of the Book of History is in verse :—

> *" The people should be cherished,*
> *And should not be downtrodden.*
> *The people are the root of a country,*
> *And if the root is firm, the country will be tranquil.*
>
> .   .   .   .
>
> *The palace a wild for lust,*
> *The country a wild for hunting,*
> *Rich wine, seductive music,*
> *Lofty roofs, carved walls,—*
> *Given any one of these,*
> *And the result can only be ruin."*

From the date of the foundation of the Hsia dynasty
the throne of the empire was transmitted from father to
son, and there were no more abdications in favour of
virtuous sages. The fourth division of the Book of
History deals with the decadence of the Hsia rulers and
their final displacement in B.C. 1766 by T'ang the Com-
pleter, founder of the Shang dynasty.   By B.C. 1122, the
Shang sovereigns had similarly lapsed from the kingly
qualities of their founder to even a lower level of degradation and vice.   Then arose one of the purest and most
venerated heroes of Chinese history, popularly known by
his canonisation as Wên Wang. He was hereditary ruler
of a principality in the modern province of Shensi, and in
B.C. 1144 he was denounced as dangerous to the throne.
He was seized and thrown into prison, where he passed
two years, occupying himself with the Book of Changes,
to which we shall presently return.   At length the
Emperor, yielding to the entreaties of the people, backed
up by the present of a beautiful concubine and some

fine horses, set him at liberty and commissioned him
to make war upon the frontier tribes. To his dying day
he never ceased to remonstrate against the cruelty and
corruption of the age, and his name is still regarded
as one of the most glorious in the annals of the empire.
It was reserved for his son, known as Wu Wang, to
overthrow the Shang dynasty and mount the throne as
first sovereign of the Chou dynasty, which was to last
for eight centuries to come. The following is a speech
by the latter before a great assembly of nobles who were
siding against the House of Shang. It is preserved
among others in the Book of History, and is assigned
to the year B.C. 1133 (Legge's translation):—

" Heaven and Earth are the parents of all creatures ;
and of all creatures man is the most highly endowed.
The sincere, intelligent, and perspicacious among men
becomes the great sovereign, and the great sovereign
is the parent of the people. But now, Shou, the king
of Shang, does not reverence Heaven above, and inflicts
calamities on the people below. He has been aban-
doned to drunkenness, and reckless in lust. He has
dared to exercise cruel oppression. Along with criminals
he has punished all their relatives. He has put men
into office on the hereditary principle. He has made
it his pursuit to have palaces, towers, pavilions, embankments, ponds, and all other extravagances, to the
most painful injury of you, the myriad people. He has
burned and roasted the loyal and good. He has ripped
up pregnant women. Great Heaven was moved with
indignation, and charged my deceased father, Wên,
reverently to display its majesty ; but he died before
the work was completed.

" On this account I, Fa, who am but a little child, have,

by means of you, the hereditary rulers of my friendly States, contemplated the government of Shang; but Shou has no repentant heart. He abides squatting on his heels, not serving God or the spirits of heaven and earth, neglecting also the temple of his ancestors, and not sacrificing in it. The victims and the vessels of millet all become the prey of wicked robbers; and still he says, 'The people are mine: the decree is mine,' never trying to correct his contemptuous mind. Now Heaven, to protect the inferior people, made for them rulers, and made for them instructors, that they might be able to be aiding to God, and secure the tranquillity of the four quarters of the empire. In regard to who are criminals and who are not, how dare I give any allowance to my own wishes?

"'Where the strength is the same, measure the virtue of the parties; where the virtue is the same, measure their righteousness.' Shou has hundreds of thousands and myriads of ministers, but they have hundreds of thousands and myriads of minds; I have three thousand ministers, but they have one mind. The iniquity of Shang is full. Heaven gives command to destroy it. If I did not comply with Heaven, my iniquity would be as great.

"I, who am a little child, early and late am filled with apprehensions. I have received charge from my deceased father, Wên; I have offered special sacrifice to God; I have performed the due services to the great Earth; and I lead the multitude of you to execute the punishment appointed by Heaven. Heaven compassionates the people. What the people desire, Heaven will be found to give effect to. Do you aid me, the one man, to cleanse for ever all within the four seas. Now is the time!—it may not be lost."

Two of the documents which form the Book of History are directed against luxury and drunkenness, to both of which the people seemed likely to give way even within measurable distance of the death of Wên Wang. The latter had enacted that wine (that is to say, ardent spirits distilled from rice) should only be used on sacrificial occasions, and then under strict supervision ; and it is laid down, almost as a general principle, that all national misfortunes, culminating in the downfall of a dynasty, may be safely ascribed to the abuse of wine.

The *Shih Ching*, or Book of Odes, is another work for the preservation of which we are indebted to Confucius. It consists of a collection of rhymed ballads in various metres, usually four words to the line, composed between the reign of the Great Yü and the beginning of the sixth century B.C. These, which now number 305, are popularly known as the " Three Hundred," and are said by some to have been selected by Confucius from no less than 3000 pieces. They are arranged under four heads, as follows :—(*a*) Ballads commonly sung by the people in the various feudal States and forwarded periodically by the nobles to their suzerain, the Son of Heaven. The ballads were then submitted to the Imperial Musicians, who were able to judge from the nature of such compositions what would be the manners and customs prevailing in each State, and to advise the suzerain accordingly as to the good or evil administration of each of his vassal rulers. (*b*) Odes sung at ordinary entertainments given by the suzerain. (*c*) Odes sung on grand occasions when the feudal nobles were gathered together. (*d*) Panegyrics and sacrificial odes.

Confucius himself attached the utmost importance to his labours in this direction. "Have you learned the Odes?" he inquired upon one occasion of his son; and on receiving an answer in the negative, immediately told the youth that until he did so he would be unfit for the society of intellectual men. Confucius may indeed be said to have anticipated the apophthegm attributed by Fletcher of Saltoun to a "very wise man," namely, that he who should be allowed to make a nation's "ballads need care little who made its laws." And it was probably this appreciation by Confucius that gave rise to an extraordinary literary craze in reference to these Odes. Early commentators, incapable of seeing the simple natural beauties of the poems, which have furnished endless household words and a large stock of phraseology to the language of the present day, and at the same time unable to ignore the deliberate judgment of the Master, set to work to read into country-side ditties deep moral and political significations. Every single one of the immortal Three Hundred has thus been forced to yield some hidden meaning and point an appropriate moral. If a maiden warns her lover not to be too rash—

> " Don't come in, sir, please !
> Don't break my willow-trees !
> Not that that would very much grieve me ;
> But alack-a-day ! what would my parents say ?
> And love you as I may,
> I cannot bear to think what that would be,"—

commentators promptly discover that the piece refers to a feudal noble whose brother had been plotting against him, and to the excuses of the former for not visiting the latter with swift and exemplary punishment.

Another independent young lady may say—

> *" If you will love me dear, my lord,*
> *I'll pick up my skirts and cross the ford,*
> *But if from your heart you turn me out . . .*
> *Well, you're not the only man about,*
> *You silly, silly, silliest lout ! "—*

still commentaries are not wanting to show that these straightforward words express the wish of the people of a certain small State that some great State would intervene and put an end to an existing feud in the ruling family. Native scholars are, of course, hide-bound in the traditions of commentators, but European students will do well to seek the meaning of the Odes within the compass of the Odes themselves.

Possibly the very introduction of these absurdities may have helped to preserve to our day a work which would otherwise have been considered too trivial to merit the attention of scholars. Chinese who are in the front rank of scholarship know it by heart, and each separate piece has been searchingly examined, until the force of exegesis can no farther go. There is one famous line which runs, according to the accepted commentary, "The muddiness of the Ching river appears from the (clearness of the) Wei river." In 1790 the Emperor Ch'ien Lung, dissatisfied with this interpretation, sent a viceroy to examine the rivers. The latter reported that the Ching was really clear and the Wei muddy, so that the wording of the line must mean "The Ching river is made muddy by the Wei river."

The following is a specimen of one of the longer of the Odes, saddled, like all the rest, with an impossible political interpretation, of which nothing more need be said :—

You seemed a guileless youth enough,
Offering for silk your woven stuff; [1]
But silk was not required by you;
I was the silk you had in view.
With you I crossed the ford, and while
We wandered on for many a mile
I said, ' I do not wish delay,
But friends must fix our wedding-day. . . .
Oh, do not let my words give pain,
But with the autumn come again.'

" And then I used to watch and wait
To see you passing through the gate;
And sometimes, when I watched in vain,
My tears would flow like falling rain;
But when I saw my darling boy,
I laughed and cried aloud for joy.
The fortune-tellers, you declared,
Had all pronounced us duly paired;
' Then bring a carriage,' I replied,
' And I'll away to be your bride.'

" The mulberry-leaf, not yet undone
By autumn chill, shines in the sun.
O tender dove, I would advise,
Beware the fruit that tempts thy eyes!
O maiden fair, not yet a spouse,
List lightly not to lovers' vows!
A man may do this wrong, and time
Will fling its shadow o'er his crime;
A woman who has lost her name
Is doomed to everlasting shame.

" The mulberry-tree upon the ground
Now sheds its yellow leaves around.
Three years have slipped away from me
Since first I shared your poverty;
And now again, alas the day!
Back through the ford I take my way.

[1] Supposed to have been stamped pieces of linen, used as a circulating
medium before the invention of coins.

My heart is still unchanged, but you
Have uttered words now proved untrue;
And you have left me to deplore
A love that can be mine no more.

" *For three long years I was your wife,*
And led in truth a toilsome life;
Early to rise and late to bed,
Each day alike passed o'er my head.
I honestly fulfilled my part,
And you—well, you have broke my heart.
The truth my brothers will not know,
So all the more their gibes will flow.
I grieve in silence and repine
That such a wretched fate is mine.

" *Ah, hand in hand to face old age !—*
Instead, I turn a bitter page.
O for the river-banks of yore;
O for the much-loved marshy shore;
The hours of girlhood, with my hair
Ungathered, as we lingered there.
The words we spoke, that seemed so true,
I little thought that I should rue;
I little thought the vows we swore
Would some day bind us two no more."

Many of the Odes deal with warfare, and with the separation of wives from their husbands; others, with agriculture and with the chase, with marriage and feasting. The ordinary sorrows of life are fully represented, and to these may be added frequent complaints against the harshness of officials, one speaker going so far as to wish he were a tree without consciousness, without home, and without family. The old-time theme of "eat, drink, and be merry" is brought out as follows:—

" *You have coats and robes,*
But you do not trail them;
You have chariots and horses,
But you do not ride in them.

> *By and by you will die,*
> *And another will enjoy them.*

> " *You have courtyards and halls,*
> *But they are not sprinkled and swept;*
> *You have bells and drums,*
> *But they are not struck.*
> *By and by you will die,*
> *And another will possess them.*

> " *You have wine and food;*
> *Why not play daily on your lute,*
> *That you may enjoy yourself now*
> *And lengthen your days?*
> *By and by you will die,*
> *And another will take your place.*"

The Odes are especially valuable for the insight they give us into the manners, and customs, and beliefs of the Chinese before the age of Confucius. How far back they extend it is quite impossible to say. An eclipse of the sun, "an event of evil omen," is mentioned in one of the Odes as a recent occurrence on a certain day which works out as the 29th August, B.C. 775; and this eclipse has been verified for that date. The following lines are from Legge's rendering of this Ode :—

> " *The sun and moon announce evil,*
> *Not keeping to their proper paths.*
> *All through the kingdom there is no proper government,*
> *Because the good are not employed.*
> *For the moon to be eclipsed*
> *Is but an ordinary matter.*
> *Now that the sun has been eclipsed,*
> *How bad it is!*"

The rainbow was regarded, not as a portent of evil, but as an improper combination of the dual forces of nature,—

> " *There is a rainbow in the east,*
> *And no one dares point at it*,"—

and is applied figuratively to women who form improper connections.

The position of women generally seems to have been very much what it is at the present day. In an Ode which describes the completion of a palace for one of the ancient princes, we are conducted through the rooms,—

> " *Here will he live, here will he sit,*
> *Here will he laugh, here will he talk*,"—

until we come to the bedchamber, where he will awake, and call upon the chief diviner to interpret his dream of bears and serpents. The interpretation (Legge) is as follows :—

> " *Sons shall be born to him :—*
> *They will be put to sleep on couches ;*
> *They will be clothed in robes ;*
> *They will have sceptres to play with ;*
> *Their cry will be loud.*
> *They will be resplendent with red knee-covers,*
> *The future princes of the land.*

> " *Daughters shall be born to him :—*
> *They will be put to sleep on the ground ;*
> *They will be clothed with wrappers ;*
> *They will have tiles to play with.*
> *It will be theirs neither to do wrong nor to do good.*
> *Only about the spirits and the food will they have to think,*
> *And to cause no sorrow to their parents.*"

The distinction thus drawn is severe enough, and it is quite unnecessary to make a comparison, as some writers on China have done, between the tile and the sceptre, as though the former were but a dirty potsherd, good enough for a girl. A tile was used in the early

ages as a weight for the spindle, and is here used merely
to indicate the direction which a girl's activities should
take.

Women are further roughly handled in an Ode which
traces the prevailing misgovernment to their interference
in affairs of State and in matters which do not lie within
their province :—

> "*A clever man builds a city,*
> *A clever woman lays one low;*
> *With all her qualifications, that clever woman*
> *Is but an ill-omened bird.*
> *A woman with a long tongue*
> *Is a flight of steps leading to calamity;*
> *For disorder does not come from heaven,*
> *But is brought about by women.*
> *Among those who cannot be trained or taught*
> *Are women and eunuchs.*"

About seventy kinds of plants are mentioned in the
Odes, including the bamboo, barley, beans, convolvulus,
dodder, dolichos, hemp, indigo, liquorice, melon, millet,
peony, pepper, plantain, scallions, sorrel, sowthistle,
tribulus, and wheat; about thirty kinds of trees, including the cedar, cherry, chestnut, date, hazel, medlar,
mulberry, oak, peach, pear, plum, and willow; about
thirty kinds of animals, including the antelope, badger,
bear, boar, elephant, fox, leopard, monkey, rat, rhino-
ceros, tiger, and wolf; about thirty kinds of birds,
including the crane, eagle, egret, magpie, oriole, swallow,
and wagtail; about ten kinds of fishes, including the
barbel, bream, carp, and tench; and about twenty kinds
of insects, including the ant, cicada, glow-worm, locust,
spider, and wasp.

Among the musical instruments of the Odes are found
the flute, the drum, the bell, the lute, and the Pandæan

pipes; among the metals are gold and iron, with an indirect allusion to silver and copper; and among the arms and munitions of war are bows and arrows, spears, swords, halberds, armour, grappling-hooks, towers on wheels for use against besieged cities, and gags for soldiers' mouths, to prevent them talking in the ranks on the occasion of night attacks.

The idea of a Supreme Being is brought out very fully in the Odes—

> "Great is God,
> Ruling in majesty."

Also,

> "How mighty is God,
> The Ruler of mankind!
> How terrible is His majesty!"

He is apparently in the form of man, for in one place we read of His footprint. He hates the oppression of great States, although in another passage we read—

> "Behold Almighty God;
> Who is there whom He hates?"

He comforts the afflicted. He is free from error. His "Way" is hard to follow. He is offended by sin. He can be appeased by sacrifice :—

> "We fill the sacrificial vessels with offerings,
> Both the vessels of wood, and those of earthenware.
> Then when the fragrance is borne on high,
> God smells the savour and is pleased."

One more quotation, which, in deference to space limits, must be the last, exhibits the husbandman of early China in a very pleasing light :—

> "The clouds form in dense masses,
> And the rain falls softly down.
> Oh, may it first water the public lands,
> And then come to our private fields!

Here shall some corn be left standing,
Here some sheaves unbound;
Here some handfuls shall be dropped,
And there some neglected ears;
These are for the benefit of the widow."

The next of the pre-Confucian works, and possibly the oldest of all, is the famous *I Ching*, or Book of Changes. It is ascribed to WÊN WANG, the virtual founder of the Chou dynasty, whose son, WU WANG, became the first sovereign of a long line, extending from B.C. 1122 to B.C. 249. It contains a fanciful system of philosophy, deduced originally from Eight Diagrams consisting of triplet combinations or arrangements of a line and a divided line, either one or other of which is necessarily repeated twice, and in two cases three times, in the same combination. Thus there may be three lines ≡≡≡, or three divided lines ≡≡ ≡≡, a divided line above or below two lines ≡≡≡ ≡≡≡, a divided line between two lines ≡≡≡, and so on, eight in all. These so-called diagrams are said to have been invented two thousand years and more before Christ by the monarch Fu Hsi, who copied them from the back of a tortoise. He subsequently increased the above simple combinations to sixty-four double ones, on the permutations of which are based the philosophical speculations of the Book of Changes. Each diagram represents some power in nature, either active or passive, such as fire, water, thunder, earth, and so on.

The text consists of sixty-four short essays, enigmatically and symbolically expressed, on important themes, mostly of a moral, social, and political character, and based upon the same number of lineal figures, each made up of six lines, some of which are whole and the others divided. The text is followed by commentaries, called the Ten Wings, probably of a later date and commonly ascribed to Confucius, who declared that were a hundred years added to his life he would devote fifty of them to a study of the *I Ching*.

The following is a specimen (Legge's translation) :—

" *Text.* This suggests the idea of one treading on the tail of a tiger, which does not bite him. There will be progress and success.

" 1. The first line, undivided, shows its subject treading his accustomed path. If he go forward, there will be no error.

" 2. The second line, undivided, shows its subject treading the path that is level and easy ;—a quiet and solitary man, to whom, if he be firm and correct, there will be good fortune.

" 3. The third line, divided, shows a one-eyed man who thinks he can see ; a lame man who thinks he can walk well ; one who treads on the tail of a tiger and is bitten. All this indicates ill-fortune. We have a mere bravo acting the part of a great ruler.

" 4. The fourth line, undivided, shows its subject treading on the tail of a tiger. He becomes full of apprehensive caution, and in the end there will be good fortune.

" 5. The fifth line, undivided, shows the resolute tread of its subject. Though he be firm and correct, there will be peril.

" 6. The sixth line, undivided, tells us to look at the whole course that is trodden, and examine the presage which that gives. If it be complete and without failure, there will be great good fortune.

" *Wing.*—In this hexagram we have the symbol of weakness treading on that of strength.

" The lower trigram indicates pleasure and satisfaction, and responds to the upper indicating strength. Hence it is said, ' He treads on the tail of a tiger, which does not bite him ; there will be progress and success.'

" The fifth line is strong, in the centre, and in its correct place. Its subject occupies the God-given position, and falls into no distress or failure ;—his action will be brilliant."

As may be readily inferred from the above extract, no one really knows what is meant by the apparent gibberish of the Book of Changes. This is freely admitted by all learned Chinese, who nevertheless hold tenaciously to the belief that important lessons could be derived from its pages if we only had the wit to understand them. Foreigners have held various theories on the subject. Dr. Legge declared that he had found the key, with the result already shown. The late Terrien de la Couperie took a bolder flight, unaccompanied by any native commentator, and discovered in this cherished volume a vocabulary of the language of the Bák tribes. A third writer regards it as a calendar of the lunar year, and so forth.

The *Li Chi*, or Book of Rites, seems to have been a compilation by two cousins, known as the Elder and the Younger TAI, who flourished in the 2nd and 1st centuries B.C. From existing documents, said to have emanated from Confucius and his disciples, the Elder Tai prepared a work in 85 sections on what may be roughly called social rites. The Younger Tai reduced these to 46 sections. Later scholars, such as Ma Jung and Chêng Hsüan, left their mark upon the work, and it was not until near the close of the 2nd century A.D.

that finality in this direction was achieved. It then became known as a *Chi* = Record, not as a *Ching* = Text, the latter term being reserved by the orthodox solely for such books as have reached us direct from the hands of Confucius. The following is an extract (Legge's translation) :—

Confucius said : "Formerly, along with Lao Tan, I was assisting at a burial in the village of Hsiang, and when we had got to the path the sun was eclipsed. Lao Tan said to me, 'Ch'iu, let the bier be stopped on the left of the road ; and then let us wail and wait till the eclipse pass away. When it is light again we will proceed.' He said that this was the rule. When we had returned and completed the burial, I said to him, 'In the progress of a bier there should be no re- turning. When there is an eclipse of the sun, we do not know whether it will pass away quickly or not ; would it not have been better to go on ?' Lao Tan said, 'When the prince of a state is going to the court of the Son of Heaven, he travels while he can see the sun. At sundown he halts and presents his offerings (to the spirit of the way). When a great officer is on a mission, he travels while he can see the sun, and at sundown he halts. Now a bier does not set forth in the early morning, nor does it rest anywhere at night ; but those who travel by starlight are only criminals and those who are hastening to the funeral rites of a parent.'"

Other specimens will be found in Chapters iii. and iv.

Until the time of the Ming dynasty, A.D. 1368, an- other and a much older work, known as the *Chou Li,* or Rites of the Chou dynasty, and dealing more with constitutional matters, was always coupled with the *Li Chi*, and formed one of the then recognised Six Classics. There is still a third work of the same class, and also of considerable antiquity, called the *I Li*. Its contents treat mostly of the ceremonial observances of everyday life.

We now come to the last of the Five Classics as at present constituted, the *Ch'un Ch'iu*, or Spring and Autumn Annals. This is a chronological record of the chief events in the State of Lu between the years B.C. 722–484, and is generally regarded as the work of Confucius, whose native State was Lu. The entries are of the briefest, and comprise notices of incursions, victories, defeats, deaths, murders, treaties, and natural phenomena.

The following are a few illustrative extracts :—

" In the 7th year of Duke Chao, in spring, the Northern Yen State made peace with the Ch'i State.

" In the 3rd month the Duke visited the Ch'u State.

" In summer, on the *chia shên* day of the 4th month (March 11th, B.C. 594), the sun was eclipsed.

" In the 7th year of Duke Chuang (B.C. 685), in summer, in the 4th moon, at midnight, there was a shower of stars like rain."

The Spring and Autumn owes its name to the old custom of prefixing to each entry the year, month, day, and season when the event recorded took place ; spring, as a commentator explains, including summer, and autumn winter. It was the work which Confucius singled out as that one by which men would know and commend him, and Mencius considered it quite as important an achievement as the draining of the empire by the Great Yü. The latter said, "Confucius completed the Spring and Autumn, and rebellious ministers and bad sons were struck with terror." Consequently, just as in the case of the Odes, native wits set to work to read into the bald text all manner of hidden meanings, each entry being supposed to contain approval or condemnation, their efforts resulting in what is now known as the praise-and-blame theory. The critics of the Han dynasty even went so far as to declare the very title elliptical for " praise life-giving like spring, and blame life-withering like autumn."

Such is the *Ch'un Ch'iu;* and if that were all, it is difficult to say how the boast of Confucius could ever have been fulfilled. But it is not all ; there is a saving clause. For bound up, so to speak, with the Spring and Autumn, and forming as it were an integral part of the work, is a commentary known as the *Tso Chuan* or Tso's Commentary. Of the writer himself, who has been canonised as the Father of Prose, and to whose pen has also been attributed the *Kuo Yü* or Episodes of the States, next to nothing is known, except that he was a disciple of Confucius ; but his glowing narrative remains, and is likely to continue to remain, one of the most precious heirlooms of the Chinese people.

What Tso did was this. He took the dry bones of these annals and clothed them with life and reality by adding a more or less complete setting to each of the events recorded. He describes the loves and hates of the heroes, their battles, their treaties, their feastings, and their deaths, in a style which is always effective, and often approaches to grandeur. Circumstances of apparently the most trivial character are expanded into

interesting episodes, and every now and again some
quaint conceit or scrap of proverbial literature is thrown
in to give a passing flavour of its own. Under the 21st
year of Duke Hsi, the Spring and Autumn has the
following exiguous entry :—

"In summer there was great drought."

To this the *Tso Chuan* adds—

"In consequence of the drought the Duke wished to
burn a witch. One of his officers, however, said to him,
'That will not affect the drought. Rather repair your
city walls and ramparts ; eat less, and curtail your expenditure ; practise strict economy, and urge the people
to help one another. That is the essential ; what have
witches to do in the matter ? If God wishes her to be
slain, it would have been better not to allow her to be
born. If she can cause a drought, burning her will only
make things worse.' The Duke took this advice, and
during that year, although there was famine, it was not
very severe."

Under the 12th year of Duke Hsüan the Spring and
Autumn says—

"In spring the ruler of the Ch'u State besieged the
capital of the Chêng State."

Thereupon the *Tso Chuan* adds a long account of the
whole business, from which the following typical paragraph is extracted :—

"In the rout which followed, a war-chariot of the Chin
State stuck in a deep rut and could not get on. Thereupon a man of the Ch'u State advised the charioteer to
take out the stand for arms. This eased it a little, but
again the horses turned round. The man then advised
that the flagstaff should be taken out and used as a lever,
and at last the chariot was extricated. 'Ah,' said the

charioteer to the man of Ch'u, 'we don't know so much about running away as the people of your worthy State.'"

The *Tso Chuan* contains several interesting passages on music, which was regarded by Confucius as an important factor in the art of government, recalling the well-known views of Plato in Book III. of his *Republic*. Apropos of disease, we read that "the ancient rulers regulated all things by music." Also that "the superior man will not listen to lascivious or seductive airs;" "he addresses himself to his lute in order to regulate his conduct, and not to delight his heart."

When the rabid old anti-foreign tutor of the late Emperor T'ung Chih was denouncing the barbarians, and expressing a kindly desire to "sleep on their skins," he was quoting the phraseology of the *Tso Chuan*.

One hero, on going into battle, told his friends that he should only hear the drum beating the signal to advance, for he would take good care not to hear the gong sounding the retreat. Another made each of his men carry into battle a long rope, seeing that the enemy all wore their hair short. In a third case, where some men in possession of boats were trying to prevent others from scrambling in, we are told that the fingers of the assailants were chopped off in such large numbers that they could be picked up in double handfuls.

Many maxims, practical and unpractical, are to be found scattered over the *Tso Chuan*, such as, "One day's leniency to an enemy entails trouble for many generations;" "Propriety forbids that a man should profit himself at the expense of another;" "The receiver is as bad as the thief;" "It is better to attack than to be attacked."

When the French fleet returned to Shanghai in 1885, after being repulsed in a shore attack at Tamsui, a local wit at once adapted a verse of doggerel found in the *Tso Chuan* :—

> " *See goggle-eyes and greedy-guts*
> *Has left his shield among the ruts ;*
> *Back from the field, back from the field*
> *He's brought his beard, but not his shield;*"

and for days every Chinaman was muttering the refrain—

> " *Yü sai, yü sai*
> *Ch'i chia fu lai.*"

There are two other commentaries on the Spring and Autumn, similar, but generally regarded as inferior, to the *Tso Chuan*. They are by KU-LIANG and KUNG-YANG, both of the fifth century B.C. The following are specimens (Legge's translation, omitting unimportant details) :—

Text.—" In spring, in the king's first month, the first day of the moon, there fell stones in Sung—five of them. In the same month, six fish-hawks flew backwards, past the capital of Sung.

The commentary of Ku-liang says, "Why does the text first say "there fell," and then "stones"? There was the falling, and then the stones.

In "six fish-hawks flying backwards past the capital of Sung," the number is put first, indicating that the birds were collected together. The language has respect to the seeing of the eyes.

The Master said, "Stones are

The commentary of Kung-yang says, "How is it that the text first says "there fell," and then "stones"?

"There fell stones" is a record of what was heard. There was heard a noise of something falling. On looking at what had fallen, it was seen to be stones. On examination it was found there were five of them.

Why does the text say "six," and then "fish-hawks"?

things without any intelligence, and fish-hawks creatures that have a little intelligence. The stones, having no intelligence, are mentioned along with the day when they fell, and the fish-hawks, having a little intelligence, are mentioned along with the month when they appeared. The superior man (Confucius) even in regard to such things and creatures records nothing rashly. His expressions about stones and fish-hawks being thus exact, how much more will they be so about men!"

"Six fish-hawks backwards flew" is a record of what was seen. When they looked at the objects, there were six. When they examined them, they were fish-hawks. When they examined them leisurely, they were flying backwards.

Sometimes these commentaries are seriously at variance with that of Tso. For instance, the text says that in B.C. 689 the ruler of the Chi State "made a great end of his State." Tso's commentary explains the words to mean that for various urgent reasons the ruler abdicated. Kung-yang, however, takes quite a different view. He explains the passage in the sense that the State in question was utterly destroyed, the population being wiped out by the ruler of another State in revenge for the death in B.C. 893 of an ancestor, who was boiled to death at the feudal metropolis in consequence of slander by a contemporary ruler of the Chi State. It is important for candidates at the public examinations to be familiar with these discrepancies, as they are frequently called upon to "discuss" such points, always with the object of establishing the orthodox and accepted interpretations.

The following episode is from Kung-yang's commentary, and is quite different from the story told by Tso in reference to the same passage :—

Text.—" In summer, in the 5th month, the Sung State made peace with the Ch'u State.

" In B.C. 587 King Chuang of Ch'u was besieging the capital of Sung. He had only rations for seven days, and if these were exhausted before he could take the city, he meant to withdraw. He therefore sent his general to climb the ramparts and spy out the condition of the besieged. It chanced that at the same time an officer of the Sung army came forth upon the ramparts, and the two met. 'How is your State getting on?' inquired the general. 'Oh, badly,' replied the officer. 'We are reduced to exchanging children for food, and their bones are chopped up for fuel.' 'That is bad indeed,' said the general; 'I had heard, however, that the besieged, while feeding their horses with bits in their mouths, kept some fat ones for exhibition to strangers. What a spirit is yours!' To this the officer replied, 'I too have heard that the superior man, seeing another's misfortune, is filled with pity, while the ignoble man is filled with joy. And in you I recognise the superior man; so I have told you our story.' 'Be of good cheer,' said the general. 'We too have only seven days' rations, and if we do not conquer you in that time, we shall withdraw.' He then bowed, and retired to report to his master. The latter said, 'We must now capture the city before we withdraw.' 'Not so,' replied the general; 'I told the officer we had only rations for seven days.' King Chuang was greatly enraged at this; but the general said, 'If a small State like Sung has officers who speak the truth, should not the State of Ch'u have such men also?' The king still wished to remain, but the general threatened to leave him, and thus peace was brought about between the two States."

CHAPTER III

THE FOUR BOOKS—MENCIUS

No Chinaman thinks of entering upon a study of the Five Classics until he has mastered and committed to memory a shorter and simpler course known as The Four Books.

The first of these, as generally arranged for students, is the *Lun Yü* or Analects, a work in twenty short chapters or books, retailing the views of Confucius on a variety of subjects, and expressed so far as possible in the very words of the Master. It tells us nearly all we really know about the Sage, and may possibly have been put together within a hundred years of his death. From its pages we seem to gather some idea, a mere *silhouette* perhaps, of the great moralist whose mission on earth was to teach duty towards one's neighbour to his fellow-men, and who formulated the Golden Rule : "What you would not others should do unto you, do not unto them!"

It has been urged by many, who should know better, that the negative form of this maxim is unfit to rank with the positive form as given to us by Christ. But of course the two are logically identical, as may be shown by the simple insertion of the word "abstain;" that is, you would not that others should abstain from certain actions in regard to yourself, which practically conveys the positive injunction.

When a disciple asked Confucius to explain charity of heart, he replied simply, " Love one another." When, however, he was asked concerning the principle that good should be returned for evil, as already enunciated by Lao Tzŭ (see ch. iv.), he replied, "What then will you return for good ? No: return good for good; for evil, justice."

He was never tired of emphasising the beauty and necessity of truth : "A man without truthfulness ! I know not how that can be."

" Let loyalty and truth be paramount with you."

" In mourning, it is better to be sincere than punctilious."

" Man is born to be upright. If he be not so, and yet live, he is lucky to have escaped."

" Riches and honours are what men desire; yet except in accordance with right these may not be enjoyed."

Confucius undoubtedly believed in a Power, unseen and eternal, whom he vaguely addressed as Heaven : "He who has offended against Heaven has none to whom he can pray." "I do not murmur against Heaven," and so on. His greatest commentator, however, Chu Hsi, has explained that by "Heaven" is meant "Abstract Right," and that interpretation is accepted by Confucianists at the present day. At the same time, Confucius strongly objected to discuss the supernatural, and suggested that our duties are towards the living rather than towards the dead.

He laid the greatest stress upon filial piety, and taught that man is absolutely pure at birth, and afterwards becomes depraved only because of his environment.

Chapter x. of the *Lun Yü* gives some singular details of the every-day life and habits of the Sage, calculated to provoke a smile among those with whom reverence for Confucius has not been a first principle from the cradle upwards, but received with loving gravity by the Chinese people at large. The following are extracts (Legge's translation) from this famous chapter :—

"Confucius, in his village, looked simple and sincere, and as if he were not able to speak. When he was in the prince's ancestral temple or in the court, he spoke minutely on every point, but cautiously.

"When he entered the palace gate, he seemed to bend his body, as if it were not sufficient to admit him.

"He ascended the daïs, holding up his robe with both his hands and his body bent; holding in his breath also, as if he dared not breathe.

"When he was carrying the sceptre of his prince, he seemed to bend his body as if he were not able to bear its weight.

"He did not use a deep purple or a puce colour in the ornaments of his dress. Even in his undress he did not wear anything of a red or reddish colour.

"He required his sleeping dress to be half as long again as his body.

"He did not eat rice which had been injured by heat or damp and turned sour, nor fish or flesh which was gone. He did not eat what was discoloured, or what was of a bad flavour, nor anything which was not in season. He did not eat meat which was not cut properly, nor what was served without its proper sauce.

"He was never without ginger when he ate. He did not eat much.

"When eating, he did not converse. When in bed, he did not speak.

"Although his food might be coarse rice and vegetable

soup, he would offer a little of it in sacrifice with a grave respectful air.

"If his mat was not straight, he did not sit on it.

"The stable being burned down when he was at Court, on his return he said, 'Has any man been hurt?' He did not ask about the horses.

"When a friend sent him a present, though it might be a carriage and horses, he did not bow. The only present for which he bowed was that of the flesh of sacrifice.

"In bed, he did not lie like a corpse. At home, he did not put on any formal deportment.

"When he saw any one in a mourning dress, though it might be an acquaintance, he would change countenance; when he saw any one wearing the cap of full dress, or a blind person, though he might be in his undress, he would salute them in a ceremonious manner.

"When he was at an entertainment where there was an abundance of provisions set before him, he would change countenance and rise up. On a sudden clap of thunder or a violent wind, he would change countenance."

Next in educational order follows the work briefly known as MENCIUS. This consists of seven books recording the sayings and doings of a man to whose genius and devotion may be traced the final triumph of Confucianism. Born in B.C. 372, a little over a hundred years after the death of the Master, Mencius was brought up under the care of his widowed mother, whose name is a household word even at the present day. As a child he lived with her at first near a cemetery, the result being that he began to reproduce in play the solemn scenes which were constantly enacted before his eyes. His mother accordingly removed to another house near the market-place, and before long the little boy forgot all about funerals and played at buying and selling goods. Once more his mother disapproved, and once more she changed her dwelling; this time to a house near a college, where he soon began to imitate the ceremonial observances in which the students were instructed, to the great joy and satisfaction of his mother.

Later on he studied under K'ung Chi, the grandson of Confucius; and after having attained to a perfect apprehension of the roms or Way of Confucius, became, at the age of about forty-five, Minister under Prince Hsüan of the Ch'i State. But the latter would not carry out his principles, and Mencius threw up his post. Thence he wandered away to several States, advising their rulers to the best of his ability, but making no very prolonged stay. He then visited Prince Hui of the Liang State, and abode there until the monarch's death in B.C. 319. After that event he returned to the State of Ch'i and resumed his old position. In B.C. 311 he once more felt himself constrained to resign office, and retired finally into private life, occupying himself during the remainder of his days in teaching and in preparing the philosophical record which now passes under his name. He lived at a time when the feudal princes were squabbling over the rival systems of federation and imperialism, and he vainly tried to put into practice at an epoch of blood and iron the gentle virtues of the Golden Age. His criterion was that of Confucius, but his teachings were on a lower plane, dealing rather with man's well-being from the point of view of political economy. He was therefore justly named by Chao Ch'i the Second Holy One or Prophet, a title under which he is still known. He was an uncompromising defender of the doctrines of Confucius, and he is considered to have effectually "snuffed out" the heterodox schools of Yang Chu and Mo Ti.

The following is a specimen of the logomachy of the day, in which Mencius is supposed to have excelled. The subject is a favourite one—human nature :—

"Kao Tzŭ said, 'Human nature may be compared with a block of wood ; duty towards one's neighbour, with a wooden bowl. To develop charity and duty towards one's neighbour out of human nature is like making a bowl out of a block of wood.'

"To this Mencius replied, 'Can you, without interfering with the natural constitution of the wood, make out of it a bowl ? Surely you must do violence to that constitution in the process of making your bowl. And by parity of reasoning you would do violence to human nature in the process of developing charity and duty towards one's neighbour. From which it follows that all men would come to regard these rather as evils than otherwise.'

"Kao Tzŭ said, 'Human nature is like rushing water, which flows east or west according as an outlet is made for it. For human nature makes indifferently for good or for evil, precisely as water makes indifferently for the east or for the west.'

"Mencius replied, 'Water will indeed flow indifferently towards the east or west ; but will it flow indifferently up or down ? It will not ; and the tendency of human nature towards good is like the tendency of water to flow down. Every man has this bias towards good, just as all water flows naturally downwards. By splashing water, you may indeed cause it to fly over your head ; and by turning its course you may keep it for use on the hillside; but you would hardly speak of such results as the nature of water. They are the results, of course, of a *force majeure*. And so it is when the nature of man is diverted towards evil.'

"Kao Tzŭ said, 'That which comes with life is nature.'

"Mencius replied, 'Do you mean that there is such a thing as nature in the abstract, just as there is whiteness in the abstract?'

"'I do,' answered Kao Tzŭ.

"'Just, for instance,' continued Mencius, 'as the whiteness of a feather is the same as the whiteness of snow, or the whiteness of snow as the whiteness of jade?'

"'I do,' answered Kao Tzŭ again.

"'In that case,' retorted Mencius, 'the nature of a dog is the same as that of an ox, and the nature of an ox the same as that of a man.'

"Kao Tzŭ said, 'Eating and reproduction of the species are natural instincts. Charity is subjective and innate; duty towards one's neighbour is objective and acquired. For instance, there is a man who is my senior, and I defer to him as such. Not because any abstract principle of seniority exists subjectively in me, but in the same way that if I see an albino, I recognise him as a white man because he is so objectively to me. Consequently, I say that duty towards one's neighbour is objective or acquired.'

"Mencius replied, 'The cases are not analogous. The whiteness of a white horse is undoubtedly the same as the whiteness of a white man; but the seniority of a horse is not the same as the seniority of a man. Does our duty to our senior begin and end with the fact of his seniority? Or does it not rather consist in the necessity of deferring to him as such?'

"Kao Tzŭ said, 'I love my own brother, but I do not love another man's brother. The distinction arises from within myself; therefore I call it subjective or innate. But I defer to a stranger who is my senior, just as I defer to a senior among my own people. The distinction comes to me from without; therefore I call it objective or acquired."

"Mencius retorted, 'We enjoy food cooked by strangers just as much as food cooked by our own people. Yet extension of your principle lands us in the conclusion that our appreciation of cooked food is also objective and acquired.'"

The following is a well-known colloquy between Mencius and a sophist of the day who tried to entangle the former in his talk :—

The sophist inquired, saying, "'Is it a rule of social etiquette that when men and women pass things from one to another they shall not allow their hands to touch?'

"'That is the rule,' replied Mencius.

"'Now suppose,' continued the sophist, 'that a man's sister-in-law were drowning, could he take hold of her hand and save her?'

"'Any one who did not do so,' said Mencius, 'would have the heart of a wolf. That men and women when passing things from one to another may not let their hands touch is a rule for general application. To save a drowning sister-in-law by taking hold of her hand is altogether an exceptional case.'"

The works of Mencius abound, like the Confucian Analects, in sententious utterances. The following examples illustrate his general bias in politics :—"The people are of the highest importance ; the gods come second ; the sovereign is of lesser weight."

"Chieh and Chou lost the empire because they lost the people, which means that they lost the confidence of the people. The way to gain the people is to gain their confidence, and the way to do that is to provide them with what they like and not with what they loathe."

This is how Mencius snuffed out the two heterodox philosophers mentioned above :—

"The systems of Yang Chu and Mo Ti fill the whole empire. If a man is not a disciple of the former, he is a disciple of the latter. But Yang Chu's egoism excludes the claim of a sovereign, while Mo Ti's universal altruism leaves out the claim of a father. And he who recognises the claim of neither sovereign nor father is a brute beast."

Yang Chu seems to have carried his egoism so far that even to benefit the whole world he would not have parted with a single hair from his body.

"The men of old knew that with life they had come but for a while, and that with death they would shortly depart again. Therefore they followed the desires of their own hearts, and did not deny themselves pleasures to which they felt naturally inclined. Fame tempted them not ; but led by their instincts alone, they took such enjoyments as lay in their path, not seeking for a name beyond the grave. They were thus out of the reach of censure ; while as for precedence among men, or length or shortness of life, these gave them no concern whatever."

Mo Ti, on the other hand, showed that under the altruistic system all calamities which men bring upon one another would altogether disappear, and that the peace and happiness of the Golden Age would be renewed.

In the *Ta Hsüeh*, or Great Learning, which forms Sect. xxxix. of the Book of Rites, and really means learning for adults, we have a short politico-ethical treatise, the authorship of which is unknown, but is usually attributed partly to Confucius, and partly to TSÊNG TS'AN, one of the most famous of his disciples. In the former portion there occurs the following well-known climax :—

"The men of old, in their desire to manifest great virtue throughout the empire, began with good government in the various States. To achieve this, it was necessary first to order aright their own families, which in turn was preceded by cultivation of their own selves, and that again by rectification of the heart, following upon sincerity of purpose which comes from extension of knowledge, this last being derived from due investigation of objective existences."

One more short treatise, known as the *Chung Yung*, which forms Ch. xxviii. of the Book of Rites, brings us to the end of the Four Books. Its title has been translated in various ways.[1] Julien rendered the term by "L'Invariable Milieu," Legge by "The Doctrine of the Mean." Its authorship is assigned to K'UNG CHI, grand-

---

[1] *Chung* means "middle," and *Yung* means "course," the former being defined by the Chinese as "that which is without deflection or bias," the latter as "that which never varies in its direction."

son of Confucius. He seems to have done little more than enlarge upon certain general principles of his grandfather in relation to the nature of man and right conduct upon earth. He seizes the occasion to pronounce an impassioned eulogium upon Confucius, concluding with the following words :—

"Therefore his fame overflows the Middle Kingdom, and reaches the barbarians of north and south. Wherever ships and waggons can go, or the strength of man penetrate ; wherever there is heaven above and earth below ; wherever the sun and moon shed their light, or frosts and dews fall,—all who have blood and breath honour and love him. Wherefore it may be said that he is the peer of God."

CHAPTER IV

MISCELLANEOUS WRITERS

NAMES of the authors who belong to this period, B.C. 600 to B.C. 200, and of the works on a variety of subjects attributed to them, would fill a long list. Many of the latter have disappeared, and others are gross forgeries, chiefly of the first and second centuries of our era, an epoch which, curiously enough, is remarkable for a similar wave of forgery on the other side of the world. As to the authors, it will be seen later on that the Chinese even went so far as to create some of these for antiquity and then write up treatises to match.

There was SUN TZŬ of the 6th century B.C. He is said to have written the *Ping Fa*, or Art of War, in thirteen sections, whereby hangs a strange tale. When he was discoursing one day with Prince Ho-lu of the Wu State, the latter said, " I have read your book and want to know if you could apply its principles to women." Sun Tzŭ replied in the affirmative, whereupon the Prince took 180 girls out of his harem and bade Sun Tzŭ deal with them as with troops. Accordingly he divided them into two companies, and at the head of each placed a favourite concubine of the Prince. But when the drums sounded for drill to begin, all the girls burst out laughing. Thereupon Sun Tzŭ, without a moment's delay, caused the two concubines in command to be beheaded. This at once restored order, and ultimately the corps was raised to a state of great efficiency.

The following is an extract from the Art of War :—

" If soldiers are not carefully chosen and well drilled to obey, their movements will be irregular. They will not act in concert. They will miss success for want of unanimity. Their retreat will be disorderly, one half fighting while the other is running away. They will not respond to the call of the gong and drum. One hundred such as these will not hold their own against ten well-drilled men.

" If their arms are not good, the soldiers might as well have none. If the cuirass is not stout and close set, the breast might as well be bare. Bows that will not carry are no more use at long distances than swords and spears. Bad marksmen might as well have no arrows. Even good marksmen, unless able to make their arrows pierce, might as well shoot with headless shafts. These are the oversights of incompetent generals. Five such soldiers are no match for one."

It is notwithstanding very doubtful if we have any genuine remains of either Sun Tzŭ, or of Kuan Tzŭ, Wu Tzŭ, Wên Tzŭ, and several other early writers on war, political philosophy, and cognate subjects. The same remark applies equally to Chinese medical literature, the bulk of which is enormous, some of it nominally dating back to legendary times, but always failing to stand the application of the simplest test.

The *Erh Ya*, or Nearing the Standard, is a work which has often been assigned to the 12th century B.C. It is a guide to the correct use of many miscellaneous terms, including names of animals, birds, plants, etc., to which are added numerous illustrations. It was first edited with commentary by Kuo P'o, of whom we shall read later on, and some Chinese critics would have us believe that the illustrations we now possess were then already in existence. But the whole question is involved in mystery. The following will give an idea of the text :—

"For metal we say *lou* (to chase) ; for wood *k'o* (to carve) ; for bone *ch'ieh* (to cut)," etc., etc.

There are some interesting remains of a writer named T'AN KUNG, who flourished in the 4th and 3rd centuries B.C., and whose work has been included in the Book of Rites. The three following extracts will give an idea of his scope :—

1. "One day Yu-tzŭ and Tzŭ-yu saw a child weeping for the loss of its parents. Thereupon the former observed, 'I never could understand why mourners should necessarily jump about to show their grief, and would long ago have got rid of the custom. Now here you have an honest expression of feeling, and that is all there should ever be.'

"'My friend,' replied Tzŭ-yu, 'the mourning ceremonial, with all its material accompaniments, is at once a check upon undue emotion and a guarantee against any lack of proper respect. Simply to give vent to the feelings is the way of barbarians. That is not our way.

"'Consider. A man who is pleased will show it in his face. He will sing. He will get excited. He will dance. So, too, a man who is vexed will look sad. He will sigh. He will beat his breast. He will jump about. The due regulation of these emotions is the function of a set ceremonial.

"'Further. A man dies and becomes an object of loathing. A dead body is shunned. Therefore, a shroud is prepared, and other paraphernalia of burial, in order that the survivors may cease to loathe. At death there is a sacrifice of wine and meat; when the funeral cortège is about to start, there is another; and after burial there is yet another. Yet no one ever saw the spirit of the departed come to taste of the food.

"'These have been our customs from remote antiquity. They have not been discarded, because, in consequence, men no more shun the dead. What you may censure in those who perform the ceremonial is no blemish in the ceremonial itself.'"

2. "When Tzŭ-chü died, his wife and secretary took counsel together as to who should be interred with him. All was settled before the arrival of his brother, Tzŭ-hêng; and then they informed him, saying, 'The deceased requires some one to attend upon him in the nether world. We must ask you to go down with his body into the grave.' 'Burial of the living with the dead,' replied Tzŭ-hêng, 'is not in accordance with established rites. Still, as you say some one is wanted to attend upon the deceased, who better fitted than his wife and secretary? If this contingency can be avoided altogether, I am willing; if not, then the duty will devolve upon you two.' From that time forth the custom fell into desuetude."

3. "When Confucius was crossing the T'ai mountain, he overheard a woman weeping and wailing beside a grave. He thereupon sent one of his disciples to ask what was the matter; and the latter addressed the

woman, saying, 'Some great sorrow must have come upon you that you give way to grief like this?' 'Indeed it is so,' replied she. 'My father-in-law was killed here by a tiger; after that, my husband; and now my son has perished by the same death.' 'But why, then,' inquired Confucius, 'do you not go away?' 'The government is not harsh,' answered the woman. 'There!' cried the Master, turning to his disciples; 'remember that. Bad government is worse than a tiger.'"

The philosopher Hsün Tzŭ of the 3rd century B.C. is widely known for his heterodox views on the nature of man, being directly opposed to the Confucian doctrine so warmly advocated by Mencius. The following passage, which hardly carries conviction, contains the gist of his argument :—

"By nature, man is evil. If a man is good, that is an artificial result. For his condition being what it is, he is influenced first of all by a desire for gain. Hence he strives to get all he can without consideration for his neighbour. Secondly, he is liable to envy and hate. Hence he seeks the ruin of others, and loyalty and truth are set aside. Thirdly, he is a slave to his animal passions. Hence he commits excesses, and wanders from the path of duty and right.

"Thus, conformity with man's natural disposition leads to all kinds of violence, disorder, and ultimate barbarism. Only under the restraint of law and of lofty moral influences does man eventually become fit to be a member of regularly organised society.

"From these premisses it seems quite clear that by nature man is evil; and that if a man is good, that is an artificial result."

The *Hsiao Ching*, or Classic of Filial Piety, is assigned partly to Confucius and partly to TSÊNG TS'AN, though it more probably belongs to a very much later date. Considering that filial piety is admittedly the keystone of Chinese civilisation, it is disappointing to find nothing more on the subject than a poor pamphlet of commonplace and ill-strung sentences, which gives the impression of having been written to fill a void. One short extract will suffice:—

"The Master said, 'There are three thousand offences against which the five punishments are directed, and there is not one of them greater than being unfilial.

"'When constraint is put upon a ruler, that is the disowning of his superiority; when the authority of the sages is disallowed, that is the disowning of all law; when filial piety is put aside, that is the disowning of the principle of affection. These three things pave the way to anarchy.'"

The *Chia Yü*, or Family Sayings of Confucius, is a work with a fascinating title, which has been ascribed by some to the immediate disciples of Confucius, but which, as it now exists, is usually thought by native scholars to have been composed by Wang Su, a learned official who died A.D. 256. There appears to have been an older work under this same title, but how far the later work is indebted to it, or based upon it, seems likely to remain unknown.

Another discredited work is the *Lü Shih Ch'un Ch'iu*, or Spring and Autumn of LÜ PU-WEI, who died B.C. 235 and was the putative sire of the First Emperor (see ch. vii.). It contains a great deal about the early history of China, some of which is no doubt based upon fact.

Lastly, among spurious books may be mentioned the

Mu T'ien Tzŭ Chuan, an account of a mythical journey by a sovereign of the Chou dynasty, supposed to have been taken about 1000 B.C. The sovereign is unfortunately spoken of by his posthumous title, and the work was evidently written up in the 3rd century A.D. to suit a statement found in Lieh Tzŭ (see chapter vi.) to the effect that the ruler in question did make some such journey to the West.

CHAPTER V

POETRY—INSCRIPTIONS

THE poetry which is representative of the period between the death of Confucius and the 2nd century B.C. is a thing apart. There is nothing like it in the whole range of Chinese literature. It illumines many a native pronouncement on the poetic art, the drift of which would otherwise remain obscure. For poetry has been defined by the Chinese as "emotion expressed in words," a definition perhaps not more inadequate than Wordsworth's "impassioned expression." "Poetry," they say, "knows no law." And again, "The men of old reckoned it the highest excellence in poetry that the meaning should lie beyond the words, and that the reader should have to think it out." Of these three canons only the last can be said to have survived to the present day. But in the fourth century B.C., Ch'ü Yüan and his school indulged in wild irregular metres which consorted well with their wild irregular thoughts. Their poetry was prose run mad. It was allusive and allegorical to a high degree, and now, but for the commentary, much of it would be quite unintelligible.

CH'Ü YÜAN is the type of a loyal Minister. He enjoyed the full confidence of his Prince until at length the jealousies and intrigues of rivals sapped his position in the State. Then it was that he composed the *Li Sao*, or Falling into Trouble, the first section of which extends to nearly 400 lines. Beginning from the birth of the writer, it describes his cultivation of virtue and his earnest endeavour to translate precept into practice. Discouraged by failure, he visits the grave of the Emperor Shun (chapter ii.), and gives himself up to prayer, until at length a phœnix-car and dragons appear, and carry him in search of his ideal away beyond the domain of mortality,—the chariot of the Sun moving slowly to light him longer on the way, the Moon leading and the Winds bringing up the rear,—up to the very palace of God. Unable to gain admission here, he seeks out a famous magician, who counsels him to stand firm and to continue his search; whereupon, surrounded by gorgeous clouds and dazzling rainbows, and amid the music of tinkling ornaments attached to his car, he starts from the Milky Way, and passing the Western Pole, reaches the sources of the Yellow River. Before long he is once again in sight of his native land, but without having discovered the object of his search.

Overwhelmed by further disappointments, and sinking still more deeply into disfavour, so that he cared no longer to live, he went forth to the banks of the Mi-lo river. There he met a fisherman who accosted him, saying, "Are you not his Excellency the Minister? What has brought you to this pass?" "The world," replied Ch'ü Yüan, "is foul, and I alone am clean. There they are all drunk, while I alone am sober. So I am dismissed." "Ah!" said the fisherman, "the true sage does not quarrel with his environment, but adapts himself to it. If, as you say, the world is foul, why not leap into the tide and make it clean? If all men are drunk, why not drink with them and teach them to avoid excess?" After some further colloquy, the fisherman rowed away; and Ch'ü Yüan, clasping a large stone in his arms, plunged into the river and was seen no more. This took place on the fifth of the fifth moon; and ever afterwards the people of Ch'u commemorated the day by an annual festival, when offerings of rice in bamboo tubes were cast into the river as a sacrifice to the spirit of their great hero. Such is the origin of the modern Dragon-Boat Festival, which is supposed to be a search for the body of Ch'ü Yüan.

A good specimen of his style will be found in the following short poem, entitled "The Genius of the Mountain." It is one of "nine songs" which, together with a number of other pieces in a similar strain, have been classed under the general heading, *Li Sao*, as above.

"Methinks there is a Genius of the hills, clad in wistaria, girdled with ivy, with smiling lips, of witching mien, riding on the red pard, wild cats galloping in the rear, reclining in a chariot, with banners of cassia, cloaked with the orchid, girt with azalea, culling the perfume of sweet flowers to leave behind a memory in the heart. But dark is the grove wherein I dwell. No light of day reaches it ever. The path thither is dangerous and difficult to climb. Alone I stand on the hill-top, while the clouds float beneath my feet, and all around is wrapped in gloom.

"Gently blows the east wind; softly falls the rain. In my joy I become oblivious of home; for who in my decline would honour me now?

"I pluck the larkspur on the hillside, amid the chaos of rock and tangled vine. I hate him who has made me an outcast, who has now no leisure to think of me.

"I drink from the rocky spring. I shade myself

beneath the spreading pine. Even though he were to recall me to him, I could not fall to the level of the world.

"Now booms the thunder through the drizzling rain. The gibbons howl around me all the long night. The gale rushes fitfully through the whispering trees. And I am thinking of my Prince, but in vain; for I cannot lay my grief."

Another leading poet of the day was SUNG YÜ, of whom we know little beyond the fact that he was nephew of Ch'ü Yüan, and like his uncle both a statesman and a poet. The following extract exhibits him in a mood not far removed from the lamentations of the *Li Sao* :—

> "*Among birds the phœnix, among fishes the leviathan*
>   *holds the chiefest place;*
> *Cleaving the crimson clouds*
>   *the phœnix soars apace,*
> *With only the blue sky above,*
>   *far into the realms of space;*
> *But the grandeur of heaven and earth*
>   *is as naught to the hedge-sparrow race.*
>
> *And the leviathan rises in one ocean*
>   *to go to rest in a second,*
> *While the depth of a puddle by a humble minnow*
>   *as the depth of the sea is reckoned.*
>
> *And just as with birds and with fishes,*
>   *so too it is with man;*
> *Here soars a phœnix,*
>   *there swims a leviathan . . .*
> *Behold the philosopher, full of nervous thought,*
>   *with a flame that never grows dim,*
> *Dwelling complacently alone;*
>   *say, what can the vulgar herd know of him?*"

As has been stated above, the poems of this school are irregular in metre ; in fact, they are only approximately metrical. The poet never ends his line in deference to a prescribed number of feet, but lengthens or shortens to suit the exigency of his thought. Similarly, he may rhyme or he may not. The reader, however, is never conscious of any want of art, carried away as he is by flow of language and rapid succession of poetical imagery.

Several other poets, such as Chia I and Tung-fang So, who cultivated this particular vein, but on a somewhat lower plane, belong to the second century B.C., thus overlapping a period which must be regarded as heralding the birth of a new style rather than occupied with the passing of the old.

It may here be mentioned that many short pieces of doubtful age and authorship—some few unquestionably old—have been rescued by Chinese scholars from various sources, and formed into convenient collections. Of such is a verse known as " Yao's Advice," Yao being the legendary monarch mentioned in chapter ii., who is associated with Shun in China's Golden Age :—

> "*With trembling heart and cautious steps*
> *Walk daily in fear of God* . . .
> *Though you never trip over a mountain,*
> *You may often trip over a clod.*"

There is also the husbandman's song, which enlarges upon the national happiness of those halcyon days :—

> " *Work, work ;—from the rising sun*
> *Till sunset comes and the day is done*
> *I plough the sod*
> *And harrow the clod,*
> *And meat and drink both come to me,*
> *So what care I for the powers that be ?*"

It seems to have been customary in early days to attach inscriptions, poetical and otherwise, to all sorts of articles for daily use. On the bath-tub of T'ang, founder of the Shang dynasty in B.C. 1766, there was said to have been written these words :—" If any one on any one day can make a new man of himself, let him do so every day." Similarly, an old metal mirror bore as its legend, " Man combs his hair every morning : why not his heart ? " And the following lines are said to be taken from an ancient wash-basin :—

> " *Oh, rather than sink in the world's foul tide*
> *I would sink in the bottomless main ;*
> *For he who sinks in the world's foul tide*
> *In noisome depths shall for ever abide,*
> *But he who sinks in the bottomless main*
> *May hope to float to the surface again.*"

In this class of verse, too, the metre is often irregular and the rhyme a mere jingle, according to the canons of the stricter prosody which came into existence later on.

CHAPTER VI

TAOISM—THE "TAO-TÊ-CHING"

THE reader is now asked to begin once more at the sixth
century B.C. So far we have dealt almost exclusively with
what may be called orthodox literature, that is to say, of
or belonging to or based upon the Confucian Canon. It
seemed advisable to get that well off our hands before
entering upon another branch, scarcely indeed as important, but much more difficult to handle. This branch
consists of the literature of Taoism, or that which has
gathered around what is known as the Tao or Way of
LAO TZŬ, growing and flourishing alongside of, though
in direct antagonism to, that which is founded upon the
criteria and doctrines of Confucius. Unfortunately it is
quite impossible to explain at the outset in what this
Tao actually consists. According to Lao Tzŭ himself,
"Those who know do not tell; those who tell do not
know." It is hoped, however, that by the time the end
of this chapter is reached, some glimmering of the meaning of Tao may have reached the minds of those who
have been patient enough to follow the argument.

Lao Tzŭ was born, according to the weight of evidence,
in the year B.C. 604. Omitting all reference to the supernatural phenomena which attended his birth and early
years, it only remains to say that we really know next to
nothing about him. There is a short biography of Lao

Tzŭ to be found in the history of Ssŭ-ma Ch'ien, to be dealt with in Book II., chapter iii., but internal evidence points to embroidery laid on by other hands. Just as it was deemed necessary by pious enthusiasts to interpolate in the work of Josephus a passage referring to Christ, so it would appear that the original note by Ssŭ-ma Ch'ien has been carefully touched up to suit the requirements of an unauthenticated meeting between Lao Tzŭ and Confucius, which has been inserted very much *à propos de bottes;* the more so, as Confucius is made to visit Lao Tzŭ with a view to information on Rites, a subject which Lao Tzŭ held in very low esteem. This biography ends with the following extraordinary episode :—

" Lao Tzŭ abode for a long time in Chou, but when he saw that the State showed signs of decay, he left. On reaching the frontier, the Warden, named Yin Hsi, said to him, 'So you are going into retirement. I beg you to write a book for me.' Thereupon Lao Tzŭ wrote a book, in two parts, on Tao and Tê,[1] extending to over 5000 words. He then went away, and no one knows where he died."

It is clear from Ssŭ-ma Ch'ien's account that he himself had never seen the book, though a dwindling minority still believe that we possess that book in the well-known *Tao-Tê-Ching*.

It must now be stated that throughout what are generally believed to be the writings of Confucius the name of Lao Tzŭ is never once mentioned.[2] It is not mentioned by Tso of the famous commentary, nor by the editors of the Confucian Analects, nor by Tsêng Ts'an,

---

[1] Tê is the exemplification of Tao.

[2] The name Lao Tan occurs in four passages in the Book of Rites, but we are expressly told that by it is not meant the philosopher Lao Tzŭ.

nor by Mencius. Chuang Tzŭ, who devoted all his energies to the exposition and enforcement of the teaching of Lao Tzŭ, never once drops even a hint that his Master had written a book. In his work will now be found an account of the meeting of Confucius and Lao Tzŭ, but it has long since been laughed out of court as a pious fraud by every competent Chinese critic. Chu Hsi, Shên Jo-shui, and many others, declare emphatically against the genuineness of the *Tao-Tê-Ching;* and scant allusion would indeed have been made to it here, were it not for the attention paid to it by several more or less eminent foreign students of the language. It is interesting as a collection of many genuine utterances of Lao Tzŭ, sandwiched however between thick wads of padding from which little meaning can be extracted except by enthusiasts who curiously enough disagree absolutely among themselves. A few examples from the real Lao Tzŭ will now be given:—

"The Way (Tao) which can be walked upon is not the eternal Way."

"Follow diligently the Way in your own heart, but make no display of it to the world."

"By many words wit is exhausted; it is better to preserve a mean."

"To the good I would be good. To the not-good I would also be good, in order to make them good."

"Recompense injury with kindness."

"Put yourself behind, and you shall be put in front."

"Abandon wisdom and discard knowledge, and the people will be benefited an hundredfold."

These last maxims are supposed to illustrate Lao Tzŭ's favourite doctrine of doing nothing, or, as it has been termed, Inaction, a doctrine inseparably associated with his name, and one which has ever exerted much fascination over the more imaginative of his countrymen. It was openly enunciated as follows :—

"Do nothing, and all things will be done."

"I do nothing, and the people become good of their own accord."

To turn to the padding, as rendered by the late Drs. Chalmers and Legge, we may take a paragraph which now passes as chapter vi. :—

CHALMERS :—" The Spirit (like perennial spring) of the valley never dies. This (Spirit) I call the abyss-mother. The passage of the abyss-mother I call the root of heaven and earth. Ceaselessly it seems to endure, and it is employed without effort."

LEGGE :—" *The valley spirit dies not, aye the same;*
The female mystery thus do we name.
Its gate, from which at first they issued forth,
Is called the root from which grew heaven and earth.
Long and unbroken does its power remain,
Used gently, and without the touch of pain."

One more example from Chalmers' translation will perhaps seal the fate of this book with readers who claim at least a minimum of sense from an old-world classic.

" *Where water abides, it is good for adaptability.*
In its heart, it is good for depth.
In giving, it is good for benevolence.
In speaking, it is good for fidelity."

That there was such a philosopher as Lao Tzŭ who lived about the time indicated, and whose sayings have come down to us first by tradition and later by written and printed record, cannot possibly be doubted. The great work of Chuang Tzŭ would be sufficient to establish this beyond cavil, while at the same time it forms a handy guide to a nearer appreciation of this elusive Tao.

CHUANG TZǓ was born in the fourth century B.C., and held a petty official post. " He wrote," says the historian Ssǔ-ma Ch'ien, "with a view to asperse the Confucian school and to glorify the mysteries of Lao Tzǔ. . . . His teachings are like an overwhelming flood, which spreads at its own sweet will. Consequently, from rulers and ministers downwards, none could apply them to any definite use."

Here we have the key to the triumph of the Tao of Confucius over the Tao of Lao Tzǔ. The latter was idealistic, the former a practical system for everyday use. And Chuang Tzǔ was unable to persuade the calculating Chinese nation that by doing nothing, all things would be done. But he bequeathed to posterity a work which, by reason of its marvellous literary beauty, has always held a foremost place. It is also a work of much originality of thought. The writer, it is true, appears chiefly as a disciple insisting upon the principles of a Master. But he has contrived to extend the field, and carry his own speculations into regions never dreamt of by Lao Tzǔ.

The whole work of Chuang Tzǔ has not come down to us, neither can all that now passes under his name be regarded as genuine. Alien hands have added, vainly indeed, many passages and several entire chapters. But a sable robe, says the Chinese proverb, cannot be eked out with dogs' tails. Lin Hsi-chung, a brilliant critic of the seventeenth century, to whose edition all students should turn, has shown with unerring touch where the lion left off and the jackals began.

The honour of the first edition really belongs to a volatile spirit of the third century A.D., named Hsiang Hsiu. He was probably the founder, at any rate a member, of a small club of bibulous poets who called themselves the Seven Sages of the Bamboo Grove. Death, however, interrupted his labours before he had finished his work on Chuang Tzŭ, and the manuscript was purloined by Kuo Hsiang, a scholar who died A.D. 312, and with some additions was issued by the latter as his own.

Before attempting to illustrate by extracts the style and scope of Chuang Tzŭ, it will be well to collect from his work a few passages dealing with the attributes of Tao. In his most famous chapter, entitled Autumn Floods, a name by which he himself is sometimes spoken of, Chuang Tzŭ writes as follows:—

"Tao is without beginning, without end." Elsewhere he says, "There is nowhere where it is not." "Tao cannot be heard; heard, it is not Tao. Tao cannot be seen; seen, it is not Tao. Tao cannot be spoken; spoken, it is not Tao. That which imparts form to forms is itself formless; therefore Tao cannot have a name (as form precedes name)."

"Tao is not too small for the greatest, nor too great for the smallest. Thus all things are embosomed therein; wide, indeed, its boundless capacity, unfathomable its depth."

"By no thoughts, by no cogitations, Tao may be known. By resting in nothing, by according in nothing, Tao may be approached. By following nothing, by pursuing nothing, Tao may be attained."

In these and many like passages Lao Tzŭ would have been in full sympathy with his disciple. So far as it is possible to deduce anything definite from the scanty traditions of the teachings of Lao Tzŭ, we seem to obtain this, that man should remain impassive under the operation of an eternal, omnipresent law (Tao), and that thus he will become in perfect harmony with his environment, and that if he is in harmony with his environment, he will thereby attain to a vague condition of general immunity. Beyond this the teachings of Lao Tzŭ would not carry us. Chuang Tzŭ, however, from simple problems, such as a drunken man falling out of a cart and not injuring himself—a common superstition among sailors—because he is unconscious and therefore in harmony with his environment, slides easily into an advanced mysticism. In his marvellous chapter on The Identity of Contraries, he maintains that from the standpoint of Tao all things are One. Positive and negative, this and that, here and there, somewhere and nowhere, right and wrong, vertical and horizontal, subjective and objective, become indistinct, as water is in water. "When subjective and objective are both without their correlates, that is the very axis of Tao. And when that axis passes through the centre at which all Infinities converge, positive and negative alike blend into an infinite One." This localisation in a Centre, and this infinite absolute represented by One, were too concrete even for Chuang Tzŭ. The One became God, and the Centre, assigned by later Taoist writers to the pole-star (see Book IV. ch. i.), became the source of all life and the haven to which such life returned after its transitory stay on earth. By ignoring the distinctions of contraries "we are embraced in the obliterating unity of God. Take no heed of time, nor of right and wrong; but passing into the realm of the Infinite, make your final rest therein."

That the idea of an indefinite future state was familiar to the mind of Chuang Tzŭ may be gathered from many passages such as the following :—

"How then do I know but that the dead repent of having previously clung to life ?

"Those who dream of the banquet, wake to lamentation and sorrow. Those who dream of lamentation and sorrow, wake to join the hunt. While they dream, they do not know that they dream. Some will even interpret the very dream they are dreaming; and only when they awake do they know it was a dream. By and by comes the Great Awakening, and then we find out that this life is really a great dream. Fools think they are awake now, and flatter themselves they know if they are really princes or peasants. Confucius and you are both dreams; and I who say you are dreams, —I am but a dream myself."

The chapter closes with a paragraph which has gained for its writer an additional epithet, Butterfly Chuang :—

"Once upon a time, I, Chuang Tzŭ, dreamt I was a butterfly, fluttering hither and thither, to all intents and purposes a butterfly. I was conscious only of following my fancies as a butterfly, and was unconscious of my individuality as a man. Suddenly, I awaked, and there I lay, myself again. Now I do not know whether I was then a man dreaming I was a butterfly, or whether I am now a butterfly dreaming I am a man."

Chuang Tzŭ is fond of paradox. He delights in dwelling on the usefulness of useless things. He shows that ill-grown or inferior trees are allowed to stand, that diseased pigs are not killed for sacrifice, and that a hunchback can not only make a good living by washing, for which a bent body is no drawback, but escapes the dreaded press-gang in time of war.

With a few illustrative extracts we must now take leave of Chuang Tzǔ, a writer who, although heterodox in the eyes of a Confucianist, has always been justly esteemed for his pointed wit and charming style.

(1.) "It was the time of autumn floods. Every stream poured into the river, which swelled in its turbid course. The banks receded so far from one another that it was impossible to tell a cow from a horse.

"Then the Spirit of the River laughed for joy that all the beauty of the earth was gathered to himself. Down with the stream he journeyed east, until he reached the ocean. There, looking eastwards and seeing no limit to its waves, his countenance changed. And as he gazed over the expanse, he sighed and said to the Spirit of the Ocean, 'A vulgar proverb says, that he who has heard but part of the truth thinks no one equal to himself. And such a one am I.

"'When formerly I heard people detracting from the learning of Confucius, or underrating the heroism of Po I, I did not believe. But now that I have looked upon your inexhaustibility — alas for me had I not reached your abode, I should have been for ever a laughing-stock to those of comprehensive enlightenment!'

"To which the Spirit of the Ocean replied, 'You cannot speak of ocean to a well-frog,—the creature of a narrower sphere. You cannot speak of ice to a summer-insect,—the creature of a season. You cannot speak of Tao to a pedagogue: his scope is too restricted. But now that you have emerged from your narrow sphere and have seen the great ocean, you know your own insignificance, and I can speak to you of great principles.'"

(2.) "Have you never heard of the frog in the old well ?—The frog said to the turtle of the eastern sea, 'Happy indeed am I ! I hop on to the rail around the well. I rest in the hollow of some broken brick. Swimming, I gather the water under my arms and shut my mouth. I plunge into the mud, burying my feet and toes ; and not one of the cockles, crabs, or tadpoles I see around me are my match. [Fancy pitting the happiness of an old well, ejaculates Chuang Tzŭ, against all the water of Ocean !] Why do you not come, sir, and pay me a visit ?'[1]

"Now the turtle of the eastern sea had not got its left leg down ere its right had already stuck fast, so it shrank back and begged to be excused. It then described the sea, saying, 'A thousand *li* would not measure its breadth, nor a thousand fathoms its depth. In the days of the Great Yü, there were nine years of flood out of ten ; but this did not add to its bulk. In the days of T'ang, there were seven years out of eight of drought ; but this did not narrow its span. Not to be affected by duration of time, not to be affected by volume of water,—such is the great happiness of the eastern sea.'

"At this the well-frog was considerably astonished, and knew not what to say next. And for one whose knowledge does not reach to the positive-negative domain, to attempt to understand me, Chuang Tzŭ, is like a

---

[1] "To the minnow, every cranny and pebble and quality and accident of its little native creek may have become familiar ; but does the minnow understand the ocean tides and periodic currents, the trade-winds. and monsoons, and moon's eclipses . . .?"—*Sartor Resartus*, Natural Supernaturalism.

mosquito trying to carry a mountain, or an ant to swim a river,—they cannot succeed."

(3.) "Chuang Tzŭ was fishing in the P'u when the prince of Ch'u sent two high officials to ask him to take charge of the administration of the Ch'u State.

"Chuang Tzŭ went on fishing, and without turning his head said, 'I have heard that in Ch'u there is a sacred tortoise which has been dead now some three thousand years. And that the prince keeps this tortoise carefully enclosed in a chest on the altar of his ancestral temple. Now would this tortoise rather be dead, and have its remains venerated, or be alive and wagging its tail in the mud?'

"'It would rather be alive,' replied the two officials, 'and wagging its tail in the mud.'

"'Begone!' cried Chuang Tzŭ. 'I too will wag my tail in the mud.'"

(4.) "Chuang Tzŭ one day saw an empty skull, bleached, but still preserving its shape. Striking it with his riding whip, he said, 'Wert thou once some ambitious citizen whose inordinate yearnings brought him to this pass?— some statesman who plunged his country in ruin, and perished in the fray?—some wretch who left behind him a legacy of shame?—some beggar who died in the pangs of hunger and cold? Or didst thou reach this state by the natural course of old age?'

"When he had finished speaking, he took the skull, and placing it under his head as a pillow, went to sleep. In the night, he dreamt that the skull appeared to him, and said, 'You speak well, sir; but all you say has reference to the life of mortals, and to mortal troubles. In death there are none of these. Would you like to hear about death?'

"Chuang Tzŭ having replied in the affirmative, the skull began :—'In death, there is no sovereign above, and no subject below. The workings of the four seasons are unknown. Our existences are bounded only by eternity. The happiness of a king among men cannot exceed that which we enjoy.'

"Chuang Tzŭ, however, was not convinced, and said, 'Were I to prevail upon God to allow your body to be born again, and your bones and flesh to be renewed, so that you could return to your parents, to your wife, and to the friends of your youth—would you be willing ?'

"At this, the skull opened its eyes wide and knitted its brows and said, ' How should I cast aside happiness greater than that of a king, and mingle once again in the toils and troubles of mortality ?'"

(5.) "The Grand Augur, in his ceremonial robes, approached the shambles and thus addressed the pigs :—

"' How can you object to die ? I shall fatten you for three months. I shall discipline myself for ten days and fast for three. I shall strew fine grass, and place you bodily upon a carved sacrificial dish. Does not this satisfy you ?'

"Then speaking from the pigs' point of view, he continued, ' It is better perhaps after all to live on bran and escape the shambles. . . .'

"' But then,' added he, speaking from his own point of view, ' to enjoy honour when alive one would readily die on a war-shield or in the headsman's basket.'

"So he rejected the pigs' point of view and adopted his own point of view. In what sense then was he different from the pigs ?"

(6.) "When Chuang Tzŭ was about to die, his disciples expressed a wish to give him a splendid funeral. But

Chuang Tzŭ said, 'With heaven and earth for my coffin and shell, with the sun, moon, and stars as my burial regalia, and with all creation to escort me to the grave,— are not my funeral paraphernalia ready to hand ?'

"'We fear,' argued the disciples, 'lest the carrion kite should eat the body of our Master'; to which Chuang Tzŭ replied, 'Above ground I shall be food for kites, below I shall be food for mole-crickets and ants. Why rob one to feed the other ?'"

The works of LIEH Tzŭ, in two thin volumes, may be procured at any Chinese book-shop. These volumes profess to contain the writings of a Taoist philosopher who flourished some years before Chuang Tzŭ, and for a long time they received considerable attention at the hands of European students, into whose minds no suspicion of their real character seems to have found its way. Gradually the work came to be looked upon as doubtful, then spurious ; and now it is known to be a forgery, possibly of the first or second century A.D. The scholar—for he certainly was one—who took the trouble to forge this work, was himself the victim of a strange delusion. He thought that Lieh Tzŭ, to whom Chuang Tzŭ devotes a whole chapter, had been a live philosopher of flesh and blood. But he was in reality nothing more than a figment of the imagination, like many others of Chuang Tzŭ's characters, though his name was less broadly allegorical than those of All-in-Extremes, and of Do-Nothing-Say-Nothing, and others. The book attributed to him is curious enough to deserve attention. It is on a lower level of thought and style than the work of Chuang Tzŭ ; still, it contains much traditional matter and many allusions not found elsewhere. To its author we owe the famous, but of course apocryphal, story of Confucius meeting two boys quarrelling about the distance of the sun from the earth. One of them said that at dawn the sun was much larger than at noon, and must consequently be much nearer; but the other retorted that at noon the sun was much hotter, and therefore nearer than at dawn. Confucius confessed himself unable to decide between them, and was jeered at by the boys as an impostor. But of all this work perhaps the most attractive portion is a short story on Dream and Reality :—

"A man of the State of Chêng was one day gathering fuel, when he came across a startled deer, which he pursued and killed. Fearing lest any one should see him, he hastily concealed the carcass in a ditch and covered it with plaintain leaves, rejoicing excessively at his good fortune. By and by, he forgot the place where he had put it, and, thinking he must have been dreaming, he set off towards home, humming over the affair on his way.

"Meanwhile, a man who had overheard his words, acted upon them, and went and got the deer. The latter, when he reached his house, told his wife, saying, 'A woodman dreamt he had got a deer, but he did not know where it was. Now I have got the deer; so his dream was a reality.' 'It is you,' replied his wife, 'who have been dreaming you saw a woodman. Did he get the deer? and is there really such a person? It is you who have got the deer: how, then, can his dream be a reality?' 'It is true,' assented the husband, 'that I have got the deer. It is therefore of little importance whether the woodman dreamt the deer or I dreamt the woodman.'

"Now when the woodman reached his home, he became much annoyed at the loss of the deer ; and in the night he actually dreamt where the deer then was, and who had got it. So next morning he proceeded to the place indicated in his dream,—and there it was. He then took legal steps to recover possession ; and when the case came on, the magistrate delivered the following judgment :—' The plaintiff began with a real deer and an alleged dream. He now comes forward with a real dream and an alleged deer. The defendant really got the deer which plaintiff said he dreamt, and is now trying to keep it ; while, according to his wife, both the woodman and the deer are but the figments of a dream, so that no one got the deer at all. However, here is a deer, which you had better divide between you.'"

HAN FEI TZŬ, who died B.C. 233, has left us fifty-five essays of considerable value, partly for the light they throw upon the connection between the genuine sayings of Lao Tzŭ and the *Tao-Tê-Ching*, and partly for the quaint illustrations he gives of the meaning of the sayings themselves. He was deeply read in law, and obtained favour in the eyes of the First Emperor (see Book II., ch. i.) ; but misrepresentations of rivals brought about his downfall, and he committed suicide in prison. We cannot imagine that he had before him the *Tao-Tê-Ching*. He deals with many of its best sayings, which may well have come originally from an original teacher, such as Lao Tzŭ is supposed to have been, but quite at random and not as if he took them from an orderly work. And what is more, portions of his own commentary have actually slipped into the *Tao-Tê-Ching* as text, showing how this book was pieced together from various sources. Again, he quotes sentences not to be found in the *Tao-Tê-Ching*. He illustrates such a simple saying as "To see small beginnings is clearness of sight," by drawing attention to a man who foresaw, when the tyrant Chou Hsin (who died B.C. 1122) took to ivory chopsticks, that the tide of luxury had set in, to bring licentiousness and cruelty in its train, and to end in downfall and death.

Lao Tzŭ said, "Leave all things to take their natural course." To this Han Fei Tzŭ adds, "A man spent three years in carving a leaf out of ivory, of such elegant and detailed workmanship that it would lie undetected among a heap of real leaves. But Lieh Tzŭ said, 'If God Almighty were to spend three years over every leaf, the trees would be badly off for foliage.'"

Lao Tzŭ said, "The wise man takes time by the forelock." Han Fei Tzŭ adds, "One day the Court physician said to Duke Huan, 'Your Grace is suffering from an affection of the muscular system. Take care, or it may become serious.' 'Oh no,' replied the Duke, 'I have nothing the matter with me;' and when the physician was gone, he observed to his courtiers, 'Doctors dearly love to treat patients who are not ill, and then make capital out of the cure.' Ten days afterwards, the Court physician again remarked, 'Your Grace has an affection of the flesh. Take care, or it may become serious.' The Duke took no notice of this, but after ten days more the physician once more observed, 'Your Grace has an affection of the viscera. Take care, or it may become serious.' Again the Duke paid no heed; and ten days later, when the physician came, he simply looked at his royal patient, and departed without saying anything. The Duke sent some one to inquire what was the matter, and to him the physician said, 'As long as the disease was in the muscles, it might have been met by fomentations and hot applications; when it was in the flesh, acupuncture might have been employed; and as long as it was in the viscera, cauterisation might have been tried; but now it is in the bones and marrow, and naught will avail.' Five days later, the Duke felt pains all over his body, and sent to summon his physician; but the physician had fled, and the Duke died. So it is that the skilful doctor attacks disease while it is still in the muscles and easy to deal with."

To clear off finally this school of early Taoist writers, it will be necessary to admit here one whose life properly belongs to the next period. Liu An, a grandson of the founder of the Han dynasty, became Prince of Huai-nan, and it is as HUAI-NAN TZŬ, the Philosopher of that ilk, that he is known to the Chinese people. He wrote an esoteric work in twenty-one chapters, which we are supposed still to possess, besides many exoteric works, such as a treatise on alchemy, none of which are extant. It is fairly certain, however, that alchemy was not known to the Chinese until between two and three centuries later, when it was introduced from the West. As to the book which passes under his name, it is difficult to assign to it any exact date. Like the work of Lieh Tzŭ, it is interesting enough in itself; and what is more important, it marks the transition of the pure and simple Way of Lao Tzŭ, etherealised by Chuang Tzŭ, to the grosser beliefs of later ages in magicians and the elixir of life. Lao Tzŭ urged his fellow-mortals to guard their vitality by entering into harmony with their environment. Chuang Tzŭ added a motive, "to pass into the realm of the Infinite and make one's final rest therein." From which it is but a step to immortality and the elixir of life.

Huai-nan Tzŭ begins with a lengthy disquisition "On the Nature of Tao," in which, as elsewhere, he deals with the sayings of Lao Tzŭ after the fashion of Han Fei Tzŭ. Thus Lao Tzŭ said, "If you do not quarrel, no one on earth will be able to quarrel with you." To this Huai-nan Tzŭ adds, that when a certain ruler was besieging an enemy's town, a large part of the wall fell down; whereupon the former gave orders to beat a retreat at once. "For," said he in reply to the remonstrances of his officers, "a gentleman never hits a man who is down. Let them rebuild their wall, and then we will renew the attack." This noble behaviour so delighted the enemy that they tendered allegiance on the spot.

Lao Tzŭ said, "Do not value the man, value his abilities." Whereupon Huai-nan Tzŭ tells a story of a general of the Ch'u State who was fond of surrounding himself with men of ability, and once even went so far as to engage a man who represented himself as a master-thief. His retainers were aghast; but shortly afterwards their State was attacked by the Ch'i State, and then, when fortune was adverse and all was on the point of being lost, the master-thief begged to be allowed to try his skill. He went by night into the enemy's camp, and stole their general's bed-curtain. This was returned next morning with a message that it had been found by one of the soldiers who was gathering fuel. The same night our master-thief stole the general's pillow, which was restored with a similar message; and the following night he stole the long pin used to secure the hair.

"Good heavens!" cried the general at a council of war, "they will have my head next." Upon which the army of the Ch'i State was withdrawn.

Among passages of general interest the following may well be quoted :—

"Once when the Duke of Lu-yang was at war with the Han State, and sunset drew near while a battle was still fiercely raging, the Duke held up his spear, and shook it at the sun, which forthwith went back three zodiacal signs."

The end of this philosopher was a tragic one. He seems to have mixed himself up in some treasonable enterprise, and was driven to commit suicide. Tradition, however, says that he positively discovered the elixir of immortality, and that after drinking of it he rose up to heaven in broad daylight. Also that, in his excitement, he dropped the vessel which had contained this elixir into his courtyard, and that his dogs and poultry sipped up the dregs, and immediately sailed up to heaven after him!

BOOK THE SECOND

THE HAN DYNASTY (B.C. 200–A.D. 200)

BOOK THE SECOND

THE HAN DYNASTY (B.C. 200–A.D. 200)

CHAPTER I

THE "FIRST EMPEROR"—THE BURNING OF THE BOOKS—MISCELLANEOUS WRITERS

NEVER has the literature of any country been more closely bound up with the national history than was that of China at the beginning of the period upon which we are now about to enter.

The feudal spirit had long since declined, and the bond between suzerain and vassal had grown weaker and weaker until at length it had ceased to exist. Then came the opportunity and the man. The ruler of the powerful State of Ch'in, after gradually vanquishing and absorbing such of the other rival States as had not already been swallowed up by his own State, found himself in B.C. 221 master of the whole of China, and forthwith proclaimed himself its Emperor. The Chou dynasty, with its eight hundred years of sway, was a thing of the past, and the whole fabric of feudalism melted easily away.

This catastrophe was by no means unexpected. Some forty years previously a politician, named Su Tai, was one day advising the King of Chao to put an end to his ceaseless hostilities with the Yen State. "This morning," said he, "when crossing the river, I saw a mussel open its shell to sun itself. Immediately an oyster-catcher thrust in his bill to eat the mussel, but the latter promptly closed its shell and held the bird fast. 'If it doesn't rain to-day or to-morrow,' cried the oyster-catcher, 'there will be a dead mussel.' 'And if you don't get out of this by to-day or to-morrow,' retorted the mussel, 'there will be a dead oyster-catcher.' Meanwhile up came a fisherman and carried off both of them. I fear lest the Ch'in State should be our fisherman."

The new Emperor was in many senses a great man, and civilisation made considerable advances during his short reign. But a single decree has branded his name with infamy, to last so long as the Chinese remain a lettered people. In B.C. 13, a trusted Minister, named Li Ssŭ, is said to have suggested an extraordinary plan, by which the claims of antiquity were to be for ever blotted out and history was to begin again with the ruling monarch, thenceforward to be famous as the First Emperor. All existing literature was to be destroyed, with the exception only of works relating to agriculture, medicine, and divination; and a penalty of branding and four years' work on the Great Wall, then in process of building, was enacted against all who refused to surrender their books for destruction. This plan was carried out with considerable vigour. Many valuable works perished; and the Confucian Canon would have been irretrievably lost but for the devotion of scholars, who at considerable risk concealed the tablets by which they set such store, and thus made possible the discoveries of the following century and the restoration of the sacred text. So many, indeed, of the literati are said to have been put to death for disobedience that melons actually grew in winter on the spot beneath which their bodies were buried.

LI SSŬ was a scholar himself, and the reputed inventor of the script known as the Lesser Seal, which was in vogue for several centuries. The following is from a memorial of his against the proscription of nobles and others from rival States :—

"As broad acres yield large crops, so for a nation to be great there should be a great population ; and for soldiers to be daring their generals should be brave. Not a single clod was added to T'ai-shan in vain : hence the huge mountain we now behold. The merest streamlet is received into the bosom of Ocean : hence the Ocean's unfathomable expanse. And wise and virtuous is the ruler who scorns not the masses below. For him, no boundaries of realm, no distinctions of nationality exist. The four seasons enrich him ; the Gods bless him ; and, like our rulers of old, no man's hand is against him."

The First Emperor died in B.C. 210,[1] and his feeble son, the Second Emperor, was put to death in 207, thus bringing their line to an end. The vacant throne was won by a quondam beadle, who established the glorious House of Han, in memory of which Chinese of the present day, chiefly in the north, are still proud to call themselves Sons of Han.

So soon as the empire settled down to comparative peace, a mighty effort was made to undo at least some of the mischief sustained by the national literature. An

---

[1] An account of the mausoleum built to receive his remains will be found in Chapter iii. of this Book.

extra impetus was given to this movement by the fact that under the First Emperor, if we can believe tradition, the materials of writing had undergone a radical change. A general, named Mêng T'ien, added to the triumphs of the sword the invention of the camel's-hair brush, which the Chinese use as a pen. The clumsy bamboo tablet and stylus were discarded, and strips of cloth or silk came into general use, and were so employed until the first century A.D., when paper was invented by Ts'ai Lun. Some say that brickdust and water did duty at first for ink. However that may be, the form of the written character underwent a corresponding change to suit the materials employed.

Meanwhile, books were brought out of their hiding-places, and scholars like K'UNG AN-KUO, a descendant of Confucius in the twelfth degree, set to work to restore the lost classics. He deciphered the text of the Book of History, which had been discovered when pulling down the old house where Confucius once lived, and transcribed large portions of it from the ancient into the later script. He also wrote a commentary on the Analects and another on the Filial Piety Classic.

CH'AO TS'O (perished B.C. 155), popularly known as Wisdom-Bag, was a statesman rather than an author. Still, many of his memorials to the throne were considered masterpieces, and have been preserved accordingly. He wrote on the military operations against the Huns, pleading for the employment of frontier tribes, "barbarians, who in point of food and skill are closely allied to the Huns." "But arms," he says, "are a curse, and war is a dread thing. For in the twinkling of an eye the mighty may be humbled, and the strong may be brought low." In an essay "On the Value of Agriculture" he writes thus :—

"Crime begins in poverty; poverty in insufficiency of food; insufficiency of food in neglect of agriculture. Without agriculture, man has no tie to bind him to the soil. Without such tie he readily leaves his birth-place and his home. He is like unto the birds of the air or the beasts of the field. Neither battlemented cities, nor deep moats, nor harsh laws, nor cruel punishments, can subdue this roving spirit that is strong within him.

"He who is cold examines not the quality of cloth; he who is hungry tarries not for choice meats. When cold and hunger come upon men, honesty and shame depart. As man is constituted, he must eat twice daily, or hunger; he must wear clothes, or be cold. And if the stomach cannot get food and the body clothes, the love of the fondest mother cannot keep her children at her side. How then should a sovereign keep his subjects gathered around him?

"The wise ruler knows this. Therefore he concentrates the energies of his people upon agriculture. He levies light taxes. He extends the system of grain storage, to provide for his subjects at times when their resources fail."

The name of LI LING (second and first centuries B.C.) is a familiar one to every Chinese schoolboy. He was a military official who was sent in command of 800 horse to reconnoitre the territory of the Huns; and returning successful from this expedition, he was promoted to a high command and was again employed against these troublesome neighbours. With a force of only 5000 infantry he penetrated into the Hun territory as far as Mount Ling-chi (?), where he was surrounded by an army of 30,000 of the Khan's soldiers; and when his troops had exhausted all their arrows, he was forced to surrender. At this the Emperor was furious; and later on, when he heard that Li Ling was training the Khan's soldiers in the art of war as then practised by the Chinese, he caused his mother, wife, and children to be put to death. Li Ling remained some twenty years, until his death, with the Huns, and was highly honoured by the Khan, who gave him his daughter to wife.

With the renegade Li Ling is associated his patriot contemporary, Su Wu, who also met with strange adventures among the Huns. Several Chinese envoys had been imprisoned by the latter, and not allowed to return; and by way of reprisal, Hun envoys had been imprisoned in China. But a new Khan had recently sent back all the imprisoned envoys, and in A.D. 100 Su Wu was despatched upon a mission of peace to return the Hun envoys who had been detained by the Chinese. Whilst at the Court of the Khan his fellow-envoys revolted, and on the strength of this an attempt was made to persuade him to throw off his allegiance and enter the service of the Huns; upon which he tried to commit suicide, and wounded himself so severely that he lay unconscious for some hours. He subsequently slew a Chinese renegade with his own hand; and then when it was found that he was not to be forced into submission, he was thrown into a dungeon and left without food for several days. He kept himself alive by sucking snow and gnawing a felt rug; and at length the Huns, thinking that he was a supernatural being, sent him away north and set him to tend sheep. Then Li Ling was ordered to try once more by briiliant offers to shake his unswerving loyalty, but all was in vain. In the year 86, peace was made with the Huns, and the Emperor asked for the return of Su Wu. To this the Huns replied that he was dead; but a former assistant to Su Wu bade the new envoy tell the Khan that the Emperor had shot a goose with a letter tied to its leg, from which he had learnt the whereabouts of his missing envoy. This story so astonished the Khan that Su Wu was released, and in B.C. 81 returned to China after a captivity of nineteen years. He had gone away in the prime of life; he returned a white-haired and broken-down old man.

Li Ling and Su Wu are said to have exchanged poems at parting, and these are to be found published in collections under their respective names. Some doubt has been cast upon the genuineness of one of those attributed to Li Ling. It was pointed out by Hung Mai, a brilliant critic of the twelfth century, that a certain word was used in the poem, which, being part of the personal name of a recent Emperor, would at that date have been taboo. No such stigma attaches to the verses by Su Wu, who further gave to his wife a parting poem, which has been preserved, promising her that if he lived he would not fail to return, and if he died he would never forget her. But most famous of all, and still a common model for students, is a letter written by Li Ling to Su Wu, after the latter's return to China, in reply to an affectionate appeal to him to return also. Its genuineness has been questioned by Su Shih of the Sung dynasty, but not by the greatest of modern critics, Lin Hsi-chung, who declares that its pathos is enough to make even the gods weep, and that it cannot possibly have come from any other hand save that of Li Ling. With this verdict the foreign student may well rest content. Here is the letter :—

"O Tzǔ-ch'ing, O my friend, happy in the enjoyment of a glorious reputation, happy in the prospect of an imperishable name,—there is no misery like exile in a far-off foreign land, the heart brimful of longing thoughts of home! I have thy kindly letter, bidding me of good cheer, kinder than a brother's words; for which my soul thanks thee.

"Ever since the hour of my surrender until now, destitute of all resource, I have sat alone with the bitterness of my grief. All day long I see none but barbarians around me. Skins and felt protect me from wind and rain. With mutton and whey I satisfy my hunger and slake my thirst. Companions with whom to while time away, I have none. The whole country is stiff with black ice. I hear naught but the moaning of the bitter autumn blast, beneath which all vegetation has disappeared. I cannot sleep at night. I turn and listen to the distant sound of Tartar pipes, to the whinnying of Tartar steeds. In the morning I sit up and listen still, while tears course down my cheeks. O Tzǔ-ch'ing, of what stuff am I, that I should do aught but grieve? The day of thy departure left me disconsolate indeed. I thought of my aged mother butchered upon the threshold of the grave. I thought of my innocent wife and child, condemned to the same cruel fate. Deserving as I might have been of Imperial censure, I am now an object of pity to all. Thy return was to honour and renown, while I remained behind with infamy and disgrace. Such is the divergence of man's destiny.

"Born within the domain of refinement and justice, I

passed into an environment of vulgar ignorance. I left behind me obligations to sovereign and family for life amid barbarian hordes; and now barbarian children will carry on the line of my forefathers. And yet my merit was great, my guilt of small account. I had no fair hearing; and when I pause to think of these things, I ask to what end I have lived? With a thrust I could have cleared myself of all blame: my severed throat would have borne witness to my resolution; and between me and my country all would have been over for aye. But to kill myself would have been of no avail: I should only have added to my shame. I therefore steeled myself to obloquy and to life. There were not wanting those who mistook my attitude for compliance, and urged me to a nobler course; ignorant that the joys of a foreign land are sources only of a keener grief.

"O Tzŭ-ch'ing, O my friend, 1 will complete the half-told record of my former tale. His late Majesty commissioned me, with five thousand infantry under my command, to carry on operations in a distant country. Five brother generals missed their way: I alone reached the theatre of war. With rations for a long march, leading on my men, I passed beyond the limits of the Celestial Land, and entered the territory of the fierce Huns. With five thousand men I stood opposed to a hundred thousand: mine jaded foot-soldiers, theirs horsemen fresh from the stable. Yet we slew their leaders, and captured their standards, and drove them back in confusion towards the north. We obliterated their very traces: we swept them away like dust: we beheaded their general. A martial spirit spread abroad among my men. With them, to die in battle was to return to their homes; while I—I venture to think that I had already accomplished something.

"This victory was speedily followed by a general rising of the Huns. New levies were trained to the use of arms, and at length another hundred thousand barbarians were arrayed against me. The Hun chieftain himself appeared, and with his army surrounded my little band, so unequal in strength,—foot-soldiers opposed to horse. Still my tired veterans fought, each man worth a thousand of the foe, as, covered with wounds, one and all struggled bravely to the fore. The plain was strewed with the dying and the dead : barely a hundred men were left, and these too weak to hold a spear and shield. Yet, when I waved my hand and shouted to them, the sick and wounded arose. Brandishing their blades, and pointing towards the foe, they dismissed the Tartar cavalry like a rabble rout. And even when their arms were gone, their arrows spent, without a foot of steel in their hands, they still rushed, yelling, onward, each eager to lead the way. The very heavens and the earth seemed to gather round me, while my warriors drank tears of blood. Then the Hunnish chieftain, thinking that we should not yield, would have drawn off his forces. But a false traitor told him all : the battle was renewed, and we were lost.

"The Emperor Kao Ti, with 300,000 men at his back, was shut up in P'ing-ch'êng. Generals he had, like clouds ; counsellors, like drops of rain. Yet he remained seven days without food, and then barely escaped with life. How much more then I, now blamed on all sides that I did not die ? This was my crime. But, O Tzŭ-ch'ing, canst thou say that I would live from craven fear of death ? Am I one to turn my back on my country and all those dear to me, allured by sordid thoughts of gain? It was not indeed without cause that I did not elect to die. I longed, as explained in my former letter, to prove my loyalty to my prince. Rather than die to no purpose, I chose to live and to establish my good name. It was better to achieve something than to perish. Of old, Fan Li did not slay himself after the battle of Hui-chi; neither did Ts'ao Mo die after the ignominy of three defeats. Revenge came at last; and thus I too had hoped to prevail. Why then was I overtaken with punishment before the plan was matured? Why were my own flesh and blood condemned before the design could be carried out? It is for this that I raise my face to Heaven, and beating my breast, shed tears of blood.

"O my friend, thou sayest that the House of Han never fails to reward a deserving servant. But thou art thyself a servant of the House, and it would ill beseem thee to say other words than these. Yet Hsiao and Fan were bound in chains; Han and P'êng were sliced to death; Ch'ao Ts'o was beheaded. Chou Po was disgraced, and Tou Ying paid the penalty with his life. Others, great in their generation, have also succumbed to the intrigues of base men, and have been overwhelmed beneath a weight of shame from which they were unable to emerge. And now, the misfortunes of Fan Li and Ts'ao Mo command the sympathies of all.

"My grandfather filled heaven and earth with the fame of his exploits—the bravest of the brave. Yet, fearing the animosity of an Imperial favourite, he slew himself in a distant land, his death being followed by the secession, in disgust, of many a brother-hero. Can this be the reward of which thou speakest?

"Thou too, O my friend, an envoy with a slender equipage, sent on that mission to the robber race, when fortune failed thee even to the last resource of the dagger. Then years of miserable captivity, all but ended by death among the wilds of the far north. Thou left us full of young life, to return a graybeard; thy old mother dead, thy wife gone from thee to another. Seldom has the like of this been known. Even the savage barbarian respected thy loyal spirit: how much more the lord of all under the canopy of the sky? A many-acred barony should have been thine, the ruler of a thousand-charioted fief! Nevertheless, they tell me 'twas but two paltry millions, and the chancellorship of the Tributary States. Not a foot of soil repaid thee for the past, while some cringing courtier gets the marquisate of ten thousand families, and each greedy parasite of the Imperial house is gratified by the choicest offices of the State. If then thou farest thus, what could I expect? I have been heavily repaid for that I did not die. Thou hast been meanly rewarded for thy unswerving devotion to thy prince. This is barely that which should attract the absent servant back to his fatherland.

"And so it is that I do not now regret the past. Wanting though I may have been in my duty to the State, the State was wanting also in gratitude towards me. It was said of old, 'A loyal subject, though not a hero, will rejoice to die for his country.' I would die joyfully even now; but the stain of my prince's ingratitude can never be wiped away. Indeed, if the brave man is not to be allowed to achieve a name, but must die like a dog in a barbarian land, who will be found to crook the back and bow the knee before an Imperial throne, where the bitter pens of courtiers tell their lying tales?

"O my friend, look for me no more. O Tzŭ-ch'ing, what shall I say ? A thousand leagues lie between us, and separate us for ever. I shall live out my life as it were in another sphere : my spirit will find its home among a strange people. Accept my last adieu. Speak for me to my old acquaintances, and bid them serve their sovereign well. O my friend, be happy in the bosom of thy family, and think of me no more. Strive to take all care of thyself ; and when time and opportunity are thine, write me once again in reply.

"Li Ling salutes thee !"

One of the Chinese models of self-help alluded to in the *San Tzŭ Ching*, the famous school primer, to be described later on, is LU WÊN-SHU (first century B.C.). The son of a village gaoler, he was sent by his father to tend sheep, in which capacity he seems to have formed sheets of writing material by plaiting rushes, and otherwise to have succeeded in educating himself. He became an assistant in a prison, and there the knowledge of law which he had picked up stood him in such good stead that he was raised to a higher position ; and then, attracting the notice of the governor, he was still further advanced, and finally took his degree, ultimately rising to the rank of governor. In B.C. 67 he submitted to the throne the following well-known memorial :—

"May it please your Majesty.

"Of the ten great follies of our predecessors, one still survives in the maladministration of justice which prevails.

"Under the Ch'ins learning was at a discount ; brute force carried everything before it. Those who cultivated a spirit of charity and duty towards their neigh-

bour were despised.   Judicial appointments were the
prizes coveted by all.   He who spoke out the truth was
stigmatised as a slanderer, and he who strove to expose
abuses was set down as a pestilent fellow.   Consequently
all who acted up to the precepts of our ancient code
found themselves out of place in their generation, and
loyal words of good advice to the sovereign remained
locked up within their bosoms, while hollow notes of
obsequious flattery soothed the monarch's ear and lulled
his heart with false images, to the exclusion of disagree-
able realities.   And so the rod of empire fell from their
grasp for ever.

"At the present moment the State rests upon the
immeasurable bounty and goodness of your Majesty.
We are free from the horrors of war, from the calamities
of hunger and cold.   Father and son, husband and wife,
are united in their happy homes.   Nothing is wanting
to make this a golden age save only reform in the
administration of justice.

"Of all trusts, this is the greatest and most sacred.
The dead man can never come back to life : that which
is once cut off cannot be joined again.   'Rather than
slay an innocent man, it were better that the guilty
escape.'   Such, however, is not the view of our judicial
authorities of to-day.   With them, oppression and severity
are reckoned to be signs of magisterial acumen and
lead on to fortune, whereas leniency entails naught
but trouble.   Therefore their chief aim is to compass
the death of their victims ; not that they entertain any
grudge against humanity in general, but simply that this
is the shortest cut to their own personal advantage.
Thus, our market-places run with blood, our criminals
throng the gaols, and many thousands annually suffer

death. These things are injurious to public morals and hinder the advent of a truly golden age.

"Man enjoys life only when his mind is at peace; when he is in distress, his thoughts turn towards death. Beneath the scourge what is there that cannot be wrung from the lips of the sufferer? His agony is overwhelming, and he seeks to escape by speaking falsely. The officials profit by the opportunity, and cause him to say what will best confirm his guilt. And then, fearing lest the conviction be quashed by higher courts, they dress the victim's deposition to suit the circumstances of the case, so that, when the record is complete, even were Kao Yao[1] himself to rise from the dead, he would declare that death still left a margin of unexpiated crime. This, because of the refining process adopted to ensure the establishment of guilt.

"Our magistrates indeed think of nothing else. They are the bane of the people. They keep in view their own ends, and care not for the welfare of the State. Truly they are the worst criminals of the age. Hence the saying now runs, 'Chalk out a prison on the ground, and no one would remain within. Set up a gaoler of wood, and he will be found standing there alone.'[2] Imprisonment has become the greatest of all misfortunes, while among those who break the law, who violate family ties, who choke the truth, there are none to be compared in iniquity with the officers of justice themselves.

"Where you let the kite rear its young undisturbed, there will the phœnix come and build its nest. Do not punish for misguided advice, and by and by valuable

---

[1] A famous Minister of Crime in the mythical ages.

[2] Contrary to what was actually the case in the Golden Age.

suggestions will flow in. The men of old said, 'Hills and jungles shelter many noxious things; rivers and marshes receive much filth; even the finest gems are not wholly without flaw. Surely then the ruler of an empire should put up with a little abuse.' But I would have your Majesty exempt from vituperation, and open to the advice of all who have aught to say. I would have freedom of speech in the advisers of the throne. I would sweep away the errors which brought the downfall of our predecessors. I would have reverence for the virtues of our ancient kings and reform in the administration of justice, to the utter confusion of those who now pervert its course. Then indeed would the golden age be renewed over the face of the glad earth, and the people would move ever onwards in peace and happiness boundless as the sky itself."

LIU HSIANG (B.C. 80–89) was a descendant of the beadle founder of the great Han dynasty. Entering into official life, he sought to curry favour with the reigning Emperor by submitting some secret works on the black art, towards which his Majesty was much inclined. The results not proving successful, he was thrown into prison, but was soon released that he might carry on the publication of the commentary on the Spring and Autumn by Ku-liang. He also revised and re-arranged the historical episodes known as the *Chan Kuo Ts'ê*, wrote treatises on government and some poetry, and compiled Biographies of Eminent Women, the first work of its kind.

His son, LIU HSIN, was a precocious boy, who early distinguished himself by wide reading in all branches of literature. He worked with his father upon the restoration of the classical texts, especially of the Book of Changes, and later on was chiefly instrumental in establishing the position of Tso's Commentary on the Spring and Autumn. He catalogued the Imperial Library, and in conjunction with his father discovered—some say compiled—the Chou Ritual.

A well-known figure in Chinese literature is YANG HSIUNG (B.C. 53–A.D. 18). As a boy he was fond of straying from the beaten track and reading whatever he could lay his hands on. He stammered badly, and consequently gave much time to meditation. He propounded an ethical criterion occupying a middle place between those insisted upon by Mencius and by Hsün K'uang, teaching that the nature of man at birth is neither good nor evil, but a mixture of both, and that development in either direction depends wholly upon environment. In glorification of the Book of Changes he wrote the *T'ai Hsüan Ching*, and to emphasise the value of the Confucian Analects he produced a philosophical treatise known as the *Fa Yen*, both between A.D. 1 and 6. On completion of this last, his most famous work, a wealthy merchant of the province was so struck by its excellence that he offered to give 100,000 *cash* if his name should merely be mentioned in it. But Yang answered with scorn that a stag in a pen or an ox in a cage would not be more out of place than the name of a man with nothing but money to recommend him in the sacred pages of a book. Liu Hsin, however, sneeringly suggested that posterity would use Yang Hsiung's work to cover pickle-jars.

Besides composing some mediocre poetry, Yang Hsiung wrote on acupuncture, music, and philology.

There is little doubt that he did not write the *Fang Yen*, a vocabulary of words and phrases used in various parts of the empire, which was steadily attributed to him until Hung Mai, a critic of the twelfth century, already mentioned in Chapter I. of this Book, made short work of his claims.

A brilliant writer who attracted much attention in his day was WANG CH'UNG (A.D. 27–97). He is said to have picked up his education at bookstalls, with the aid of a superbly retentive memory. Only one of his works is extant, the *Lun Hêng*, consisting of eighty-five essays on a variety of subjects. In these he tilts against the errors of the age, and exposes even Confucius and Mencius to free and searching criticisms. He is consequently ranked as a heterodox thinker. He showed that the soul could neither exist after death as a spirit nor exercise any influence upon the living. When the body decomposes, the soul, a phenomenon inseparable from vitality, perishes with it. He further argued that if the souls of human beings were immortal, those of animals would be immortal likewise; and that space itself would not suffice to contain the countless shades of the men and creatures of all time.

MA JUNG (A.D. 79–166) was popularly known as the Universal Scholar. His learning in Confucian lore was profound, and he taught upwards of one thousand pupils. He introduced the system of printing notes or comments in the body of the page, using for that purpose smaller characters cut in double columns; and it was by a knowledge of this fact that a clever critic of the T'ang dynasty was able to settle the spuriousness of an early edition of the *Tao-Tê-Ching* with double-column commentary, which had been attributed to Ho Shang Kung, a writer of the second century B.C.

TS'AI YUNG (A.D. 133–192), whose tippling propensities earned for him the nickname of the Drunken Dragon, is chiefly remembered in connection with literature as superintending the work of engraving on stone the authorised text of the Five Classics. With red ink he wrote these out on forty-six tablets for the workmen to cut. The tablets were placed in the Hung-tu College, and fragments of them are said to be still in existence.

The most famous of the pupils who sat at the feet of Ma Jung was CHÊNG HSÜAN (A.D. 127–200). He is one of the most voluminous of all the commentators upon the Confucian classics. He lived for learning. The very slave-girls of his household were highly educated, and interlarded their conversation with quotations from the Odes. He was nevertheless fond of wine, and is said to have been able to take three hundred cups at a sitting without losing his head. Perhaps it may be as well to add that a Chinese cup holds about a thimbleful. As an instance of the general respect in which he was held, it is recorded that at his request the chief of certain rebels spared the town of Kao-mi (his native place), marching forward by another route. In A.D. 200 Confucius appeared to him in a vision, and he knew by this token that his hour was at hand. Consequently, he was very loth to respond to a summons sent to him from Chi-chou in Chihli by the then powerful Yüan Shao. He set out indeed upon the journey, but died on the way.

It is difficult to bring the above writers, representatives of a class, individually to the notice of the reader. Though each one wandered into by-paths of his own, the common

lode-star was Confucianism—elucidation of the Confucian
Canon. For although, with us, commentaries upon the
classics are not usually regarded as literature, they are
so regarded by the Chinese, who place such works in the
very highest rank, and reward successful commentators
with the coveted niche in the Confucian temple.

CHAPTER II

POETRY

AT the beginning of the second century B.C., poetry was still composed on the model of the *Li Sao*, and we are in possession of a number of works assigned to Chia I (B.C. 199–168), Tung-fang So (*b.* B.C. 160), Liu Hsiang, and others, all of which follow on the lines of Ch'ü Yüan's great poem.   But gradually, with the more definite establishment of what we may call classical influence, poets went back to find their exemplars in the Book of Poetry, which came as it were from the very hand of Confucius himself.   Poems were written in metres of four, five, and seven words to a line.   Ssŭ-ma Hsiang-ju (*d.* B.C. 117), a gay Lothario who eloped with a young widow, made such a name with his verses that he was summoned to Court, and appointed by the Emperor to high office.   His poems, however, have not survived.

MEI SHÊNG (*d.* B.C. 140), who formed his style on Ssŭ-ma, has the honour of being the first to bring home to his fellow-countrymen the extreme beauty of the five-word metre.   From him modern poetry may be said to date.   Many specimens of his workmanship are extant :—

> (1.) "*Green grows the grass upon the bank,*
> *The willow-shoots are long and lank ;*
> *A lady in a glistening gown*
> *Opens the casement and looks down*

The roses on her cheek blush bright,
Her rounded arm is dazzling white;
A singing-girl in early life,
And now a careless roué's wife. . . .
Ah, if he does not mind his own,
He'll find some day the bird has flown!"

(2.) *" The red hibiscus and the reed,*
The fragrant flowers of marsh and mead,
All these I gather as I stray,
As though for one now far away.
I strive to pierce with straining eyes
The distance that between us lies.
Alas that hearts which beat as one
Should thus be parted and undone!"

LIU HÊNG (*d.* B.C. 157) was the son by a concubine of
the founder of the Han dynasty, and succeeded in B.C. 180
as fourth Emperor of the line. For over twenty years
he ruled wisely and well. He is one of the twenty-four
classical examples of filial piety, having waited on his sick
mother for three years without changing his clothes. He
was a scholar, and was canonised after death by a title
which may fairly be rendered "Beauclerc." The following is a poem which he wrote on the death of his illustrious father, who, if we can accept as genuine the remains
attributed to him, was himself also a poet:—

" I look up, the curtains are there as of yore;
I look down, and there is the mat on the floor;
These things I behold, but the man is no more.

" To the infinite azure his spirit has flown,
And I am left friendless, uncared-for, alone,
Of solace bereft, save to weep and to moan.

" The deer on the hillside caressingly bleat,
And offer the grass for their young ones to eat,
While birds of the air to their nestlings bring meat

" *But I a poor orphan must ever remain,*
  My heart, still so young, overburdened with pain
  For him I shall never set eyes on again.

" *'Tis a well-worn old saying, which all men allow,*
  That grief stamps the deepest of lines on the brow :
  Alas for my hair, it is silvery now !

" *Alas for my father, cut off in his pride !*
  Alas that no more I may stand by his side !
  Oh, where were the gods when that great hero died ?"

The literary fame of the Beauclerc was rivalled, if not surpassed, by his grandson, LIU CH‘Ê (B.C. 156–87), who succeeded in B.C. 140 as sixth Emperor of the Han dynasty. He was an enthusiastic patron of literature. He devoted great attention to music as a factor in national life. He established important religious sacrifices to heaven and earth. He caused the calendar to be reformed by his grand astrologer, the historian SSŬ-MA CH‘IEN, from which date accurate chronology may be almost said to begin. His generals carried the Imperial arms into Central Asia, and for many years the Huns were held in check. Notwithstanding his enlightened policy, the Emperor was personally much taken up with the magic and mysteries which were being gradually grafted on to the Tao of Lao Tzŭ, and he encouraged the numerous quacks who pretended to have discovered the elixir of life. The following are specimens of his skill in poetry :—

" *The autumn blast drives the white scud in the sky,*
  Leaves fade, and wild geese sweeping south meet the eye ;
  The scent of late flowers fills the soft air above,
  My heart full of thoughts of the lady I love.
  In the river the barges for revel-carouse
  Are lined by white waves which break over their bows ;

Their oarsmen keep time to the piping and drumming. . . .
Yet joy is as naught
Alloyed by the thought
That youth slips away and that old age is coming."

The next lines were written upon the death of a harem favourite, to whom he was fondly attached :—

" *The sound of rustling silk is stilled,*
With dust the marble courtyard filled ;
No footfalls echo on the floor,
Fallen leaves in heaps block up the door. . . .
For she, my pride, my lovely one, is lost,
And I am left, in hopeless anguish tossed."

A good many anonymous poems have come down to us from the first century B.C., and some of these contain here and there quaint and pleasing conceits, as, for instance—

" *Man reaches scarce a hundred, yet his tears*
Would fill a lifetime of a thousand years."

The following is a poem of this period, the author of which is unknown :—

" *Forth from the eastern gate my steeds I drive,*
And lo ! a cemetery meets my view ;
Aspens around in wild luxuriance thrive,
The road is fringed with fir and pine and yew.
Beneath my feet lie the forgotten dead,
Wrapped in a twilight of eternal gloom ;
Down by the Yellow Springs their earthy bed,
And everlasting silence is their doom.
How fast the lights and shadows come and go !
Like morning dew our fleeting life has passed ;
Man, a poor traveller on earth below,
Is gone, while brass and stone can still outlast.

Time is inexorable, and in vain
Against his might the holiest mortal strives ;
Can we *then hope this precious boon to gain,*
By strange elixirs to prolong our lives ? . . .
Oh, rather quaff good liquor while we may,
And dress in silk and satin every day ! "

Women now begin to appear in Chinese literature. The Lady PAN was for a long time chief favourite of the Emperor who ruled China B.C. 32–6. So devoted was his Majesty that he even wished her to appear alongside of him in the Imperial chariot. Upon which she replied, " Your handmaid has heard that wise rulers of old were always accompanied by virtuous ministers, but never that they drove out with women by their side." She was ultimately supplanted by a younger and more beautiful rival, whereupon she forwarded to the Emperor one of those fans, round or octagonal frames of bamboo with silk stretched over them,[1] which in this country are called " fire-screens," inscribed with the following lines :—

" *O fair white silk, fresh from the weaver's loom,*
Clear as the frost, bright as the winter snow—
See ! friendship fashions out of thee a fan,
Round as the round moon shines in heaven above,
At home, abroad, a close companion thou,
Stirring at every move the grateful gale.
And yet I fear, ah me ! that autumn chills,
Cooling the dying summer's torrid rage,
Will see thee laid neglected on the shelf,
All thought of bygone days, like them bygone."

The phrase " autumn fan " has long since passed into the language, and is used figuratively of a deserted wife.

[1] The folding fan, invented by the Japanese, was not known in China until the eleventh century A.D., when it was introduced through Korea.

CHAPTER III

HISTORY—LEXICOGRAPHY

So far as China is concerned, the art of writing history may be said to have been created during the period under review. SSU-MA CH'IEN, the so-called Father of History, was born about B.C. 145. At the age of ten he was already a good scholar, and at twenty set forth upon a round of travel which carried him to all parts of the empire. In B.C. 110 his father died, and he stepped into the hereditary post of grand astrologer. After devoting some time and energy to the reformation of the calendar, he now took up the historical work which had been begun by his father, and which was ultimately given to the world as the Historical Record. It is a history of China from the earliest ages down to about one hundred years before the Christian era, in one hundred and thirty chapters, arranged under five headings, as follows:—(1) Annals of the Emperors; (2) Chronological Tables; (3) Eight chapters on Rites, Music, the Pitch-pipes, the Calendar, Astrology, Imperial Sacrifices, Watercourses, and Political Economy; (4) Annals of the Feudal Nobles; and (5) Biographies of many of the eminent men of the period, which covers nearly three thousand years. In such estimation is this work justly held that its very words have been counted, and found to number 526,500 in all. It must be borne in mind that these characters were, in all probability, scratched with a stylus on bamboo tablets, and that previous to this there was no such thing as a history on a general and comprehensive plan; in fact, nothing beyond mere local annals in the style of the Spring and Autumn.

Since the Historical Record, every dynasty has had its historian, their works in all cases being formed upon the model bequeathed by Ssŭ-ma Ch'ien. The Twenty-four Dynastic Histories of China were produced in 1747 in a uniform series bound up in 219 large volumes, and together show a record such as can be produced by no other country in the world.

The following are specimens of Ssŭ-ma Ch'ien's style :—

(1.) "When the House of Han arose, the evils of their predecessors had not passed away. Husbands still went off to the wars. The old and the young were employed in transporting food. Production was almost at a standstill, and money became scarce. So much so, that even the Son of Heaven had not carriage-horses of the same colour; the highest civil and military authorities rode in bullock-carts, and the people at large knew not where to lay their heads.

"At this epoch, the coinage in use was so heavy and cumbersome that the people themselves started a new issue at a fixed standard of value. But the laws were too lax, and it was impossible to prevent grasping persons from coining largely, buying largely, and then holding against a rise in the market. The consequence was that prices went up enormously. Rice sold at 10,000 *cash* per picul; a horse cost 100 ounces of silver. But by and by, when the empire was settling down to tranquillity, his Majesty Kao Tsu gave orders that no trader should wear silk nor ride in a carriage; besides which, the imposts levied upon this class were greatly increased, in order to keep them down. Some years later these restrictions were withdrawn; still, however, the descendants of traders were disqualified from holding any office connected with the State.

"Meanwhile, certain levies were made on a scale calculated to meet the exigencies of public expenditure; while the land-tax and customs revenue were regarded by all officials, from the Emperor downwards, as their own personal emolument. Grain was forwarded by water to the capital for the use of the officials there, but the quantity did not amount to more than a few hundred thousand piculs every year.

"Gradually the coinage began to deteriorate and light coins to circulate; whereupon another issue followed, each piece being marked 'half an ounce.' But at length the system of private issues led to serious abuses, resulting first of all in vast sums of money accumulating in the hands of individuals; finally, in rebellion, until the country was flooded with the coinage of the rebels, and it became necessary to enact laws against any such issues in the future.

"At this period the Huns were harassing our northern frontier, and soldiers were massed there in large bodies; in consequence of which food became so scarce that the authorities offered certain rank and titles of honour to those who would supply a given quantity of grain. Later on, drought ensued in the west, and in order to meet necessities of the moment, official rank was again made a marketable commodity, while those who broke the laws were allowed to commute their penalties by money payments. And now horses began to reappear in official stables, and in palace and hall signs of an ampler luxury were visible once more.

"Thus it was in the early days of the dynasty, until some seventy years after the accession of the House of Han. The empire was then at peace. For a long time there had been neither flood nor drought, and a season of plenty had ensued. The public granaries were well stocked; the Government treasuries were full. In the capital, strings of *cash* were piled in myriads, until the very strings rotted, and their tale could no longer be told. The grain in the Imperial storehouses grew mouldy year by year. It burst from the crammed granaries, and lay about until it became unfit for human food. The streets were thronged with horses belonging to the people, and on the highroads whole droves were to be seen, so that it became necessary to prohibit the public use of mares. Village elders ate meat and drank wine. Petty government clerkships and the like lapsed from father to son; the higher offices of State were treated as family heirlooms. For there had gone abroad a spirit of self-respect and of reverence for the law, while a sense of charity and of duty towards one's neighbour kept men aloof from disgrace and shame.

"At length, under lax laws, the wealthy began to use their riches for evil purposes of pride and self-aggrandisement and oppression of the weak. Members of the Imperial family received grants of land, while from the highest to the lowest, every one vied with his neighbour in lavishing money on houses, and appointments, and apparel, altogether beyond the limit of his means. Such is the everlasting law of the sequence of prosperity and decay.

"Then followed extensive military preparations in

various parts of the empire; the establishment of a tradal route with the barbarians of the south-west, for which purpose mountains were hewn through for many miles. The object was to open up the resources of those remote districts, but the result was to swamp the inhabitants in hopeless ruin. Then, again, there was the subjugation of Korea; its transformation into an Imperial dependency; with other troubles nearer home. There was the ambush laid for the Huns, by which we forfeited their alliance, and brought them down upon our northern frontier. Nothing, in fact, but wars and rumours of wars from day to day. Money was constantly leaving the country. The financial stability of the empire was undermined, and its impoverished people were driven thereby into crime. Wealth had been frittered away, and its renewal was sought in corruption. Those who brought money in their hands received appointments under government. Those who could pay escaped the penalties of their guilt. Merit had to give way to money. Shame and scruples of conscience were laid aside. Laws and punishments were administered with severer hand. From this period must be dated the rise and growth of official venality."

(2.) "The Odes have it thus :—'We may gaze up to the mountain's brow: we may travel along the great road;' signifying that although we cannot hope to reach the goal, still we may push on thitherwards in spirit.

"While reading the works of Confucius, I have always fancied I could see the man as he was in life; and when I went to Shantung I actually beheld his carriage, his robes, and the material parts of his ceremonial usages. There were his descendants practising the old rites in their ancestral home, and I lingered on, unable to tear myself away. Many are the princes and prophets that the world has seen in its time, glorious in life, forgotten in death. But Confucius, though only a humble member of the cotton-clothed masses, remains among us after many generations. He is the model for such as would be wise. By all, from the Son of Heaven down to the meanest student, the supremacy of his principles is fully and freely admitted. He may indeed be pronounced the divinest of men."

(3.) "In the 9th moon the First Emperor was buried in Mount Li, which in the early days of his reign he had caused to be tunnelled and prepared with that view. Then, when he had consolidated the empire, he employed his soldiery, to the number of 700,000, to bore down to the Three Springs (that is, until water was reached), and there a foundation of bronze[1] was laid and the sarcophagus placed thereon. Rare objects and costly jewels were collected from the palaces and from the various officials, and were carried thither and stored in vast quantities. Artificers were ordered to construct mechanical cross-bows, which, if any one were to enter, would immediately discharge their arrows. With the aid of quicksilver, rivers were made, the Yang-tsze, the Hoang-ho, and the great ocean, the metal being poured from one into the other by machinery. On the roof were delineated the constellations of the sky, on the floor the geographical divisions of the earth. Candles were made from the fat of the man-fish (walrus), calculated to last for a very long time.

"The Second Emperor said, 'It is not fitting that the concubines of my late father who are without children

---

[1] Variant " firm," *i.e.* was firmly laid.

should leave him now;' and accordingly he ordered them to accompany the dead monarch to the next world, those who thus perished being many in number.

"When the interment was completed, some one suggested that the workmen who had made the machinery and concealed the treasure knew the great value of the latter, and that the secret would leak out. Therefore, so soon as the ceremony was over, and the path giving access to the sarcophagus had been blocked up at its innermost end, the outside gate at the entrance to this path was let fall, and the mausoleum was effectually closed, so that not one of the workmen escaped. Trees and grass were then planted around, that the spot might look like the rest of the mountain."

The history by Ssŭ-ma Ch'ien stops about 100 years before Christ. To carry it on from that point was the ambition of a scholar named Pan Piao (A.D. 3–54), but he died while still collecting materials for his task. His son, PAN KU, whose scholarship was extensive and profound, took up the project, but was impeached on the ground that he was altering the national records at his own discretion, and was thrown into prison. Released on the representations of a brother, he continued his work; however, before its completion he became involved in a political intrigue and was again thrown into prison, where he died. The Emperor handed the unfinished history to PAN CHAO, his gifted sister, who had been all along his assistant, and by her it was brought to completion down to about the Christian era, where the occupancy of the throne by a usurper divides the Han dynasty into two distinct periods. This lady was also the author of a volume of moral advice to young women, and of many poems and essays.

Lexicography, which has since been so widely cultivated by the Chinese, was called into being by a famous
scholar named HSÜ SHÊN (*d.* A.D. 120). Entering upon
an official career, he soon retired and devoted the rest of
his life to books. He was a deep student of the Five
Classics, and wrote a work on the discrepancies in the
various criticisms of these books. But it is by his *Shuo
Wên* that he is now known. This was a collection, with
short explanatory notes, of all the characters—about ten
thousand—which were to be found in Chinese literature
as then existing, written in what is now known as the
Lesser Seal style. It is the oldest Chinese dictionary of
which we have any record, and has hitherto formed the
basis of all etymological research. It is arranged under
540 radicals or classifiers, that is to say, specially
selected portions of characters which indicate to some
extent the direction in which lies the sense of the whole
character, and its chief object was to exhibit the pictorial
features of Chinese writing.

CHAPTER IV

BUDDHISM

THE introduction of Buddhism into China must now be considered, especially under its literary aspect.

So early as B.C. 217 we read of Buddhist priests, Shih-li-fang and others, coming to China. The "First Emperor" seems to have looked upon them with suspicion. At any rate, he threw them into prison, from which, we are told, they were released in the night by a golden man or angel. Nothing more was heard of Buddhism until the Emperor known as Ming Ti, in consequence, it is said, of a dream in which a foreign god appeared to him, sent off a mission to India to see what could be learnt upon the subject of this barbarian religion. The mission, which consisted of eighteen persons, returned about A.D. 67, accompanied by two Indian Buddhists named Kashiapmadanga and Gobharana. These two settled at Lo-yang in Honan, which was then the capital, and proceeded to translate into Chinese the Sûtra of Forty-two Sections—the beginning of a long line of such. Soon afterwards the former died, but the seed had been sown, and a great rival to Taoism was about to appear on the scene.

Towards the close of the second century A.D. another Indian Buddhist, who had come to reside at Ch'ang-an in Shensi, translated the *sûtra* known as the Lotus of the

Good Law, and Buddhist temples were built in various parts of China. By the beginning of the fourth century Chinese novices were taking the vows required for the Buddhist priesthood, and monasteries were endowed for their reception.

In A.D. 399 FA HSIEN started on his great pedestrian journey from the heart of China overland to India, his object being to procure copies of the Buddhist Canon, statues, and relics. Those who accompanied him at starting either turned back or died on the way, and he finally reached India with only one companion, who settled there and never returned to China. After visiting various important centres, such as Magadha, Patna, Benares, and Buddha-Gaya, and effecting the object of his journey, he took passage on a merchant-ship, and reached Ceylon. There he found a large junk which carried him to Java, whence, after surviving many perils of the sea, he made his way on board another junk to the coast of Shantung, disembarking in A.D. 414 with all his treasures at the point now occupied by the German settlement of Kiao-chow.

The narrative of his adventurous journey, as told by himself, is still in existence, written in a crabbed and difficult style. His itinerary has been traced, and nearly all the places mentioned by him have been identified. The following passage refers to the desert of Gobi, which the travellers had to cross :—

"In this desert there are a great many evil spirits and hot winds. Those who encounter the latter perish to a man. There are neither birds above nor beasts below. Gazing on all sides, as far as the eye can reach, in order to mark the track, it would be impossible to succeed but for the rotting bones of dead men which point the way."

Buddha-Gaya, the scene of recent interesting explorations conducted by the late General Cunningham, was visited by Fa Hsien, and is described by him as follows :—

"The pilgrims now arrived at the city of Gaya, also a complete waste within its walls. Journeying about three more miles southwards, they reached the place where the Bôdhisatva formerly passed six years in self-mortification. It is very woody. From this point going west a mile, they arrived at the spot where Buddha entered the water to bathe, and a god pressed down the branch of a tree to pull him out of the pool. Also, by going two-thirds of a mile farther north, they reached the place where the two lay-sisters presented Buddha with congee made with milk. Two-thirds of a mile to the north of this is the place where Buddha, sitting on a stone under a great tree and facing the east, ate it. The tree and the stone are both there still, the latter being about six feet in length and breadth by over two feet in height. In Central India the climate is equable ; trees will live several thousand, and even so much as ten thousand years. From this point going north-east half a yojana, the pilgrims arrived at the cave where the Bôdhisatva, having entered, sat down cross-legged with his face to the west, and reflected as follows: 'If I attain perfect wisdom, there should be some miracle in token thereof.' Whereupon the silhouette of Buddha appeared upon the stone, over three feet in length, and is plainly visible to this day. Then heaven and earth quaked mightily, and the gods who were in space cried out, saying, 'This is not the place where past and future Buddhas have attained and should attain perfect wisdom. The proper spot is beneath the Bô tree, less than half a yojana to the south-west of this.' When the gods had uttered these words, they proceeded to lead the way with singing in order to conduct him thither. The Bôdhisatva got up and followed, and when thirty paces from the tree a god gave him the *kus'a* grass. Having accepted this, he went on fifteen paces farther, when five hundred dark-coloured birds came and flew three times round him, and departed. The Bôdhisatva went on to the Bô tree, and laying down his *kus'a* grass, sat down with his face to the east. Then Mara, the king of the devils, sent three beautiful women to approach from the north and tempt him; he himself approaching from the south with the same object. The Bôdhisatva pressed the ground with his toes, whereupon the infernal army retreated in confusion, and the three women became old. At the above-mentioned place where Buddha suffered mortification for six years, and on all these other spots, men of after ages have built pagodas and set up images, all of which are still in existence. Where Buddha, having attained perfect wisdom, contemplated the tree for seven days, experiencing the joys of emancipation; where Buddha walked backwards and forwards, east and west, under the Bô tree for seven days; where the gods produced a jewelled chamber and worshipped Buddha for seven days; where the blind dragon Muchilinda enveloped Buddha for seven days; where Buddha sat facing the east on a square stone beneath the nyagrodha tree, and Brahmâ came to salute him; where the four heavenly kings offered their alms-bowls; where the five hundred traders gave him cooked rice and honey; where he converted the brothers Kasyapa with their disciples to the number of one thousand souls—on all these spots stûpas have been raised."

The following passage refers to Ceylon, called by Fa Hsien the Land of the Lion, that is, Singhala, from the name of a trader who first founded a kingdom there :—

"This country had originally no inhabitants ; only devils and spirits and dragons lived in it, with whom the merchants of neighbouring countries came to trade. When the exchange of commodities took place, the devils and spirits did not appear in person, but set out their valuables with the prices attached. Then the merchants, according to the prices, bought the things and carried them off. But from the merchants going backwards and forwards and stopping on their way, the attractions of the place became known to the inhabitants of the neighbouring countries, who also went there, and thus it became a great nation. The temperature is very agreeable in this country ; there is no distinction of summer and winter. The trees and plants are always green, and cultivation of the soil is carried on as men please, without regard to seasons."

Meanwhile, the Indian Kumarajiva, one of the Four Suns of Buddhism, had been occupied between A.D. 405 and 412 in dictating Chinese commentaries on the Buddhist Canon to some eight hundred priests. He also wrote a *shâstra* on Reality and Appearance, and translated the Diamond Sûtra, which has done more to popularise Buddhism with the educated classes than all the material parts of this religion put together. Chinese poets and philosophers have drawn inspiration and instruction from its pages, and the work might now almost be classed as a national classic. Here are two short extracts :—

(1.) "Buddha said, O Subhuti, tell me after thy wit, can a man see the Buddha in the flesh ?

"He cannot, O World-Honoured, and for this reason : The Buddha has declared that flesh has no objective existence.

"Then Buddha told Subhūti, saying, All objective existences are unsubstantial and unreal. If a man can see clearly that they are so, then can he see the Buddha."

(2.) "Buddha said, O Subhūti, if one man were to collect the seven precious things from countless galaxies of worlds, and bestow all these in charity, and another virtuous man, or virtuous woman, were to become filled with the spirit, and held fast by this *sûtra*, preaching it ever so little for the conversion of mankind, I say unto you that the happiness of this last man would far exceed the happiness of that other man.

"Conversion to what ? To the disregard of objective existences, and to absolute quiescence of the individual. And why ? Because every external phenomenon is like a dream, like a vision, like a bubble, like shadow, like dew, like lightning, and should be regarded as such."

In A.D. 520 Bôdhidharma came to China, and was received with honour. He had been the son of a king in Southern India. He taught that religion was not to be learnt from books, but that man should seek and find the Buddha in his own heart. Just before his arrival Sung Yün had been sent to India to obtain more Buddhist books, and had remained two years in Kandahar, returning with 175 volumes.

Then, in 629, HSÜAN TSANG set out for India with the same object, and also to visit the holy places of Buddhism. He came back in 645, bringing with him 657 Buddhist books, besides many images and pictures and 150 relics. He spent the rest of his life translating these books, and also, like Fa Hsien, wrote a narrative of his travels.

This brings us down to the beginning of the T'ang dynasty, when Buddhism had acquired, in spite of much opposition and even persecution, what has since proved to be a lasting hold upon the masses of the Chinese people.

BOOK THE THIRD

MINOR DYNASTIES (A.D. 200—600)

BOOK THE THIRD

MINOR DYNASTIES (A.D. 200—600)

CHAPTER I

POETRY—MISCELLANEOUS LITERATURE

THE centuries which elapsed between A.D. 200 and 600 were not favourable to the development and growth of a national literature. During a great part of the time the empire was torn by civil wars; there was not much leisure for book-learning, and few patrons to encourage it. Still the work was carried on, and many great names have come down to us.

The dark years between A.D. 196 and 221, which witnessed the downfall of the House of Han, were illumined by the names of seven writers, now jointly known as the Seven Scholars of the Chien-An period. They were all poets. There was HSÜ KAN, who fell under the influence of Buddhism and translated into Chinese the *Pranyamûla shâstra tikâ* of Nâgârdjuna. The following lines are by him :—

> " *O floating clouds that swim in heaven above,*
> *Bear on your wings these words to him I love. . . .*
> *Alas ! you float along nor heed my pain,*
> *And leave me here to love and long in vain !*

I see other dear ones to their homes return,
And for his coming shall not I too yearn?
Since my lord left—ah me, unhappy day!—
My mirror's dust has not been brushed away;
My heart, like running water, knows no peace,
But bleeds and bleeds forever without cease."

There was K'UNG JUNG, a descendant of Confucius in the twentieth degree, and a most precocious child. At ten years of age he went with his father to Lo-yang, where Li Ying, the Dragon statesman, was at the height of his political reputation. Unable from the press of visitors to gain admission, he told the doorkeeper to inform Li Ying that he was a connection, and thus succeeded in getting in. When Li Ying asked him what the connection was, he replied, "My ancestor Confucius and your ancestor Lao Tzŭ were friends engaged in the quest for truth, so that you and I may be said to be of the same family." Li Ying was astonished, but Ch'ên Wei said, "Cleverness in youth does not mean brilliancy in later life," upon which K'ung Jung remarked, "You, sir, must evidently have been very clever as a boy." Entering official life, he rose to be Governor of Po-hai in Shantung; but he incurred the displeasure of the great Ts'ao Ts'ao, and was put to death with all his family. He was an open-hearted man, and fond of good company. "If my halls are full of guests," he would say, "and my bottles full of wine, I am happy."

The following is a specimen of his poetry :—

> " *The wanderer reaches home with joy*
> *From absence of a year and more :*
> *His eye seeks a beloved boy—*
> *His wife lies weeping on the floor.*

" They whisper he is gone. The glooms
 Of evening fall ; beyond the gate
A lonely grave in outline looms
 To greet the sire who came too late.

" Forth to the little mound he flings,
 Where wild-flowers bloom on every side. . . .
His bones are in the Yellow Springs,
 His flesh like dust is scattered wide.

" ' O child, who never knew thy sire,
 For ever now to be unknown,
Ere long thy wandering ghost shall tire
 Of flitting friendless and alone.

" ' O son, man's greatest earthly boon,
 With thee I bury hopes and fears.'
He bowed his head in grief, and soon
 His breast was wet with rolling tears.

" Life's dread uncertainty he knows,
 But oh for this untimely close !"

There was WANG TS'AN (A.D. 177–217), a learned man who wrote an *Ars Poetica*, not, however, in verse. A youth of great promise, he excelled as a poet, although the times were most unfavourable to success. It has been alleged, with more or less truth, that all Chinese poetry is pitched in the key of melancholy ; that the favourite themes of Chinese poets are the transitory character of life with its partings and other ills, and the inevitable approach of death, with substitution of the unknown for the known. Wang Ts'an had good cause for his lamentations. He was forced by political disturbances to leave his home at the capital and seek safety in flight. There, as he tells us,

" Wolves and tigers work their own sweet will."

On the way he finds

" Naught but bleached bones covering the plain ahead,"

and he comes across a famine-stricken woman who had thrown among the bushes a child she was unable to feed. Arriving at the Great River, the setting sun brings his feelings to a head :—

> " Streaks of light still cling to the hill-tops,
>   While a deeper shade falls upon the steep slopes ;
>   The fox makes his way to his burrow,
>   Birds fly back to their homes in the wood,
>   Clear sound the ripples of the rushing waves,
>   Along the banks the gibbons scream and cry,
>   My sleeves are fluttered by the whistling gale,
>   The lapels of my robe are drenched with dew.
>   The livelong night I cannot close my eyes.
>   I arise and seize my guitar,
>   Which, ever in sympathy with man's changing moods,
>   Now sounds responsive to my grief."

But music cannot make him forget his kith and kin—

> " Most of them, alas! are prisoners,
>   And weeping will be my portion to the end.
>   With all the joyous spots in the empire,
>   Why must I remain in this place?
>   Ah, like the grub in smartweed, I am growing insensible
>   to bitterness."

By the last line he means to hint " how much a long communion tends to make us what we are."

There was YING YANG, who, when his own political career was cut short, wrote a poem with a title which may be interpreted as " Regret that a Bucephalus should stand idle."

There was LIU CHÊNG, who was put to death for daring to cast an eye upon one of the favourites of the great general Ts'ao Ts'ao, virtual founder of the House of Wei. CH'ÊN LIN and YÜAN YÜ complete the tale.

To these seven names an eighth and a ninth are added

by courtesy: those of Ts'ao Ts'ao above mentioned, and of his third son, Ts'ao Chih, the poet. The former played a remarkable part in Chinese history. His father had been adopted as son by the chief eunuch of the palace, and he himself was a wild young man much given to coursing and hawking. He managed, however, to graduate at the age of twenty, and, after distinguishing himself in a campaign against insurgents, raised a volunteer force to purge the country of various powerful chieftains who threatened the integrity of the empire. By degrees the supreme power passed into his hands, and he caused the weak Emperor to raise his daughter to the rank of Empress. He is popularly regarded as the type of a bold bad Minister and of a cunning unscrupulous rebel. His large armies are proverbial, and at one time he is said to have had so many as a million of men under arms. As an instance of the discipline which prevailed in his camp, it is said that he once condemned himself to death for having allowed his horse to shy into a field of grain, in accordance with his own severe regulations against any injury to standing crops. However, in lieu of losing his head, he was persuaded to satisfy his sense of justice by cutting off his hair. The following lines are from a song by him, written in an abrupt metre of four words to the line:—

> " *Here is wine, let us sing;*
> *For man's life is short,*
> *Like the morning dew,*
> *Its best days gone by.*
> *But though we would rejoice,*
> *Sorrows are hard to forget,*
> *What will make us forget them?*
> *Wine, and only wine.*"

After Ts'ao Ts'ao's death came the epoch of the Three

Kingdoms, the romantic story of which is told in the famous novel to be mentioned later on. Ts'ao Ts'ao's eldest son became the first Emperor of one of these, the Wei Kingdom, and Ts'AO CHĪH, the poet, occupied an awkward position at court, an object of suspicion and dislike. At ten years of age he already excelled in composition, so much so that his father thought he must be a plagiarist; but he settled the question by producing off-hand poems on any given theme. "If all the talent of the world," said a contemporary poet, "were represented by ten, Ts'ao Chih would have eight, I should have one, and the rest of mankind one between them." There is a story that on one occasion, at the bidding of his elder brother, probably with mischievous intent, he composed an impromptu stanza while walking only seven steps. It has been remembered more for its point than its poetry :—

> " *A fine dish of beans had been placed in the pot*
> *With a view to a good mess of pottage all hot.*
> *The beanstalks, aflame, a fierce heat were begetting,*
> *The beans in the pot were all fuming and fretting.*
> *Yet the beans and the stalks were not born to be foes ;*
> *Oh, why should these hurry to finish off those ?* "

The following extract from a poem of his contains a very well-known maxim, constantly in use at the present day :—

> " *The superior man takes precautions,*
> *And avoids giving cause for suspicion.*
> *He will not pull up his shoes in a melon-field,*
> *Nor under a plum-tree straighten his hat.*
> *Brothers- and sisters-in-law may not join hands,*
> *Elders and youngers may not walk abreast ;*
> *By toil and humility the handle is grasped ;*
> *Moderate your brilliancy, and difficulties disappear.* "

During the third century A.D. another and more mercurial set of poets, also seven in number, formed themselves into a club, and became widely famous as the Seven Sages of the Bamboo Grove. Among these was LIU LING, a hard drinker, who declared that to a drunken man "the affairs of this world appear but as so much duckweed on a river." He wished to be always accompanied by a servant with wine, followed by another with a spade, so that he might be buried where he fell. On one occasion, yielding to the entreaties of his wife, he promised to "swear off," and bade her prepare the usual sacrifices of wine and meat. When all was ready, he prayed, saying, "O God, who didst give to Liu Ling a reputation through wine, he being able to consume a gallon at a sitting and requiring a quart to sober him again, listen not to the words of his wife, for she speaketh not truth." Thereupon he drank up the sacrificial wine, and was soon as drunk as ever. His bias was towards the Tao of Lao Tzŭ, and he was actually plucked for his degree in consequence of an essay extolling the heterodox doctrine of Inaction. The following skit exhibits this Taoist strain to a marked degree :—

"An old gentleman, a friend of mine (that is, himself), regards eternity as but a single day, and whole centuries as but an instant of time. The sun and moon are the windows of his house; the cardinal points are the boundaries of his domain. He wanders unrestrained and free; he dwells within no walls. The canopy of heaven is his roof; his resting-place is the lap of earth. He follows his fancy in all things. He is never for a moment without a wine-flask in one hand, a goblet in the other. His only thought is wine: he knows of naught beyond.

"Two respectable philanthropists, hearing of my friend's weakness, proceeded to tax him on the subject; and with many gestures of disapprobation, fierce scowls, and gnashing of teeth, preached him quite a sermon on the rules of propriety, and sent his faults buzzing round his head like a swarm of bees.

"When they began, the old gentleman filled himself another bumper; and sitting down, quietly stroked his beard and sipped his wine by turns, until at length he lapsed into a semi-inebriate state of placid enjoyment, varied by intervals of absolute unconsciousness or of partial return to mental lucidity. His ears were beyond the reach of thunder; he could not have seen a mountain. Heat and cold existed for him no more. He knew not even the workings of his own mind. To him, the affairs of this world appeared but as so much duckweed on a river; while the two philanthropists at his side looked like two wasps trying to convert a caterpillar" (into a wasp, as the Chinese believe is done).

Another was HSI K'ANG, a handsome young man, seven feet seven inches in height, who was married—a doubtful boon—into the Imperial family. His favourite study was alchemistic research, and he passed his days sitting under a willow-tree in his courtyard and experimenting in the transmutation of metals, varying his toil with music and poetry, and practising the art of breathing with a view to securing immortality. Happening, however, to offend by his want of ceremony one of the Imperial princes, who was also a student of alchemy, he was denounced to the Emperor as a dangerous person and a traitor, and condemned to death. Three thousand disciples offered each one to take the place of their beloved master, but their request was not granted. He met his fate with fortitude, calmly watching the shadows thrown by the sun and playing upon his lute.

The third was HSIANG HSIU, who also tried his hand at alchemy, and whose commentary on Chuang Tzŭ was stolen, as has been already stated, by Kuo Hsiang.

The fourth was YÜAN HSIEN, a wild harum-scarum fellow, but a performer on the guitar and a great authority on the theory of music. He and his uncle, both poverty-stricken, lived on one side of the road, while a wealthier branch of the family lived on the other side. On the seventh of the seventh moon the latter put out all their grand fur robes and fine clothes to air, as is customary on that day; whereupon Yüan Hsien on his side forked up a pair of the short breeches, called calf-nose drawers, worn by the common coolies, explaining to a friend that he was a victim to the tyranny of custom.

The fifth was YÜAN CHI, another musician, whose harpsichords became the "Strads" of China. He entered the army and rose to a high command, and then exchanged his post for one where he had heard there was a better cook. He was a model of filial piety, and when his mother died he wept so violently that he brought up several pints of blood. Yet when Chi Hsi went to condole with him, he showed only the whites of his eyes (that is, paid no attention to him); while Chi Hsi's brother, who carried along with him a jar of wine and a guitar, was welcomed with the pupils. His best-known work is a political and allegorical poem in thirty-eight stanzas averaging about twelve lines to each. The allusions in this are so skilfully veiled as to be quite unrecognisable without a commentary, such concealment being absolutely necessary for the protection of the author in the troublous times during which he wrote.

The sixth was WANG JUNG, who could look at the sun without being dazzled, and lastly there was SHAN T'AO, a follower of Taoist teachings, who was spoken of as "uncut jade" and as "gold ore."

Later on, in the fourth century, comes FU MI, of whom nothing is known beyond his verses, of which the following is a specimen :—

> " *Thy chariot and horses*
> *have gone, and I fret*
> *And long for the lover*
> *I ne'er can forget.*
>
> *O wanderer, bound*
> *in far countries to dwell,*
> *Would I were thy shadow !—*
> *I'd follow thee well ;*
>
> *And though clouds and though darkness*
> *my presence should hide,*
> *In the bright light of day*
> *I would stand by thy side !* "

We now reach a name which is still familiar to all students of poetry in the Middle Kingdom. T'AO CH'IEN (A.D. 365–427), or T'ao Yüan-ming as he was called in early life, after a youth of poverty obtained an appointment as magistrate. But he was unfitted by nature for official life ; all he wanted, to quote his own prayer, was "length of years and depth of wine." He only held the post for eighty-three days, objecting to receive a superior officer with the usual ceremonial on the ground that "he could not crook the hinges of his back for five pecks of rice a day," such being the regulation pay of a magistrate. He then retired into private life and occupied himself with poetry, music, and the culture of flowers, especially chrysanthemums, which are inseparably associated with his name. In the latter pursuit he was seconded by his wife, who worked in the back garden while he worked in the front. His retirement from office is the subject of the following piece, of the poetical-prose class, which, in point of style, is considered one of the masterpieces of the language :—

"Homewards I bend my steps. My fields, my gardens, are choked with weeds: should I not go ? My soul has led a bondsman's life: why should I remain to pine ? But I will waste no grief upon the past ; I will devote my energies to the future. I have not wandered far astray. I feel that I am on the right track once again.

"Lightly, lightly, speeds my boat along, my garments fluttering to the gentle breeze. I inquire my route as I go. I grudge the slowness of the dawning day. From afar I descry my old home, and joyfully press onwards in my haste. The servants rush forth to meet me; my children cluster at the gate. The place is a wilderness; but there is the old pine-tree and my chrysanthemums. I take the little ones by the hand, and pass in. Wine is brought in full jars, and I pour out in brimming cups. I gaze out at my favourite branches. I loll against the window in my new-found freedom. I look at the sweet children on my knee.

"And now I take my pleasure in my garden. There is a gate, but it is rarely opened. I lean on my staff as I wander about or sit down to rest. I raise my head and contemplate the lovely scene. Clouds rise, unwilling, from the bottom of the hills; the weary bird seeks its nest again. Shadows vanish, but still I linger around my lonely pine. Home once more! I'll have no friendships to distract me hence. The times are out of joint for me ; and what have I to seek from men ? In the pure enjoyment of the family circle I will pass my days, cheering my idle hours with lute and book. My husbandmen will tell me when spring-time is nigh, and when there will be work in the furrowed fields. Thither I shall repair by cart or by boat, through the deep gorge, over the dizzy cliff, trees bursting merrily into leaf, the streamlet swelling from its tiny source. Glad is this renewal of life in due season; but for me, I rejoice that my journey is over. Ah, how short a time it is that we are here! Why then not set our hearts at rest, ceasing to trouble whether we remain or go? What boots it to wear out the soul with anxious thoughts? I want not wealth; I want not power; heaven is beyond my hopes. Then let me stroll through the bright hours as they pass, in my garden among my flowers; or I will mount the hill and sing my song, or weave my verse beside the limpid brook. Thus will I work out my allotted span, content with the appointments of Fate, my spirit free from care."

The "Peach-blossom Fountain" of T'ao Ch'ien is a well-known and charming allegory, a form of literature much cultivated by Chinese writers. It tells how a fisherman lost his way among the creeks of a river, and came upon a dense and lovely grove of peach-trees in full bloom, through which he pushed his boat, anxious to see how far the grove extended.

"He found that the peach-trees ended where the water began, at the foot of a hill; and there he espied what seemed to be a cave with light issuing from it. So he made fast his boat, and crept in through a narrow entrance, which shortly ushered him into a new world of level country, of fine houses, of rich fields, of fine pools, and of luxuriance of mulberry and bamboo.

Highways of traffic ran north and south; sounds of crowing cocks and barking dogs were heard around; the dress of the people who passed along or were at work in the fields was of a strange cut; while young and old alike appeared to be contented and happy."

He is told that the ancestors of these people had taken refuge there some five centuries before to escape the troublous days of the "First Emperor," and that there they had remained, cut off completely from the rest of the human race. On his returning home the story is noised abroad, and the Governor sends out men to find this strange region, but the fisherman is never able to find it again. The gods had permitted the poet to go back for a brief span to the peach-blossom days of his youth.

One critic speaks of T'ao Ch'ien as "drunk with the fumes of spring." Another says, "His heart was fixed upon loyalty and duty, while his body was content with leisure and repose. His emotions were real, his scenery was real, his facts were real, and his thoughts were real. His workmanship was so exceedingly fine as to appear natural; his adze and chisel (*labor limae*) left no traces behind."

Much of his poetry is political, and bristles with allusions to events which are now forgotten, mixed up with thoughts and phrases which are greatly admired by his countrymen. Thus, when he describes meeting with an old friend in a far-off land, such a passage as this would be heavily scored by editor or critic with marks of commendation :—

> "*Ere words be spoke, the heart is drunk;*
> *What need to call for wine?*"

The following is one of his occasional poems :—

> *A scholar lives on yonder hill,*
>   *His clothes are rarely whole to view,*
> *Nine times a month he eats his fill,*
>   *Once in ten years his hat is new.*
> *A wretched lot !—and yet the while*
> *He ever wears a sunny smile.*
>
> *Longing to know what like was he,*
>   *At dawn my steps a path unclosed*
> *Where dark firs left the passage free*
>   *And on the eaves the white clouds dozed.*
>
> *But he, as spying my intent,*
>   *Seized his guitar and swept the strings ;*
> *Up flew a crane towards heaven bent,*
>   *And now a startled pheasant springs. . . .*
> *Oh, let me rest with thee until*
> *The winter winds again blow chill !*"

PAO CHAO was an official and a poet who perished, A.D. 466, in a rebellion. Some of his poetry has been preserved :—

> *" What do these halls of jasper mean,*
>   *and shining floor,*
> *Where tapestries of satin screen*
>   *window and door ?*
> *A lady on a lonely seat,*
>   *embroidering*
> *Fair flowers which seem to smell as sweet*
>   *as buds in spring.*
> *Swallows flit past, a zephyr shakes*
>   *the plum-blooms down ;*
> *She draws the blind, a goblet takes*
>   *her thoughts to drown.*
> *And now she sits in tears, or hums,*
>   *nursing her grief*
> *That in her life joy rarely comes*
>   *to bring relief. . .*

Oh, for the humble turtle's flight,
my mate and I;
Not the lone crane far out of sight
beyond the sky!"

The original name of a striking character who, in A.D. 502, placed himself upon the throne as first Emperor of the Liang dynasty, was HSIAO YEN. He was a devout Buddhist, living upon priestly fare and taking only one meal a day; and on two occasions, in 527 and 529, he actually adopted the priestly garb. He also wrote a Buddhist ritual in ten books. Interpreting the Buddhist commandment "Thou shalt not kill" in its strictest sense, he caused the sacrificial victims to be made of dough. The following short poem is from his pen :—

" Trees grow, not alike,
by the mound and the moat;
Birds sing in the forest
with varying note;
Of the fish in the river
some dive and some float.
The mountains rise high
and the waters sink low,
But the why and the wherefore
we never can know."

Another well-known poet who lived into the seventh century is HSIEH TAO-HÊNG. He offended Yang Ti, the second Emperor of the Sui dynasty, by writing better verses than his Majesty, and an excuse was found for putting him to death. One of the most admired couplets in the language is associated with his name though not actually by him, its author being unknown. To amuse a party of friends Hsieh Tao-hêng had written impromptu,

" A week in the spring to the exile appears
Like an absence from home of a couple of years."

A "southerner" who was present sneered at the shallowness of the conceit, and immediately wrote down the following :—

> "*If home, with the wild geese of autumn,*
> *we're going,*
> *Our hearts will be off ere the spring flowers*
> *are blowing.*"

An official of the Sui dynasty was FU I (A.D. 554–639), who became Historiographer under the first Emperor of the T'ang dynasty. He had a strong leaning towards Taoism, and edited the *Tao-Tê-Ching*. At the same time he presented a memorial asking that the Buddhist religion might be abolished ; and when Hsiao Yü, a descendant of Hsiao Yen (above), questioned him on the subject, he said, "You were not born in a hollow mulberry-tree ; yet you respect a religion which does not recognise the tie between father and son !" He urged that at any rate priests and nuns should be compelled to marry and bring up families, and not escape from contributing their share to the revenue, adding that Hsiao Yü by defending their doctrines showed himself no better than they were. At this Hsiao Yü held up his hands, and declared that hell was made for such men as Fu I. The result was that severe restrictions were placed for a short time upon the teachers of Buddhism. The Emperor T'ai Tsung once got hold of a Tartar priest who could "charm people into unconsciousness, and then charm them back to life again," and spoke of his powers to Fu I. The latter said confidently, "He will not be able to charm me ;" and when put to the test, the priest completely failed. He was the originator of epitaphs, and wrote his own, as follows :—

" Fu I loved the green hills and the white clouds . . .
Alas ! he died of drink."

WANG CHI of the sixth and seventh centuries A.D., was a wild and unconventional spirit, with a fatal fondness for wine, which caused his dismissal from office. His capacity for liquor was boundless, and he was known as the Five-bottle Scholar. In his lucid intervals he wrote much beautiful prose and verse, which may still be read with pleasure. The following is from an account of his visit to Drunk-Land, the story of which is told with all due gravity and in a style modelled upon that which is found in ordinary accounts of strange outlandish nations :—

"This country is many thousand miles from the Middle Kingdom. It is a vast, boundless plain, without mountains or undulations of any kind. The climate is equable, there being neither night, nor day, nor cold, nor heat. The manners and customs are everywhere the same.

"There are no villages nor congregations of persons. The inhabitants are ethereal in disposition, and know neither love, hate, joy, nor anger. They inhale the breeze and sip the dew, eating none of the five cereals. Calm in repose, slow of gait, they mingle with birds, beasts, fishes, and scaly creatures, ignorant of boats, chariots, weapons, or implements in general.

"The Yellow Emperor went on a visit to the capital of Drunk-Land, and when he came back, he was quite out of conceit with the empire, the government of which seemed to him but paltry trifling with knotted cords.

"Yüan Chi, T'ao Ch'ien,[1] and some others, about ten in all, made a trip together to Drunk-Land, and sank,

---

[1] Here the poet makes a mistake. These two were not contemporaries.

never to rise again. They were buried where they fell, and now in the Middle Kingdom they are dubbed Spirits of Wine.

"Alas, I could not bear that the pure and peaceful domain of Drunk-Land should come to be regarded as a preserve of the ancients. So I went there myself."

The period closes with the name of the Emperor known as Yang Ti, already mentioned in connection with the poet Hsieh Tao-hêng. The murderer, first of his elder brother and then of his father, he mounted the throne in A.D. 605, and gave himself up to extravagance and debauchery. The trees in his park were supplied in winter with silken leaves and flowers, and birds were almost exterminated to provide a sufficient supply of down for his cushions. After reigning for thirteen years this unlikely patron of literature fell a victim to assassination. Yet in spite of his otherwise disreputable character, Yang Ti prided himself upon his literary attainments. He set one hundred scholars to work editing a collection of classical, medical, and other treatises ; and it was under his reign, in A.D. 606, that the examination for the second or "master of arts" degree was instituted.

CHAPTER II

CLASSICAL SCHOLARSHIP

IN the domains of classical and general literature HUANG-
FU MI (A.D. 215-282) occupies an honourable place.
Beginning life at the ploughtail, by perseverance he
became a fine scholar, and adopted literature as a pro-
fession. In spite of severe rheumatism he was never
without a book in his hand, and became so absorbed
in his work that he would forget all about meals and
bedtime. He was called the Book-Debauchee, and once
when he wished to borrow works from the Emperor
Wu Ti of the Chin dynasty, whose proffers of office he
had refused, his Majesty sent him back a cart-load to
go on with. He produced essays, poetry, and several
important biographical works. His work on the Spring
and Autumn Annals had also considerable vogue.

SUN SHU-JAN, of about the same date, distinguished
himself by his works on the Confucian Canon, and wrote
on the *Erh Ya*.

HSÜN HSÜ (*d.* A.D. 289) aided in drawing up a Penal
Code for the newly-established Chin dynasty, took a
leading part in editing the Bamboo Annals, which had
just been discovered in Honan, provided a preface to
the *Mu T'ien Tzŭ Chuan*, and also wrote on music.

KUO HSIANG (*d.* A.D. 312) occupied himself chiefly
with the philosophy of Lao Tzŭ and with the writings

of Chuang Tzŭ. It was said of him that his conversation was like the continuous downflow of a rapid, or the rush of water from a sluice.

KUO P'O (*d.* A.D. 324) was a scholar of great repute. Besides editing various important classical works, he was a brilliant exponent of the doctrines of Taoism and the reputed founder of the art of geomancy as applied to graves, universally practised in China at the present day. He was also learned in astronomy, divination, and natural philosophy.

FAN YEH, executed for treason in A.D. 445, is chiefly famous for his history of the Han dynasty from about the date of the Christian era, when the dynasty was interrupted, as has been stated, by a usurper, down to the final collapse two hundred years later.

SHÊN YO (A.D. 441–513), another famous scholar, was the son of a Governor of Huai-nan, whose execution in A.D. 453 caused him to go for a time into hiding. Poor and studious, he is said to have spent the night in repeating what he had learnt by day, as his mother, anxious on account of his health, limited his supply of oil and fuel. Entering official life, he rose to high office, from which he retired in ill-health, loaded with honours. Personally, he was remarkable for having two pupils to his left eye. He was a strict teetotaller, and lived most austerely. He had a library of twenty thousand volumes. He was the author of the histories of the Chin, Liu Sung, and Ch'i dynasties. He is said to have been the first to classify the four tones. In his autobiography he writes, "The poets of old, during the past thousand years, never hit upon this plan. I alone discovered its advantages." The Emperor Wu Ti of the Liang dynasty one day said to him, "Come, tell me, what are these famous four tones?" "They are whatever your Majesty pleases to make them," replied Shên Yo, skilfully selecting for his answer four characters which illustrated, and in the usual order, the four tones in question.

HSIAO T'UNG (A.D. 501–531) was the eldest son of Hsiao Yen, the founder of the Liang dynasty, whom he predeceased. Before he was five years old he was reported to have learned the Classics by heart, and his later years were marked by great literary ability, notably in verse-making. Handsome and of charming manners, mild and forbearing, he was universally loved. In 527 he nursed his mother through her last illness, and his grief for her death impaired his naturally fine constitution, for it was only at the earnest solicitation of his father that he consented either to eat or drink during the period of mourning. Learned men were sure of his patronage, and his palace contained a large library. A lover of nature, he delighted to ramble with scholars about his beautiful park, to which he declined to add the attraction of singing-girls. When the price of grain rose in consequence of the war with Wei in 526, he lived on the most frugal fare; and throughout his life his charities were very large and kept secret, being distributed by trusty attendants who sought out all cases of distress. He even emptied his own wardrobe for the benefit of the poor, and spent large sums in burying the outcast dead. Against forced labour on public works he vehemently protested. To his father he was most respectful, and wrote to him when he himself was almost at the last gasp, in the hope of concealing his danger. But he is remembered now not so much for his virtues as for his initiation of a new department in literature. A year before his death he completed the *Wên Hsüan*, the first published collection of choice works, whole or in part, of a large number of authors. These were classified under such heads as poetry of various kinds, essays, inscriptions, memorials, funeral orations, epitaphs, and prefaces.

The idea thus started was rapidly developed, and has been continued down to modern times. Huge collections of works have from time to time been reprinted in uniform editions, and many books which might otherwise have perished have been preserved for grateful posterity. The Record of the Buddhistic Kingdoms by Fa Hsien may be quoted as an example.

BOOK THE FOURTH

THE T'ANG DYNASTY (A.D. 600–900)

BOOK THE FOURTH

THE T'ANG DYNASTY (A.D. 600–900)

CHAPTER I

POETRY

THE T'ang dynasty is usually associated in Chinese minds with much romance of love and war, with wealth, culture, and refinement, with frivolity, extravagance, and dissipation, but most of all with poetry. China's best efforts in this direction were chiefly produced within the limits of its three hundred years' duration, and they have been carefully preserved as finished models for future poets of all generations.

"Poetry," says a modern Chinese critic, "came into being with the Odes, developed with the *Li Sao*, burst forth and reached perfection under the T'angs. Some good work was indeed done under the Han and Wei dynasties; the writers of those days seemed to have material in abundance, but language inadequate to its expression."

The "Complete Collection of the Poetry of the T'ang Dynasty," published in 1707, contains 48,900 poems of all kinds, arranged in 900 books, and filling thirty good-sized volumes. Some Chinese writers divide the dynasty into three poetical periods, called Early, Glorious, and

Late ; and they profess to detect in the works assigned to each the corresponding characteristics of growth, fulness, and decay. Others insert a Middle period between the last two, making four periods in all. For general purposes, however, it is only necessary to state, that since the age of the Hans the meanings of words had gradually come to be more definitely fixed, and the structural arrangement more uniform and more polished. Imagination began to come more freely into play, and the language to flow more easily and more musically, as though responsive to the demands of art. A Chinese poem is at best a hard nut to crack, expressed as it usually is in lines of five or seven monosyllabic root-ideas, without inflection, agglutination, or grammatical indication of any kind, the connection between which has to be inferred by the reader from the logic, from the context, and least perhaps of all from the syntactical arrangement of the words. Then, again, the poet is hampered not only by rhyme but also by tone. For purposes of poetry the characters in the Chinese language are all ranged under two tones, as *flats* and *sharps*, and these occupy fixed positions just as dactyls, spondees, trochees, and anapæsts in the construction of Latin verse. As a consequence, the natural order of words is often entirely sacrificed to the exigencies of tone, thus making it more difficult than ever for the reader to grasp the sense. In a stanza of the ordinary five-character length the following tonal arrangement would appear :—

Sharp	*sharp*	*flat*	*flat*	*sharp*
Flat	*flat*	*sharp*	*sharp*	*flat*
Flat	*flat*	*flat*	*sharp*	*sharp*
Sharp	*sharp*	*sharp*	*flat*	*flat.*

The effect produced by these tones is very marked and pleasing to the ear, and often makes up for the faultiness of the rhymes, which are simply the rhymes of the Odes as heard 2500 years ago, many of them of course being no longer rhymes at all. Thus, there is as much artificiality about a stanza of Chinese verse as there is about an Alcaic stanza in Latin. But in the hands of the most gifted this artificiality is altogether concealed by art, and the very trammels of tone and rhyme become transfigured, and seem to be necessary aids and adjuncts to success. Many works have been published to guide the student in his admittedly difficult task. The first rule in one of these seems so comprehensive as to make further perusal quite unnecessary. It runs thus :— "Discard commonplace form ; discard commonplace ideas ; discard commonplace phrasing ; discard commonplace words ; discard commonplace rhymes."

A long poem does not appeal to the Chinese mind. There is no such thing as an epic in the language, though, of course, there are many pieces extending to several hundred lines. Brevity is indeed the soul of a Chinese poem, which is valued not so much for what it says as for what it suggests. As in painting, so in poetry suggestion is the end and aim of the artist, who in each case may be styled an impressionist. The ideal length is twelve lines, and this is the limit set to candidates at the great public examinations at the present day, the Chinese holding that if a poet cannot say within such compass what he has to say it may very well be left unsaid. The eight-line poem is also a favourite, and so, but for its extreme difficulty, is the four-line epigram, or "stop-short," so called because of its abruptness, though, as the critics explain, "it is

only the words which stop, the sense goes on," some
train of thought having been suggested to the reader.
The latter form of verse was in use so far back as the
Han dynasty, but only reached perfection under the
T'angs. Although consisting of only twenty or twenty-
eight words, according to the measure employed, it is
just long enough for the poet to introduce, to develop,
to embellish, and to conclude his theme in accordance
with certain established laws of composition. The third
line is considered the most troublesome to produce,
some poets even writing it first; the last line should
contain a "surprise" or *dénouement*. We are, in fact,
reminded of the old formula, "Omne epigramma sit
instar apis," &c., better known in its English dress:—

> "*The qualities rare in a bee that we meet*
> *In an epigram never should fail;*
> *The body should always be little and sweet,*
> *And a sting should be left in the tail.*"

The following is an early specimen, by an anonymous
writer, of the four-line poem :—

> "*The bright moon shining overhead,*
> *The stream beneath the breeze's touch,*
> *Are pure and perfect joys indeed,—*
> *But few are they who think them such.*"

Turning now to the almost endless list of poets from
which but a scanty selection can be made, we may
begin with WANG PO (A.D. 648–676), a precocious boy
who wrote verses when he was six. He took his degree
at sixteen, and was employed in the Historical Department, but was dismissed for satirising the cock-fighting
propensities of the Imperial princes. He filled up his
leisure by composing many beautiful poems. He never

meditated on these beforehand, but after having prepared a quantity of ink ready for use, he would drink himself tipsy and lie down with his face covered up. On waking he would seize his pen and write off verses, not a word in which needed to be changed; whence he acquired the sobriquet of Belly-Draft, meaning that his drafts, or rough copies, were all prepared inside. And he received so many presents of valuable silks for writing these odes, that it was said "he spun with his mind." These lines are from his pen :—

> "*Near these islands a palace*
>   *was built by a prince,*
> *But its music and song*
>   *have departed long since ;*
> *The hill-mists of morning*
>   *sweep down on the halls,*
> *At night the red curtains*
>   *lie furled on the walls.*
> *The clouds o'er the water*
>   *their shadows still cast,*
> *Things change like the stars :*
>   *how few autumns have passed*
> *And yet where is that prince ?*
>   *where is he ?—No reply,*
> *Save the plash of the stream*
>   *rolling ceaselessly by.*"

A still more famous contemporary of his was CH'ÊN TZŬ-ANG (A.D. 656–698), who adopted somewhat sensational means of bringing himself to the notice of the public. He purchased a very expensive guitar which had been for a long time on sale, and then let it be known that on the following day he would perform upon it in public. This attracted a large crowd ; but when Ch'ên arrived he informed his auditors that he had something in his pocket worth much more than the guitar. Thereupon he dashed the instrument into a thousand pieces, and forthwith began handing round copies of his own writings. Here is a sample, directed against the Buddhist worship of idols, the "Prophet" representing any divinely-inspired teacher of the Confucian school:—

> *On Self the Prophet never rests his eye,*
>   *His to relieve the doom of humankind;*
> *No fairy palaces beyond the sky,*
>   *Rewards to come, are present to his mind.*
>
> *And I have heard the faith by Buddha taught*
>   *Lauded as pure and free from earthly taint;*
> *Why then these carved and graven idols, fraught*
>   *With gold and silver, gems, and jade, and paint?*
>
> *The heavens that roof this earth, mountain and dale,*
>   *All that is great and grand, shall pass away;*
> *And if the art of gods may not prevail,*
>   *Shall man's poor handiwork escape decay?*
>
> *Fools that ye are! In this ignoble light*
> *The true faith fades and passes out of sight."*

As an official, Ch'ên Tzŭ-ang once gained great *kudos* by a truly Solomonic decision. A man, having slain the murderer of his father, was himself indicted for murder. Ch'ên Tzŭ-ang caused him to be put to death, but at the same time conferred an honorific distinction upon his village for having produced so filial a son.

Not much is known of SUNG CHIH-WÊN (*d.* A.D. 710), at any rate to his good. On one occasion the Emperor was so delighted with some of his verses that he took off the Imperial robe and placed it on the poet's shoulders. This is one of his poems:—

> *"The dust of the morn*
>   *had been laid by a shower,*
>   *And the trees by the bridge*
>   *were all covered with flower,*

When a white palfrey passed
            with a saddle of gold,
And a damsel as fair
            as the fairest of old.

But she veiled so discreetly
            her charms from my eyes
That the boy who was with her
            quite felt for my sighs;
And although not a light-o'-love
            reckoned, I deem,
It was hard that this vision
            should pass like a aream."

MÊNG HAO-JAN (A.D. 689–740) gave no sign in his youth of the genius that was latent within him. He failed at the public examinations, and retired to the mountains as a recluse. He then became a poet of the first rank, and his writings were eagerly sought after. At the age of forty he went up to the capital, and was one day conversing with his famous contemporary, Wang Wei, when suddenly the Emperor was announced. He hid under a couch, but Wang Wei betrayed him, the result being a pleasant interview with his Majesty. The following is a specimen of his verse :—

" *The sun has set behind the western slope,*
    The eastern moon lies mirrored in the pool;
With streaming hair my balcony I ope,
    And stretch my limbs out to enjoy the cool.
Loaded with lotus-scent the breeze sweeps by,
    Clear dripping drops from tall bamboos I hear,
I gaze upon my idle lute and sigh;
    Alas, no sympathetic soul is near .
And so I doze, the while before mine eyes
Dear friends of other days in dream-clad forms arise."

Equally famous as poet and physician was WANG WEI (A.D. 699–759). After a short spell of official life, he too retired into seclusion and occupied himself with poetry and with the consolations of Buddhism, in which he was a firm believer. His lines on bidding adieu to Mêng Hao-jan, when the latter was seeking refuge on the mountains, are as follows :—

> " *Dismounted, o'er wine*
> *we had said our last say ;*
> *Then I whisper, ' Dear friend,*
> *tell me, whither away ? '*
> *' Alas ! ' he replied,*
> *' I am sick of life's ills,*
> *And I long for repose*
> *on the slumbering hills.*
> *But oh seek not to pierce*
> *where my footsteps may stray :*
> *The white clouds will soothe me*
> *for ever and ay.' "*

The accompanying "stop-short" by the same writer is generally thought to contain an effective surprise in the last line :—

> " *Beneath the bamboo grove, alone,*
> *I seize my lute and sit and croon ;*
> *No ear to hear me, save mine own :*
> *No eye to see me—save the moon.*"

Wang Wei has been accused of loose writing and incongruous pictures. A friendly critic defends him as follows :—" For instance, there is Wang Wei, who introduces bananas into a snow-storm. When, however, we come to examine such points by the light of scholarship, we see that his mind had merely passed into subjective relationship with the things described. Fools say he did not know heat from cold."

A skilled poet, and a wine-bibber and gambler to boot, was Ts'UI HAO, who graduated about A.D. 730.

He wrote a poem on the Yellow-Crane pagoda which until quite recently stood on the bank of the Yang-tsze near Hankow, and was put up to mark the spot where Wang Tzŭ-ch'iao, who had attained immortality, went up to heaven in broad daylight six centuries before the Christian era. The great Li Po once thought of writing on the theme, but he gave up the idea so soon as he had read these lines by Ts'ui Hao :—

> " *Here a mortal once sailed*
> *up to heaven on a crane,*
> *And the Yellow-Crane Kiosque,*
> *will for ever remain ;*
> *But the bird flew away*
> *and will come back no more,*
> *Though the white clouds are there*
> *as the white clouds of yore.*
>
> *Away to the east*
> *lie fair forests of trees,*
> *From the flowers on the west*
> *comes a scent-laden breeze,*
> *Yet my eyes daily turn*
> *to their far-away home,*
> *Beyond the broad River,*
> *its waves, and its foam.*"

By general consent LI PO himself (A.D. 705–762) would probably be named as China's greatest poet. His wild Bohemian life, his gay and dissipated career at Court, his exile, and his tragic end, all combine to form a most effective setting for the splendid flow of verse which he never ceased to pour forth. At the early age of ten he wrote a " stop-short " to a firefly :—

> " *Rain cannot quench thy lantern's light,*
> *Wind makes it shine more brightly bright ;*
> *Oh why not fly to heaven afar,*
> *And twinkle near the moon—a star ?*"

Li Po began by wandering about the country, until at length, with five other tippling poets, he retired to the mountains. For some time these Six Idlers of the Bamboo Grove drank and wrote verses to their hearts' content. By and by Li Po reached the capital, and on the strength of his poetry was introduced to the Emperor as a "banished angel." He was received with open arms, and soon became the spoilt child of the palace. On one occasion, when the Emperor sent for him, he was found lying drunk in the street; and it was only after having his face well mopped with cold water that he was fit for the Imperial presence. His talents, however, did not fail him. With a lady of the seraglio to hold his ink-slab, he dashed off some of his most impassioned lines; at which the Emperor was so overcome that he made the powerful eunuch Kao Li-shih go down on his knees and pull off the poet's boots. On another occasion, the Emperor, who was enjoying himself with his favourite lady in the palace grounds, called for Li Po to commemorate the scene in verse. After some delay the poet arrived, supported between two eunuchs. "Please your Majesty," he said, "I have been drinking with the Prince and he has made me drunk, but I will do my best." Thereupon two of the ladies of the harem held up in front of him a pink silk screen, and in a very short time he had thrown off no less than ten eight-line stanzas, of which the following, describing the life of a palace favourite, is one :—

> "*Oh, the joy of youth spent*
> *in a gold-fretted hall,*
> *In the Crape-flower Pavilion,*
> *the fairest of all,*

My tresses for head-dress
  with gay garlands girt,
Carnations arranged
  o'er my jacket and skirt !
Then to wander away
  in the soft-scented air,
And return by the side
  of his Majesty's chair . . .
But the dance and the song
  will be o'er by and by,
And we shall dislimn
  like the rack in the sky."

As time went on, Li Po fell a victim to intrigue, and left the Court in disgrace. It was then that he wrote—

" My whitening hair would make a long, long rope,
  Yet would not fathom all my depth of woe."

After more wanderings and much adventure, he was drowned on a journey, from leaning one night too far over the edge of a boat in a drunken effort to embrace the reflection of the moon. Just previously he had indited the following lines :—

" An arbour of flowers
  and a kettle of wine :
Alas ! in the bowers
  no companion is mine.
Then the moon sheds her rays
  on my goblet and me,
And my shadow betrays
  we're a party of three.

" Though the moon cannot swallow
  her share of the grog,
And my shadow must follow
  wherever I jog,—
Yet their friendship I'll borrow
  and gaily carouse,
And laugh away sorrow
  while spring-time allows.

> " *See the moon,—how she glances*
> *response to my song ;*
> *See my shadow,—it dances*
> *so lightly along !*
> *While sober I feel*
> *you are both my good friends ;*
> *When drunken I reel,*
> *our companionship ends.*
> *But we'll soon have a greeting*
> *without a good-bye,*
> *At our next merry meeting*
> *away in the sky.*"

His control of the "stop-short" is considered to be perfect :—

> (1.) " *The birds have all flown to their roost in the tree,*
> *The last cloud has just floated lazily by ;*
> *But we never tire of each other, not we,*
> *As we sit there together,—the mountains*
> *and I.*"

> (2.) " *I wake, and moonbeams play around my bed,*
> *Glittering like hoar-frost to my wondering eyes ;*
> *Up towards the glorious moon I raise my head,*
> *Then lay me down,—and thoughts of*
> *home arise.*"

The following are general extracts :—

A PARTING.

> (1.) " *The river rolls crystal as clear as the sky,*
> *To blend far away with the blue waves of ocean ;*
> *Man alone, when the hour of departure is nigh,*
> *With the wine-cup can soothe his emotion.*
>
> " *The birds of the valley sing loud in the sun,*
> *Where the gibbons their vigils will shortly be keeping :*
> *I thought that with tears I had long ago done,*
> *But now I shall never cease weeping.*"

(2.) "*Homeward at dusk the clanging rookery*
　　　　wings its eager flight;
Then, chattering on the branches, all
　　　are pairing for the night.
Plying her busy loom, a high-born
　　　dame is sitting near,
And through the silken window-screen
　　　their voices strike her ear.
She stops, and thinks of the absent spouse
　　　she may never see again;
And late in the lonely hours of night
　　　her tears flow down like rain."

(3.) "*What is life after all but a dream?*
　　　And why should such pother be made?
Better far to be tipsy, I deem,
　　　And doze all day long in the shade.

"*When I wake and look out on the lawn,*
　　　I hear midst the flowers a bird sing;
I ask, 'Is it evening or dawn?'
　　　The mango-bird whistles, ''Tis spring.'

"*Overpower'd with the beautiful sight,*
　　　Another full goblet I pour,
And would sing till the moon rises bright—
　　　But soon I'm as drunk as before."

(4.) "*You ask what my soul does away in the sky,*
I inwardly smile but I cannot reply;
Like the peach-blossoms carried away by the stream,
I soar to a world of which you cannot dream."

One more extract may be given, chiefly to exhibit what is held by the Chinese to be of the very essence of real poetry,—suggestion. A poet should not dot his *i*'s. The Chinese reader likes to do that for himself, each according to his own fancy. Hence such a poem as the following, often quoted as a model in its own particular line :—

> "*A tortoise I see*
> *on a lotus-flower resting:*
> *A bird 'mid the reeds*
> *and the rushes is nesting;*
> *A light skiff propelled*
> *by some boatman's fair daughter,*
> *Whose song dies away*
> *o'er the fast-flowing water.*"

Another poet of the same epoch, of whom his countrymen are also justly proud, is TU FU (A.D. 712–770). He failed to distinguish himself at the public examinations, at which verse-making counts so much, but had nevertheless such a high opinion of his own poetry that he prescribed it as a cure for malarial fever. He finally obtained a post at Court, which he was forced to vacate in the rebellion of 755. As he himself wrote in political allegory—

> "*Full with the freshets of the spring the torrent rushes on;*
> *The ferry-boat swings idly, for the ferry-man is gone.*"

After further vain attempts to make an official career, he took to a wandering life, was nearly drowned by an inundation, and was compelled to live for ten days on roots. Being rescued, he succumbed next day to the effects of eating roast-beef and drinking white wine to excess after so long a fast. These are some of his poems:—

> (1.) "*The setting sun shines low upon my door*
> *Ere dusk enwraps the river fringed with spring;*
> *Sweet perfumes rise from gardens by the shore,*
> *And smoke, where crews their boats to anchor bring.*
>
> "*Now twittering birds are roosting in the bower,*
> *And flying insects fill the air around. . . .*
> *O wine, who gave to thee thy subtle power?*
> *A thousand cares in one small goblet drowned!*"

(2.) " *A petal falls !—the spring begins to fail,*
 And my heart saddens with the growing gale.
 Come then, ere autumn spoils bestrew the ground,
 Do not forget to pass the wine-cup round.
 Kingfishers build where man once laughed elate,
 And now stone dragons guard his graveyard gate !
 Who follows pleasure, he alone is wise ;
 Why waste our life in deeds of high emprise ?"

(3.) " *My home is girdled by a limpid stream,*
 And there in summer days life's movements pause,
 Save where some swallow flits from beam to beam,
 And the wild sea-gull near and nearer draws.

 " *The goodwife rules a paper board for chess,*
 The children beat a fish-hook out of wire ;
 My ailments call for physic more or less,
 What else should this poor frame of mine require ?"

(4.) " *Alone I wandered o'er the hills*
 to seek the hermit's den,
 While sounds of chopping rang around
 the forest's leafy glen.
 I passed on ice across the brook,
 which had not ceased to freeze,
 As the slanting rays of afternoon
 shot sparkling through the trees.

 " *I found he did not joy to gloat*
 o'er fetid wealth by night,
 But, far from taint, to watch the deer
 in the golden morning light. . . .
 My mind was clear at coming ;
 but now I've lost my guide,
 And rudderless my little bark
 is drifting with the tide !"

(5.) " *From the Court every eve to the pawnshop I pass,*
 To come back from the river the drunkest of men ;
 As often as not I'm in debt for my glass ;—
 Well, few of us live to be threescore and ten.

> *The butterfly flutters from flower to flower,*
> *The dragon-fly sips and springs lightly away,*
> *Each creature is merry its brief little hour,*
> *So let us enjoy our short life while we may."*

Here is a specimen of his skill with the "stop-short," based upon a disease common to all Chinese, poets or otherwise,—nostalgia :—

> *" White gleam the gulls across the darkling tide,*
> *On the green hills the red flowers seem to burn ;*
> *Alas ! I see another spring has died. . . .*
> *When will it come—the day of my return?"*

Of the poet CHANG CH'IEN not much is known. He graduated in 727, and entered upon an official career, but ultimately betook himself to the mountains and lived as a hermit. He is said to have been a devotee of Taoism. The following poem, however, which deals with *dhyâna*, or the state of mental abstraction in which all desire for existence is shaken off, would make it seem as if his leanings had been Buddhistic. It gives a perfect picture, so far as it goes, of the Buddhist retreat often to be found among mountain peaks all over China, visited by pilgrims who perform religious exercises or fulfil vows at the feet of the World-Honoured, and by contemplative students eager to shake off the "red dust" of mundane affairs :—

> *" The clear dawn creeps into the convent old,*
> *The rising sun tips its tall trees with gold,*
> *As, darkly, by a winding path I reach*
> *Dhyâna's hall, hidden midst fir and beech.*
> *Around these hills sweet birds their pleasure take,*
> *Man's heart as free from shadows as this lake ;*
> *Here worldly sounds are hushed, as by a spell,*
> *Save for the booming of the altar bell."*

There can be little doubt of the influence of Buddhism

upon the poet TS'ÊN TS'AN, who graduated about 750, as witness his lines on that faith :—

> *" A shrine whose eaves in far-off cloudland hide :*
> *I mount, and with the sun stand side by side.*
> *The air is clear ; I see wide forests spread*
> *And mist-crowned heights where kings of old lie dead.*
> *Scarce o'er my threshold peeps the Southern Hill ;*
> *The Wei shrinks through my window to a rill. . . .*
> *O thou Pure Faith, had I but known thy scope,*
> *The Golden God[1] had long since been my hope !"*

WANG CHIEN took the highest degree in 775, and rose to be Governor of a District. He managed, however, to offend one of the Imperial clansmen, in consequence of which his official career was abruptly cut short. He wrote a good deal of verse, and was on terms of intimacy with several of the great contemporary poets. In the following lines, the metre of which is irregular, he alludes to the extraordinary case of a soldier's wife who spent all her time on a hill-top looking down the Yangtsze, watching for her husband's return from the wars. At length—

> *" Where her husband she sought,*
> *By the river's long track,*
> *Into stone she was wrought,*
> *And can never come back ;*
> *'Mid the wind and the rain-storm for ever and ay,*
> *She appeals to each home-comer passing that way."*

The last line makes the stone figure, into which the unhappy woman was changed, appear to be asking of every fresh arrival news of the missing man. That is the skill of the artist, and is inseparably woven into the original.

---

[1] Alluding to the huge gilt images of Buddha to be seen in all temples.

Passing over many poets equally well known with some of those already cited, we reach a name undoubtedly the most venerated of all those ever associated in any way with the great mass of Chinese literature. HAN YÜ (A.D. 768–824), canonised and usually spoken of as Han Wên-kung, was not merely a poet, but a statesman of the first rank, and philosopher to boot. He rose from among the humblest of the people to the highest offices of State. In 803 he presented a memorial protesting against certain extravagant honours with which the Emperor Hsien Tsung proposed to receive a bone of Buddha. The monarch was furious, and but for the intercession of friends it would have fared badly with the bold writer. As it was, he was banished to Ch'ao-chou Fu in Kuangtung, where he set himself to civilise the rude inhabitants of those wild parts. In a temple at the summit of the neighbouring range there is to be seen at this day a huge picture of the Prince of Literature, as he has been called by foreigners from his canonisation, with the following legend attached :—
"Wherever he passed, he purified." He is even said to have driven away a huge crocodile which was devastating the watercourses in the neighbourhood ; and the denunciatory ultimatum which he addressed to the monster and threw into the river, together with a pig and a goat, is still regarded as a model of Chinese composition. It was not very long ere he was recalled to the capital and reinstated in office ; but he had been delicate all his life and had grown prematurely old, and was thus unable to resist a severe illness which came upon him. His friend and contemporary, Liu Tsung-yüan, said that he never ventured to open the works of Han Yü without first washing his hands in rose-water.

His writings, especially his essays, are often of the very highest order, leaving nothing to be desired either in originality or in style. But it is more than all for his pure and noble character, his calm and dignified patriotism, that the Chinese still keep his memory green. The following lines were written by Su Tung-p'o, nearly 300 years after his death, for a shrine which had just been put up in honour of the dead teacher by the people of Ch'ao-chou Fu :—

> " *He rode on the dragon to the white cloud domain;*
> *He grasped with his hand the glory of the sky;*
> *Robed with the effulgence of the stars,*
> *The wind bore him delicately to the throne of God.*
> *He swept away the chaff and husks of his generation.*
> *He roamed over the limits of the earth.*
> *He clothed all nature with his bright rays,*
> *The third in the triumvirate of genius.*[1]
> *His rivals panted after him in vain,*
> *Dazed by the brilliancy of the light.*
> *He cursed Buddha; he offended his prince;*
> *He journeyed far away to the distant south;*
> *He passed the grave of Shun, and wept over the daughters of Yao.*
> *The water-god went before him and stilled the waves.*
> *He drove out the fierce monster as it were a lamb.*
> *But above, in heaven, there was no music, and God was sad,*
> *And summoned him to his place beside the Throne.*
> *And now, with these poor offerings, I salute him;*
> *With red lichees and yellow plantain fruit.*
> *Alas! that he did not linger awhile on earth,*
> *But passed so soon, with streaming hair, into the great unknown.*"

Han Yü wrote a large quantity of verse, frequently playful, on an immense variety of subjects, and under his touch the commonplace was often transmuted into wit. Among other pieces there is one on his teeth, which seemed to drop out at regular intervals, so that he

---

[1] The other two were Li Po and Tu Fu.

could calculate roughly what span of life remained to him. Altogether, his poetry cannot be classed with that of the highest order, unlike his prose writings, extracts from which will be given in the next chapter. The following poem is a specimen of his lighter vein :—

> " To stand upon the river-bank
>   and snare the purple fish,
> My net well cast across the stream,
>   was all that I could wish.
> Or lie concealed and shoot the geese
>   that scream and pass apace,
> And pay my rent and taxes with
>   the profits of the chase.
> Then home to peace and happiness,
>   with wife and children gay,
> Though clothes be coarse and fare be hard,
>   and earned from day to day.
> But now I read and read, scarce knowing
>   what 'tis all about,
> And, eager to improve my mind,
>   I wear my body out.
> I draw a snake and give it legs,
>   to find I've wasted skill,
> And my hair grows daily whiter
>   as I hurry towards the hill.[1]
> I sit amid the sorrows
>   I have brought on my own head,
> And find myself estranged from all,
>   among the living dead.
> I seek to drown my consciousness
>   in wine, alas ! in vain :
> Oblivion passes quickly
>   and my griefs begin again.
> Old age comes on, and yet withholds
>   the summons to depart. . . .
> So I'll take another bumper
>   just to ease my aching heart."

---

[1] Graves are placed by preference on some hillside.

Humane treatment of the lower animals is not generally supposed to be a characteristic of the Chinese. They have no Society for the Prevention of Cruelty to Animals, which may perhaps account for some of their shortcomings in this direction. Han Yü was above all things of a kindly, humane nature, and although the following piece cannot be taken seriously, it affords a useful index to his general feelings :—

> *" Oh, spare the busy morning fly,*
> *Spare the mosquitos of the night !*
> *And if their wicked trade they ply,*
> *Let a partition stop their flight.*

> *" Their span is brief from birth to death ;*
> *Like you, they bite their little day ;*
> *And then, with autumn's earliest breath,*
> *Like you, too, they are swept away."*

The following lines were written on the way to his place of exile in Kuangtung :—

> *" Alas ! the early season flies,*
> *Behold the remnants of the spring !*
> *My boat in landlocked water lies,*
> *At dawn I hear the wild birds sing.*

> *" Then, through clouds lingering on the slope,*
> *The rising sun breaks on to me,*
> *And thrills me with a fleeting hope,—*
> *A prisoner longing to be free.*

> *" My flowing tears are long since dried,*
> *Though care clings closer than it did.*
> *But stop ! All care we lay aside*
> *When once they close the coffin lid."*

Another famous poet, worthy to be mentioned even after Han Yü, was Po Chü-i (A.D. 772–846). As a child he was most precocious, knowing a considerable number of the written characters at the early age of seven months, after having had each one pointed out only once by his nurse. He graduated at the age of seventeen, and rose to high office in the State, though at one period of his life he was banished to a petty post, which somewhat disgusted him with officialdom. To console himself, he built a retreat at Hsiang-shan, by which name he is sometimes called; and there, together with eight congenial companions, he gave himself up to poetry and speculations upon a future life. To escape recognition and annoyance, all names were dropped, and the party was generally known as the Nine Old Gentlemen of Hsiang-shan. This reaching the ears of the Emperor, he was transferred to be Governor of Chung-chou; and on the accession of Mu Tsung in 821 he was sent as Governor to Hangchow. There he built one of the great embankments of the beautiful Western Lake, still known as Po's Embankment. He was subsequently Governor of Soochow, and finally rose in 841 to be President of the Board of War. His poems were collected by Imperial command and engraved upon tablets of stone, which were set up in a garden he had made for himself in imitation of his former beloved retreat at Hsiang-shan. He disbelieved in the genuineness of the *Tao-Té-Ching*, and ridiculed its preposterous claims as follows:—

> " ' *Who know, speak not; who speak, know naught,*'
>   *Are words from Lao Tzŭ's lore.*
>   *What then becomes of Lao Tzŭ's own*
>   ' *Five thousand words and more*' ? "

Here is a charming poem from his pen, which tells

the story of a poor lute-girl's sorrows. This piece is ranked very high by the commentator Lin Hsi-chung, who points out how admirably the wording is adapted to echo the sense, and declares that such workmanship raises the reader to that state of mental ecstasy known to the Buddhists as *samâdhi*, and can only be produced once in a thousand autumns. The "guest" is the poet himself, setting out a second time for his place of banishment, as mentioned above, from a point about half-way thither, where he had been struck down by illness :—

"By night, at the riverside, adieus were spoken : beneath the maple's flower-like leaves, blooming amid autumnal decay. Host had dismounted to speed the parting guest, already on board his boat. Then a stirrup-cup went round, but no flute, no guitar, was heard. And so, ere the heart was warmed with wine, came words of cold farewell beneath the bright moon, glittering over the bosom of the broad stream . . . when suddenly across the water a lute broke forth into sound. Host forgot to go, guest lingered on, wondering whence the music, and asking who the performer might be. At this, all was hushed, but no answer given. A boat approached, and the musician was invited to join the party. Cups were refilled, lamps trimmed again, and preparations for festivity renewed. At length, after much pressing, she came forth, hiding her face behind her lute ; and twice or thrice sweeping the strings, betrayed emotion ere her song was sung. Then every note she struck swelled with pathos deep and strong, as though telling the tale of a wrecked and hopeless life, while with bent head and rapid finger she poured forth her soul in melody. Now softly, now slowly, her plectrum sped to and fro ; now this air, now that ; loudly, with the crash of falling rain ; softly, as the murmur of whispered words ; now loud and soft together, like the patter of pearls and pearlets dropping upon a marble dish. Or liquid, like the warbling of the mango-bird in the bush ; trickling, like the streamlet on its downward course. And then, like the torrent, stilled by the grip of frost, so for a moment was the music lulled, in a passion too deep for sound. Then, as bursts the water from the broken vase, as clash the arms upon the mailed horseman, so fell the plectrum once more upon the strings with a slash like the rent of silk.

"Silence on all sides : not a sound stirred the air. The autumn moon shone silver athwart the tide, as with a sigh the musician thrust her plectrum beneath the strings and quietly prepared to take leave. 'My childhood,' said she, 'was spent at the capital, in my home near the hills. At thirteen, I learnt the guitar, and my name was enrolled among the *primas* of the day. The *maëstro* himself acknowledged my skill : the most beauteous of women envied my lovely face. The youths of the neighbourhood vied with each other to do me honour : a single song brought me I know not how many costly bales. Golden ornaments and silver pins were smashed, blood-red skirts of silk were stained with wine, in oft-times echoing applause. And so I laughed on from year to year, while the spring breeze and autumn moon swept over my careless head.

"'Then my brother went away to the wars : my mother died. Nights passed and mornings came ; and with them my beauty began to fade. My doors were no longer thronged ; but few cavaliers remained. So I took a husband and became a trader's wife. He was all for gain, and little recked of separation from me. Last month he went off to buy tea, and I remained behind, to wander in my lonely boat on moon-lit nights over the cold wave, thinking of the happy days gone by, my reddened eyes telling of tearful dreams.'

"The sweet melody of the lute had already moved my soul to pity, and now these words pierced me to the heart again. 'O lady,' I cried, 'we are companions in misfortune, and need no ceremony to be friends. Last year I quitted the Imperial city, and fever-stricken reached this spot, where in its desolation, from year's end to year's end, no flute or guitar is heard. I live by the marshy river-bank, surrounded by yellow reeds and stunted bamboos. Day and night no sounds reach my ears save the blood-stained note of the nightjar, the gibbon's mournful wail. Hill songs I have, and village pipes with their harsh discordant twang. But now that I listen to thy lute's discourse, methinks 'tis the music of the gods. Prithee sit down awhile and sing to us yet again, while I commit thy story to writing.'

"Grateful to me (for she had been standing long), the lute-girl sat down and quickly broke forth into another song, sad and soft, unlike the song of just now. Then all her hearers melted into tears unrestrained ; and none flowed more freely than mine, until my bosom was wet with weeping."

Perhaps the best known of all the works of Po Chü-i is a narrative poem of some length entitled "The Everlasting Wrong." It refers to the ignominious downfall of the Emperor known as Ming Huang (A.D. 685–762), who himself deserves a passing notice. At his accession to the throne in 712, he was called upon to face an attempt on the part of his aunt, the T'ai-p'ing Princess, to displace him; but this he succeeded in crushing, and entered upon what promised to be a glorious reign. He began with economy, closing the silk factories and forbidding the palace ladies to wear jewels or embroideries, considerable quantities of which were actually burnt. Until 740 the country was fairly prosperous. The administration was improved, the empire was divided into fifteen provinces, and schools were established in every village. The Emperor was a patron of literature, and himself a poet of no mean capacity. He published an edition of the Classic of Filial Piety, and caused the text to be engraved on four tablets of stone, A.D. 745. His love of war, however, and his growing extravagance, led to increased taxation. Fond of music, he founded a college for training youth of both sexes in this art. He surrounded himself by a brilliant Court, welcoming such men as the poet Li Po, at first for their talents alone, but afterwards for their readiness to participate in scenes of revelry and dissipation provided for the amusement of the Imperial concubine, the ever-famous Yang Kuei-fei. Eunuchs were appointed to official posts, and the grossest forms of religious superstition were encouraged. Women ceased to veil themselves as of old. Gradually the Emperor left off concerning himself with affairs of State; a serious rebellion broke out, and his Majesty sought safety in flight to Ssŭch'uan, returning only after having abdicated in favour of his son. The accompanying poem describes the rise of Yang Kuei-fei, her tragic fate at the hands of the soldiery, and her subsequent communication with her heart-broken lover from the world of shadows beyond the grave :—

ENNUI.—*His Imperial Majesty, a slave to beauty,*
  longed for a " subverter of empires ;" [1]
For years he had sought in vain
  to secure such a treasure for his palace. . . .

BEAUTY.—*From the Yang family came a maiden,*
  just grown up to womanhood,
Reared in the inner apartments,
  altogether unknown to fame.
But nature had amply endowed her
  with a beauty hard to conceal,
And one day she was summoned
  to a place at the monarch's side.
Her sparkling eye and merry laughter
  fascinated every beholder,
And among the powder and paint of the harem
  her loveliness reigned supreme.
In the chills of spring, by Imperial mandate,
  she bathed in the Hua-ch'ing Pool,
Laving her body in the glassy wavelets
  of the fountain perennially warm.
Then, when she came forth, helped by attendants,
  her delicate and graceful movements
Finally gained for her gracious favour,
  captivating his Majesty's heart.

REVELRY.—*Hair like a cloud, face like a flower,*
  headdress which quivered as she walked,
Amid the delights of the Hibiscus Pavilion
  she passed the soft spring nights.
Spring nights, too short alas ! for them,
  albeit prolonged till dawn,—
From this time forth no more audiences
  in the hours of early morn.
Revels and feasts in quick succession,
  ever without a break,
She chosen always for the spring excursion,
  chosen for the nightly carouse.

---

[1] Referring to a famous beauty of the Han dynasty, one glance from whom would overthrow a city, two glances an empire.

Three thousand peerless beauties adorned
　　　the apartments of the monarch's harem,
Yet always his Majesty reserved
　　　his attentions for her alone.
Passing her life in a "golden house," [1]
　　　with fair girls to wait on her,
She was daily wafted to ecstasy
　　　on the wine fumes of the banquet-hall.
Her sisters and her brothers, one and all,
　　　were raised to the rank of nobles.
Alas! for the ill-omened glories
　　　which she conferred on her family.
For thus it came about that fathers and mothers
　　　through the length and breadth of the empire
Rejoiced no longer over the birth of sons,
　　　but over the birth of daughters.
In the gorgeous palace
　　　piercing the grey clouds above,
Divine music, borne on the breeze,
　　　is spread around on all sides;
Of song and the dance
　　　to the guitar and flute,
All through the live long day,
　　　his Majesty never tires.
But suddenly comes the roll
　　　of the fish-skin war-drums,
Breaking rudely upon the air
　　　of the "Rainbow Skirt and Feather Jacket.

FLIGHT.—*Clouds of dust envelop*
　　　the lofty gates of the capital.
A thousand war-chariots and ten thousand horses
　　　move towards the south-west.
Feathers and jewels among the throng,
　　　onwards and then a halt.
A hundred li beyond the western gate,
　　　leaving behind them the city walls,

---

[1] Referring to A-chiao, one of the consorts of an Emperor of the Han dynasty. "Ah," said the latter when a boy, "if I could only get A-chiao, I would have a golden house to keep her in."

The soldiers refuse to advance;
    nothing remains to be done
Until she of the moth-eyebrows
    perishes in sight of all.
On the ground lie gold ornaments
    with no one to pick them up,
Kingfisher wings, golden birds,
    and hairpins of costly jade.
The monarch covers his face,
    powerless to save;
And as he turns to look back,
    tears and blood flow mingled together.

EXILE.—*Across vast stretches of yellow sand*
    with whistling winds,
Across cloud-capped mountain-tops
    they make their way.
Few indeed are the travellers
    who reach the heights of Mount Omi;
The bright gleam of the standards
    grows fainter day by day.
Dark the Ssŭch'uan waters,
    dark the Ssŭch'uan hills;
Daily and nightly his Majesty
    is consumed by bitter grief.
Travelling along, the very brightness
    of the moon saddens his heart,
And the sound of a bell through the evening rain
    severs his viscera in twain.

RETURN.—*Time passes, days go by, and once again*
    he is there at the well-known spot,
And there he lingers on, unable
    to tear himself wholly away.
But from the clods of earth
    at the foot of the Ma-wei hill,
No sign of her lovely face appears,
    only the place of death.
The eyes of sovereign and minister meet,
    and robes are wet with tears,
Eastward they depart and hurry on
    to the capital at full speed.

HOME.—*There is the pool and there are the flowers,*
as of old.
There is the hibiscus of the pavilion,
there are the willows of the palace.
In the hibiscus he sees her face,
in the willow he sees her eyebrows :
How in the presence of these
should tears not flow,—
In spring amid the flowers
of the peach and plum,
In autumn rains when the leaves
of the wu t'ung *fall?*
To the south of the western palace
are many trees,
And when their leaves cover the steps,
no one now sweeps them away.
The hair of the Pear-Garden musicians
is white as though with age ;
The guardians of the Pepper Chamber[1]
seem to him no longer young.
Where fireflies flit through the hall,
he sits in silent grief ;
Alone, the lamp-wick burnt out,
he is still unable to sleep.
Slowly pass the watches,
for the nights are now too long,
And brightly shine the constellations,
as though dawn would never come.
Cold settles upon the duck-and-drake tiles,[2]
and thick hoar-frost,
The kingfisher coverlet is chill,
with none to share its warmth.
Parted by life and death,
time still goes on,
But never once does her spirit come back
to visit him in dreams.

---

[1] A fancy name for the women's apartments in the palace.

[2] The mandarin duck and drake are emblems of conjugal fidelity. The allusion is to ornaments on the roof.

SPIRIT-LAND.—*A Taoist priest of Lin-ch'ung,*
of the Hung-tu school,
Was able, by his perfect art, to summon
the spirits of the dead.
Anxious to relieve the fretting mind
of his sovereign,
This magician receives orders
to urge a diligent quest.
Borne on the clouds, charioted upon ether,
he rushes with the speed of lightning
High up to heaven, low down to earth,
seeking everywhere.
Above, he searches the empyrean;
below, the Yellow Springs,
But nowhere in these vast areas
can her place be found.
At length he hears of an Isle of the Blest
away in mid-ocean,
Lying in realms of vacuity,
dimly to be descried.
There gaily decorated buildings
rise up like rainbow clouds,
And there many gentle and beautiful Immortals
pass their days in peace.
Among them is one whose name
sounds upon lips as Eternal,
And by her snow-white skin and flower-like face
he knows that this is she.
Knocking at the jade door
at the western gate of the golden palace,
He bids a fair waiting-maid announce him
to her mistress, fairer still.
She, hearing of this embassy
sent by the Son of Heaven,
Starts up from her dreams
among the tapestry curtains.
Grasping her clothes and pushing away the pillow,
she arises in haste,
And begins to adorn herself
with pearls and jewels.

Her cloud-like coiffure, dishevelled,
        shows that she has just risen from sleep,
And with her flowery head-dress awry,
        she passes into the hall.
The sleeves of her immortal robes
        are filled out by the breeze,
As once more she seems to dance
        to the " Rainbow Skirt and Feather Jacket."
Her features are fixed and calm,
        though myriad tears fall,
Wetting a spray of pear-bloom,
        as it were with the raindrops of spring.
Subduing her emotions, restraining her grief,
        she tenders thanks to his Majesty,
Saying how since they parted
        she has missed his form and voice ;
And how, although their love on earth
        has so soon come to an end,
The days and months among the Blest
        are still of long duration.
And now she turns and gazes
        towards the abode of mortals,
But cannot discern the Imperial city
        lost in the dust and haze.
Then she takes out the old keepsakes,
        tokens of undying love,
A gold hairpin, an enamel brooch,
        and bids the magician carry these back.
One half of the hairpin she keeps,
        and one half of the enamel brooch,
Breaking with her hands the yellow gold,
        and dividing the enamel in two.
" Tell him," she said, " to be firm of heart,
        as this gold and enamel,
And then in heaven or on earth below
        we two may meet once more."
At parting, she confided to the magician
        many earnest messages of love,
Among the rest recalling a pledge
        mutually understood ;

How on the seventh day of the seventh moon,
*   in the Hall of Immortality,*
At midnight, when none were near,
*   he had whispered in her ear,*
" I swear that we will ever fly
*   like the one-winged birds,*[1]
Or grow united like the tree
*   with branches which twine together."*[2]
Heaven and Earth, long-lasting as they are,
*   will some day pass away;*
But this great wrong shall stretch out for ever,
*   endless, for ever and ay.*

A precocious and short-lived poet was LI HO, of the ninth century. He began to write verses at the age of seven. Twenty years later he met a strange man riding on a hornless dragon, who said to him, " God Almighty has finished his Jade Pavilion, and has sent for you to be his secretary." Shortly after this he died. The following is a specimen of his poetry :—

" With flowers on the ground like embroidery spread,
At twenty, the soft glow of wine in my head,
My white courser's bit-tassels motionless gleam
While the gold-threaded willow scent sweeps o'er the stream.
Yet until she has smiled, all these flowers yield no ray;
When her tresses fall down the whole landscape is gay;
My hand on her sleeve as I gaze in her eyes,
A kingfisher hairpin will soon be my prize."

CHANG CHI, who also flourished in the ninth century, was eighty years old when he died. He was on terms of close friendship with Han Yü, and like him, too, a vigorous opponent of both Buddhism and Taoism. The following is his most famous poem, the beauty of which, says a commentator, lies beyond the words :—

---

[1] Each bird having only one wing, must always fly with a mate.
[2] Such a tree was believed to exist, and has often been figured by the Chinese.

> " *Knowing, fair sir, my matrimonial thrall,*
>   *Two pearls thou sentest me, costly withal.*
>   *And I, seeing that Love thy heart possessed,*
>   *I wrapped them coldly in my silken vest.*
>
> " *For mine is a household of high degree,*
>   *My husband captain in the King's army;*
>   *And one with wit like thine should say,*
>   ' *The troth of wives is for ever and ay.*'
>
> " *With thy two pearls I send thee back two tears:*
>   *Tears—that we did not meet in earlier years.*"

Many more poets of varying shades of excellence must here be set aside, their efforts often brightened by those quaint conceits which are so dear to the Chinese reader, but which approach so perilously near to bathos when they appear in foreign garb. A few specimens, torn from their setting, may perhaps have an interest of their own. Here is a lady complaining of the leaden-footed flight of time as marked by the water-clock:—

> " *It seems that the clepsydra*
>   *has been filled up with the sea,*
>   *To make the long, long night appear*
>   *an endless night to me!* "

The second line in the next example is peculiarly characteristic:—

> " *Dusk comes, the east wind blows, and birds*
>   *pipe forth a mournful sound;*
>   *Petals, like nymphs from balconies,*
>   *come tumbling to the ground.*"

The next refers to candles burning in a room where two friends are having a last talk on the night before parting for a long period:—

> " *The very wax sheds sympathetic tears,*
>   *And gutters sadly down till dawn appears.*"

This last is from a friend to a friend at a distance :—

> *" Ah, when shall we ever snuff candles again,*
> *And recall the glad hours of that evening of rain ?"*

A popular poet of the ninth century was LI SHÊ, especially well known for the story of his capture by highwaymen. The chief knew him by name and called for a sample of his art, eliciting the following lines, which immediately secured his release :—

> *" The rainy mist sweeps gently*
> *   o'er the village by the stream,*
> *When from the leafy forest glades*
> *   the brigand daggers gleam. . . .*
> *And yet there is no need to fear,*
> *   nor step from out their way,*
> *For more than half the world consists*
> *   of bigger rogues than they ! "*

A popular physician in great request, as well as a poet, was MA TZŬ-JAN (*d.* A.D. 880). He studied Taoism in a hostile sense, as would appear from the following poem by him ; nevertheless, according to tradition, he was ultimately taken up to heaven alive :—

> *" In youth I went to study TAO*
> *   at its living fountain-head,*
> *And then lay tipsy half the day*
> *   upon a gilded bed.*
> *' What oaf is this,' the Master cried,*
> *   ' content with human lot ?'*
> *And bade me to the world get back*
> *   and call myself a sot.*
> *But wherefore seek immortal life*
> *   by means of wondrous pills ?*
> *Noise is not in the market-place,*
> *   nor quiet on the hills.*

> *The secret of perpetual youth*
> *is already known to me :*
> *Accept with philosophic calm*
> *whatever fate may be."*

HSÜ AN-CHÊN, of the ninth century, is entitled to a place among the T'ang poets, if only for the following piece :—

> " *When the Bear athwart was lying,*
> *And the night was just on dying,*
> *And the moon was all but gone,*
> *How my thoughts did ramble on !*

> " *Then a sound of music breaks*
> *From a lute that some one wakes,*
> *And I know that it is she,*
> *The sweet maid next door to me.*

> " *And as the strains steal o'er me*
> *Her moth-eyebrows rise before me,*
> *And I feel a gentle thrill*
> *That her fingers must be chill.*

> " *But doors and locks between us*
> *So effectually screen us*
> *That I hasten from the street*
> *And in dreamland pray to meet."*

The following lines by TU CH'IN-NIANG, a poetess of the ninth century, are included in a collection of 300 gems of the T'ang dynasty :—

> " *I would not have thee grudge those robes*
> *which gleam in rich array,*
> *But I would have thee grudge the hours*
> *of youth which glide away.*
> *Go, pluck the blooming flower betimes,*
> *lest when thou com'st again*
> *Alas ! upon the withered stem*
> *no blooming flowers remain !"*

It is time perhaps to bring to a close the long list, which might be almost indefinitely lengthened. Ssŭ-K'UNG T U (A.D. 834–908) was a secretary in the Board of Rites, but he threw up his post and became a hermit. Returning to Court in 905, he accidentally dropped part of his official insignia at an audience,—an unpardonable breach of Court etiquette,—and was allowed to retire once more to the hills, where he ultimately starved himself to death through grief at the murder of the youthful Emperor. He is commonly known as the Last of the T'angs; his poetry, which is excessively difficult to understand, ranking correspondingly high in the estimation of Chinese critics. The following philosophical poem, consisting of twenty-four apparently unconnected stanzas, is admirably adapted to exhibit the form under which pure Taoism commends itself to the mind of a cultivated scholar:—

i.—ENERGY—ABSOLUTE.

" *Expenditure of force leads to outward decay,*
Spiritual existence means inward fulness.
Let us revert to Nothing and enter the Absolute,
Hoarding up strength for Energy.
Freighted with eternal principles,
Athwart the mighty void,
Where cloud-masses darken,
And the wind blows ceaseless around,
Beyond the range of conceptions,
Let us gain the Centre,
And there hold fast without violence,
Fed from an inexhaustible supply."

ii.—TRANQUIL REPOSE.

" *It dwells in quietude, speechless,*
Imperceptible in the cosmos,
Watered by the eternal harmonies,
Soaring with the lonely crane.

It is like a gentle breeze in spring,
Softly bellying the flowing robe ;
It is like the note of the bamboo flute,
Whose sweetness we would fain make our own.
Meeting by chance, it seems easy of access,
Seeking, we find it hard to secure.
Ever shifting in semblance,
It shifts from the grasp and is gone."

iii.—SLIM—STOUT.

" Gathering the water-plants
From the wild luxuriance of spring,
Away in the depth of a wild valley
Anon I see a lovely girl.
With green leaves the peach-trees are loaded,
The breeze blows gently along the stream,
Willows shade the winding path,
Darting orioles collect in groups.
Eagerly I press forward
As the reality grows upon me. . . .
'Tis the eternal theme
Which, though old, is ever new."

iv.—CONCENTRATION.

" Green pines and a rustic hut,
The sun sinking through pure air,
I take off my cap and stroll alone,
Listening to the song of birds.
No wild geese fly hither,
And she is far away ;
But my thoughts make her present
As in the days gone by.
Across the water dark clouds are whirled,
Beneath the moonbeams the eyots stand revealed,
And sweet words are exchanged
Though the great River rolls between."

v.—HEIGHT—ANTIQUITY.

" Lo the Immortal, borne by spirituality,
His hand grasping a lotus flower,

Away to Time everlasting,
Trackless through the regions of Space!
With the moon he issues from the Ladle,[1]
Speeding upon a favourable gale;
Below, Mount Hua looms dark,
And from it sounds a clear-toned bell.
Vacantly I gaze after his vanished image,
Now passed beyond the bounds of mortality. . . .
Ah, the Yellow Emperor and Yao,
They, peerless, are his models."

vi.—REFINEMENT.

" A jade kettle with a purchase of spring,[2]
A shower on the thatched hut
Wherein sits a gentle scholar,
With tall bamboos growing right and left,
And white clouds in the newly-clear sky,
And birds flitting in the depths of trees.
Then pillowed on his lute in the green shade,
A waterfall tumbling overhead,
Leaves dropping, not a word spoken,
The man placid, like a chrysanthemum,
Noting down the flower-glory of the season,—
A book well worthy to be read."

vii.—WASH—SMELT.

" As iron from the mines,
As silver from lead,
So purify thy heart,
Loving the limpid and clean.
Like a clear pool in spring,
With its wondrous mirrored shapes,
So make for the spotless and true,
And, riding the moonbeam, revert to the Spiritual.
Let your gaze be upon the stars of heaven,[3]
Let your song be of the hiding hermit ;[3]
Like flowing water is our to-day,
Our yesterday, the bright moon."[4]

---

[1] The Great Bear.   [2] Wine which makes man see spring at all seasons.
[3] Emblems of purity.
[4] Our previous state of existence at the eternal Centre to which the moon belongs.

viii.—STRENGTH.

" *The mind as though in the void,*
  The vitality as though of the rainbow,
  Among the thousand-ell peaks of Wu,
  Flying with the clouds, racing with the wind;
  Drink of the spiritual, feed on force,
  Store them for daily use, guard them in your heart,
  Be like Him in His might,[1]
  For this is to preserve your energy;
  Be a peer of Heaven and Earth,
  A co-worker in Divine transformation. . . .
  Seek to be full of these,
  And hold fast to them alway."

ix.—EMBROIDERIES.

" *If the mind has wealth and rank,*
  One may make light of yellow gold.
  Rich pleasures pall ere long,
  Simple joys deepen ever.
  A mist-cloud hanging on the river bank,
  Pink almond-flowers along the bough,
  A flower-girt cottage beneath the moon,
  A painted bridge half seen in shadow,
  A golden goblet brimming with wine,
  A friend with his hand on the lute. . . .
  Take these and be content;
  They will swell thy heart beneath thy robe."

x.—THE NATURAL.

" *Stoop, and there it is;*
  Seek it not right and left.
  All roads lead thither,—
  One touch and you have spring![2]
  As though coming upon opening flowers,
  As though gazing upon the new year,
  Verily I will not snatch it,
  Forced, it will dwindle away.

---

[1] The Power who, without loss of force, causes things to be what they are—God.

[2] Alluding to the art of the painter.

I will be like the hermit on the hill,
Like duckweed gathered on the stream,[1]
And when emotions crowd upon me,
I will leave them to the harmonies of heaven."

xi.—SET FREE.

" Joying in flowers without let,
Breathing the empyrean,
Through TAO reverting to ether,
And there to be wildly free,
Wide-spreading as the wind of heaven,
Lofty as the peaks of ocean,
Filled with a spiritual strength,
All creation by my side,
Before me the sun, moon, and stars,
The phœnix following behind.
In the morning I whip up my leviathans
And wash my feet in Fusang."[2]

xii.—CONSERVATION.

" Without a word writ down,
All wit may be attained.
If words do not affect the speaker,
They seem inadequate to sorrow.[3]
Herein is the First Cause,
With which we sink or rise,
As wine in the strainer mounts high,
As cold turns back the season of flowers.
The wide-spreading dust-motes in the air,
The sudden spray-bubbles of ocean,
Shallow, deep, collected, scattered,—
You grasp ten thousand, and secure one."

xiii.—ANIMAL SPIRITS.

" That they might come back unceasingly,
That they might be ever with us !—

---

[1] A creature of chance, following the doctrine of Inaction.
[2] Variously identified with Saghalien, Mexico, and Japan.
[3] . . . Si vis me flere dolendum est
Primum ipsi tibi. . . .

The bright river, unfathomable,
The rare flower just opening,
The parrot of the verdant spring,
The willow-trees, the terrace,
The stranger from the dark hills,
The cup overflowing with clear wine. . . .
Oh, for life to be extended,
With no dead ashes of writing,
Amid the charms of the Natural,—
Ah, who can compass it?"

xiv.—CLOSE WOVEN.

" In all things there are veritable atoms,
Though the senses cannot perceive them,
Struggling to emerge into shape
From the wondrous workmanship of God.
Water flowing, flowers budding,
The limpid dew evaporating,
An important road, stretching far,
A dark path where progress is slow. . . .
So words should not shock,
Nor thought be inept.
But be like the green of spring,
Like snow beneath the moon." [1]

xv.—SECLUSION

" Following our own bent,
Enjoying the Natural, free from curb,
Rich with what comes to hand,
Hoping some day to be with God.
To build a hut beneath the pines,
With uncovered head to pore over poetry,
Knowing only morning and eve,
But not what season it may be. . . .
Then, if happiness is ours,
Why must there be action?
If of our own selves we can reach this point,
Can we not be said to have attained?"

---

[1] Each invisible atom of which combines to produce a perfect whole.

xvi.—FASCINATION.

"Lovely is the pine-grove,
 With the stream eddying below,
 A clear sky and a snow-clad bank,
 Fishing-boats in the reach beyond.
 And she, like unto jade,
 Slowly sauntering, as I follow through the dark wood,
 Now moving on, now stopping short,
 Far away to the deep valley. . . .
 My mind quits its tenement, and is in the past,
 Vague, and not to be recalled,
 As though before the glow of the rising moon,
 As though before the glory of autumn."

xvii.—IN TORTUOUS WAYS.

"I climbed the T'ai-hsing mountain
 By the green winding path,
 Vegetation like a sea of jade,
 Flower-scent borne far and wide.
 Struggling with effort to advance,
 A sound escaped my lips,
 Which seemed to be back ere 'twas gone,
 As though hidden but not concealed.[1]
 The eddying waters rush to and fro,
 Overhead the great rukh soars and sails;
 TAO does not limit itself to a shape,
 But is round and square by turns."

xviii.—ACTUALITIES.

"Choosing plain words
 To express simple thoughts,
 Suddenly I happened upon a recluse,
 And seemed to see the heart of TAO.
 Beside the winding brook,
 Beneath dark pine-trees' shade,
 There was one stranger bearing a faggot,
 Another listening to the lute.

---

[1] Referring to an echo.

And so, where my fancy led me,
Better than if I had sought it,
I heard the music of heaven,
Astounded by its rare strains."

xix.—DESPONDENT.

" A gale ruffles the stream
And trees in the forest crack;
My thoughts are bitter as death,
For she whom I asked will not come.
A hundred years slip by like water,
Riches and rank are but cold ashes,
TAO is daily passing away,
To whom shall we turn for salvation?
The brave soldier draws his sword,
And tears flow with endless lamentation;
The wind whistles, leaves fall,
And rain trickles through the old thatch."

xx.—FORM AND FEATURE.

" After gazing fixedly upon expression and substance
The mind returns with a spiritual image,
As when seeking the outlines of waves,
As when painting the glory of spring.
The changing shapes of wind-swept clouds,
The energies of flowers and plants,
The rolling breakers of ocean,
The crags and cliffs of mountains,
All these are like mighty TAO,
Skilfully woven into earthly surroundings. . . .
To obtain likeness without form,
Is not that to possess the man?"

xxi.—THE TRANSCENDENTAL.

" Not of the spirituality of the mind,
Nor yet of the atoms of the cosmos,
But as though reached upon white clouds,
Borne thither by pellucid breezes.
Afar, it seems at hand,
Approach, 'tis no longer there;

Sharing the nature of TAO,
It shuns the limits of mortality.
It is in the piled-up hills, in tall trees,
In dark mosses, in sunlight rays. . . .
Croon over it, think upon it;
Its faint sound eludes the ear."

xxii.—ABSTRACTION.

" Without friends, longing to be there,
Alone, away from the common herd,
Like the crane on Mount Hou,
Like the cloud at the peak of Mount Hua.
In the portrait of the hero
The old fire still lingers;
The leaf carried by the wind
Floats on the boundless sea.
It would seem as though not to be grasped,
But always on the point of being disclosed.
Those who recognise this have already attained;
Those who hope, drift daily farther away."

xxiii.—ILLUMINED.

" Life stretches to one hundred years,
And yet how brief a span;
Its joys so fleeting,
Its griefs so many!
What has it like a goblet of wine,
And daily visits to the wistaria arbour,
Where flowers cluster around the eaves,
And light showers pass overhead?
Then when the wine-cup is drained,
To stroll about with staff of thorn;
For who of us but will some day be an ancient? . . .
Ah, there is the South Mountain in its grandeur!" [1]

xxiv.—MOTION.

" Like a whirling water-wheel,
Like rolling pearls,—
Yet how are these worthy to be named?
They are but illustrations for fools.

---

[1] This remains, while all other things pass **away.**

There is the mighty axis of Earth,
The never-resting pole of Heaven;
Let us grasp their clue,
And with them be blended in One,
Beyond the bounds of thought,
Circling for ever in the great Void,
An orbit of a thousand years,—
Yes, this is the key to my theme."

CHAPTER II

CLASSICAL AND GENERAL LITERATURE

THE classical scholarship of the T'ang dynasty was neither very original nor very profound. It is true that the second Emperor founded a College of Learning, but its members were content to continue the traditions of the Hans, and comparatively little was achieved in the line of independent research. Foremost among the names in the above College stands that of LU YÜAN-LANG (550–625). He had been Imperial Librarian under the preceding dynasty, and later on distinguished himself by his defence of Confucianism against both Buddhist and Taoist attacks. He published a valuable work on the explanations of terms and phrases in the Classics and in Taoist writers.

Scarcely less eminent as a scholar was WEI CHÊNG (581–643), who also gained great reputation as a military commander. He was appointed President of the Commission for drawing up the history of the previous dynasty, and he was, in addition, a poet of no mean order. At his death the Emperor said, "You may use copper as a mirror for the person; you may use the past as a mirror for politics; and you may use man as a mirror to guide one's judgment in ordinary affairs. These three mirrors I have always carefully cherished; but now that Wei Chêng is gone, I have lost one of them."

Another well-known scholar is YEN SHIH-KU (579–645). He was employed upon a recension of the Classics, and also upon a new and annotated edition of the history of the Han dynasty; but his exegesis in the former case caused dissatisfaction, and he was ordered to a provincial post. Although nominally reinstated before this degradation took effect, his ambition was so far wounded that he ceased to be the same man. He lived henceforth a retired and simple life.

LI PO-YAO (565–648) was so sickly a child, and swallowed so much medicine, that his grandmother insisted on naming him Po-yao = Pharmacopœia, while his precocious cleverness earned for him the sobriquet of the Prodigy. Entering upon a public career, he neglected his work for gaming and drink, and after a short spell of office he retired. Later on he rose once more, and completed the History of the Northern Ch'i Dynasty.

A descendant of Confucius in the thirty-second degree, and a distinguished scholar and public functionary, was K'UNG YING-TA (574–648). He wrote a commentary on the Book of Odes, and is credited with certain portions of the History of the Sui Dynasty. Besides this, he is responsible for comments and glosses on the Great Learning and on the Doctrine of the Mean.

Lexicography was perhaps the department of pure scholarship in which the greatest advances were made. Dictionaries on the phonetic system, based upon the work of Lu Fa-yen of the sixth century, came very much into vogue, as opposed to those on the radical system initiated by Hsü Shên. Not that the splendid work of the latter was allowed to suffer from neglect. LI YANG-PING, of the eighth century, devoted much time and labour to improving and adding to its pages. The latter was a Government official, and when filling a post as magistrate in 763, he is said to have obtained rain during a drought by threatening the City God with the destruction of his temple unless his prayers were answered within three days.

CHANG CHIH-HO (eighth century), author of a work on the conservation of vitality, was of a romantic turn of mind and especially fond of Taoist speculations. He took office under the Emperor Su Tsung of the T'ang dynasty, but got into some trouble and was banished. Soon after this he shared in a general pardon ; whereupon he fled to the woods and mountains and became a wandering recluse, calling himself the Old Fisherman of the Mists and Waters. He spent his time in angling, but used no bait, his object not being to catch fish. When asked why he roamed about, Chang answered and said, " With the empyrean as my home, the bright moon my constant companion, and the four seas my inseparable friends,—what mean you by *roaming?* " And when a friend offered him a comfortable home instead of his poor boat, he replied, " I prefer to follow the gulls into cloudland, rather than to bury my eternal self beneath the dust of the world."

The author of the *T'ung Tien,* an elaborate treatise on the constitution, still extant, was TU YU (*d.* 812). It is divided into eight sections under Political Economy, Examinations and Degrees, Government Offices, Rites, Music, Military Discipline, Geography, and National Defences.

Among writers of general prose literature, LIU TSUNG-YÜAN (773–819) has left behind him much that for purity of style and felicity of expression has rarely been surpassed. Besides being poet, essayist, and calligraphist, he was a Secretary in the Board of Rites. There he became involved in a conspiracy, and was banished to a distant spot, where he died. His views were deeply tinged with Buddhist thought, for which he was often severely censured, once in a letter by his friend and master, Han Yü. These few lines are part of his reply on the latter occasion :—

"The features I admire in Buddhism are those which are coincident with the principles enunciated in our own sacred books. And I do not think that, even were the holy sages of old to revisit the earth, they would fairly be able to denounce these. Now, Han Yü objects to the Buddhist commandments. He objects to the bald pates of the priests, their dark robes, their renunciation of domestic ties, their idleness, and life generally at the expense of others. So do I. But Han Yü misses the kernel while railing at the husk. He sees the lode, but not the ore. I see both ; hence my partiality for this faith.

"Again, intercourse with men of this religion does not necessarily imply conversion. Even if it did, Buddhism admits no envious rivalry for place or power. The majority of its adherents love only to lead a simple life of contemplation amid the charms of hill and stream. And when I turn my gaze towards the hurry-scurry of the age, in its daily race for the seals and tassels of office, I ask myself if I am to reject those in order to take my place among the ranks of these.

"The Buddhist priest, Hao-ch'u, is a man of placid temperament and of passions subdued. He is a fine scholar. His only joy is to muse o'er flood and fell, with occasional indulgence in the delights of composition. His family follow in the same path. He is independent of all men, and no more to be compared with those heterodox sages of whom we make so much than with the vulgar herd of the greedy, grasping world around us."

On this the commentator remarks, that one must have the genius of Han Yü to condemn Buddhism, the genius of Liu Tsung-yüan to indulge in it.

Here is a short study on a great question :—

"Over the western hills the road trends away towards the north, and on the farther side of the pass separates into two. The westerly branch leads to nowhere in particular ; but if you follow the other, which takes a north-easterly turn, for about a quarter of a mile, you will find that the path ends abruptly, while the stream forks to enclose a steep pile of boulders. On the summit of this pile there is what appears to be an elegantly built look-out tower ; below, as it were a battlemented wall, pierced by a city gate, through which one gazes into darkness. A stone thrown in here falls with a splash suggestive of water, and the reverberations of this sound are audible for some time. There is a way round from behind up to the top, whence nothing is seen far and wide except groves of fine straight trees, which, strange to say, are grouped symmetrically, as if by an artist's hand.

"Now, I have always had my doubts about the existence of a God, but this scene made me think He really must exist. At the same time, however, I began to wonder why He did not place it in some worthy centre of civilisation, rather than in this out-of-the-way barbarous region, where for centuries there has been no one to enjoy its beauty. And so, on the other hand, such waste of labour and incongruity of position disposed me to think that there cannot be a God after all."

One favourite piece is a letter which Liu Tsung-yüan writes in a bantering style to congratulate a well-to-do literary man on having lost everything in a fire, especially, as he explains, if the victim has been "utterly and irretrievably beggared." It will give such a rare opportunity, he points out, to show the world that there was no connection whatever between worldly means and literary reputation.

A well-known satirical piece by Liu Tsung-yüan is entitled "Catching Snakes," and is directed against the hardships of over-taxation :—

"In the wilds of Hu-kuang there is an extraordinary kind of snake, having a black body with white rings. Deadly fatal, even to the grass and trees it may chance to touch ; in man, its bite is absolutely incurable. Yet, if caught and prepared, when dry, in the form of cakes, the flesh of this snake will soothe excitement, heal leprous sores, remove sloughing flesh, and expel evil spirits. And so it came about that the Court physician, acting under Imperial orders, exacted from each family a return of two of these snakes every year ; but as few persons were able to comply with the demand, it was subsequently made known that the return of snakes was to be considered in lieu of the usual taxes. Thereupon there ensued a general stampede among the people of those parts."

It turned out, however, that snake-catching was actually less deadly than paying such taxes as were exacted from those who dared not face its risks and elected to contribute in the ordinary way. One man, whose father and grandfather had both perished from snake-bites, declared that after all he was better off than his neighbours, who were ground down and beggared by the iniquities of the tax-gatherer. "Harsh tyrants," he explained, "sweep down upon us, and throw everybody and everything, even to the brute beasts, into paroxysms of terror and disorder. But I,—I get up in the morning and look into the jar where my snakes are kept ; and if they are still there, I lie down at night in peace. At the appointed time, I take care that they are fit to be handed in ; and when that is done, I retire to enjoy the produce of my farm and complete the allotted span of my existence. Only twice a year have I to risk my life : the rest is peaceful enough and not to be compared with the daily round of annoyance which falls to the share of my fellow-villagers."

A similar satire on over-government introduces a deformed gardener called Camel-back. This man was extraordinarily successful as a nurseryman :—

"One day a customer asked him how this was so ; to which he replied, 'Old Camel-back cannot make trees live or thrive. He can only let them follow their natural tendencies. Now in planting trees, be careful to set the root straight, to smooth the earth around them, to use good mould, and to ram it down well. Then, don't touch them ; don't think about them ; don't go and look at them ; but leave them alone to take care of themselves, and nature will do the rest. I only avoid trying to make my trees grow. I have no special method of cultivation, no special means for securing luxuriance of growth. I only don't spoil the fruit. I have no way of getting it either early or in abundance. Other gardeners set with bent root and neglect the mould. They heap up either too much earth or too little. Or if not this, then they become too fond of and too anxious about their trees, and are for ever running backwards and forwards to see how they are growing ; sometimes scratching them to make sure they are still alive, or shaking them about to see if they are sufficiently firm in the ground ; thus constantly interfering with the natural bias of the tree, and turning their affection and care into an absolute bane and a curse. I only don't do these things. That's all.'

"'Can these principles you have just now set forth be applied to government ?' asked his listener. 'Ah !' replied Camel-back, 'I only understand nursery-gardening : government is not my trade. Still, in the village where I live, the officials are for ever issuing all kinds of orders, as if greatly compassionating the people, though really to their utter injury. Morning and night the underlings come round and say, 'His Honour bids us urge on your ploughing, hasten your planting, and superintend your harvest. Do not delay with your spinning and weaving. Take care of your children. Rear poultry and pigs. Come together when the drum beats. Be ready at the sound of the rattle.' Thus are we poor people badgered from morn till eve. We have not a moment to ourselves. How could any one flourish and develop naturally under such conditions ?'"

In his prose writings Han Yü showed even more variety of subject than in his verse. His farewell words to his dead friend Liu Tsung-yüan, read, according to Chinese custom, by the side of the bier or at the grave, and then burnt as a means of communicating them to the deceased, are widely known to his countrymen :—

"Alas ! Tzŭ-hou, and hast thou come to this pass ?—

Fool that I am! is it not the pass to which mortals have ever come? Man is born into the world like a dream: what need has he to take note of gain or loss? While the dream lasts, he may sorrow or may joy; but when the awakening is at hand, why cling regretfully to the past?

"'Twere well for all things an they had no worth. The excellence of its wood is the bane of the tree. And thou, whose early genius knew no curb, weaver of the jewelled words, thou wilt be remembered when the imbeciles of fortune and place are forgot.

"The unskilful bungler hacks his hands and streams with sweat, while the expert craftsman looks on with folded arms. O my friend, thy work was not for this age; though I, a bungler, have found employment in the service of the State. Thou didst know thyself above the common herd; but when in shame thou didst depart never to return, the Philistines usurped thy place.

"Alas! Tzŭ-hou, now thou art no more. But thy last wish, that I should care for thy little son, is still ringing sadly in my ears. The friendships of the day are those of self-interest alone. How can I feel sure that I shall live to carry out thy behest? I did not arrogate to myself this duty. Thou thyself hast bidden me to the task; and, by the Gods above, I will not betray thy trust.

"Thou hast gone to thy eternal home, and wilt not return. With these sacrifices by thy coffin's side, I utter an affectionate farewell."

The following passages are taken from his essay on the Way or Method of Confucianism:—

"Had there been no sages of old, the race of man would have long since become extinct. Men have not fur and feathers and scales to adjust the temperature of their bodies; neither have they claws and fangs to aid them in the struggle for food. Hence their organisation, as follows:—The sovereign issues commands. The minister carries out these commands, and makes them known to the people. The people produce grain and flax and silk, fashion articles of everyday use, and interchange commodities, in order to fulfil their obligations to their rulers. The sovereign who fails to issue his commands loses his *raison d'être;* the minister who fails to carry out his sovereign's commands, and to make them known to the people, loses his *raison d'être;* the people who fail to produce grain and flax and silk, fashion articles of everyday use, and interchange commodities, in order to fulfil their obligations to their rulers, should lose their heads."

· · · · · · ·

"And if I am asked what Method is this, I reply that it is what I call *the* Method, and not merely a method like those of Lao Tzŭ and Buddha. The Emperor Yao handed it down to the Emperor Shun; the Emperor Shun handed it down to the Great Yü; and so on until it reached Confucius, and lastly Mencius, who died without transmitting it to any one else. Then followed the heterodox schools of Hsün and Yang, wherein much that was essential was passed over, while the criterion was vaguely formulated. In the days before Chou Kung, the Sages were themselves rulers; hence they were able to secure the reception of their Method. In the days after Chou Kung, the Sages were all high officers of State; hence its duration through a long period of time.

"And now, it will be asked, what is the remedy? I answer that unless these false doctrines are rooted out, the true faith will not prevail. Let us insist that the followers of Lao Tzŭ and Buddha behave themselves like ordinary mortals. Let us burn their books. Let us turn their temples into dwelling-houses. Let us make manifest the Method of our ancient kings, in order that men may be led to embrace its teachings."

Of the character of Han Yü's famous ultimatum to the crocodile, which all Chinese writers have regarded as a real creature, though probably the name is but an allegorical veil, the following extract may suffice :—

"O Crocodile! thou and I cannot rest together here. The Son of Heaven has confided this district and this people to my charge; and thou, O goggle-eyed, by disturbing the peace of this river and devouring the people and their domestic animals, the bears, the boars, and deer of the neighbourhood, in order to batten thyself and reproduce thy kind,—thou art challenging me to a struggle of life and death. And I, though of weakly frame, am I to bow the knee and yield before a crocodile ? No! I am the lawful guardian of this place, and I would scorn to decline thy challenge, even were it to cost me my life.

"Still, in virtue of my commission from the Son of Heaven, I am bound to give fair warning; and thou, O crocodile, if thou art wise, will pay due heed to my words. There before thee lies the broad ocean, the domain alike of the whale and the shrimp. Go thither and live in peace. It is but the journey of a day."

The death of a dearly loved nephew, comparatively near to him in age, drew from Han Yü a long and pathetic "In Memoriam," conveyed, as mentioned above, to the ears of the departed through the medium of fire and smoke. These are two short extracts :—

"The line of my noble-hearted brother has indeed been

prematurely cut off. Thy pure intelligence, hope of the family, survives not to continue the traditions of his house. Unfathomable are the appointments of what men call Heaven : inscrutable are the workings of the unseen : unknowable are the mysteries of eternal truth : unrecognisable those who are destined to attain to old age !

"Henceforth my grey hairs will grow white, my strength fail. Physically and mentally hurrying on to decay, how long before I shall follow thee ? If there is knowledge after death, this separation will be but for a little while. If there is not knowledge after death, so will this sorrow be but for a little while, and then no more sorrow for ever."

.   .   .   .

"O ye blue heavens, when shall my sorrow have end ? Henceforth the world has no charms. I will get me a few acres on the banks of the Ying, and there await the end, teaching my son and thy son, if haply they may grow up,—my daughter and thy daughter, until their day of marriage comes. Alas ! though words fail, love endureth. Dost thou hear, or dost thou not hear ? Woe is me : Heaven bless thee !"

Of all Han Yü's writings in prose or in verse, there was not one which caused anything like the sensation produced by his memorial to the Emperor on the subject of Buddha's bone. The fact was, Buddhism was making vast strides in popular esteem, and but for some such bold stand as was made on this occasion by a leading man, the prestige of Confucianism would have received a staggering blow. Here is an extract from this fiery document, which sent its author into exile and nearly cost him his life :—

"Your servant has now heard that instructions have been issued to the priestly community to proceed to

Fêng-hsiang and receive a bone of Buddha, and that from a high tower your Majesty will view its introduction into the Imperial Palace ; also that orders have been sent to the various temples, commanding that the relic be received with the proper ceremonies. Now, foolish though your servant may be, he is well aware that your Majesty does not do this in the vain hope of deriving advantages therefrom ; but that in the fulness of our present plenty, and in the joy which reigns in the heart of all, there is a desire to fall in with the wishes of the people in the celebration at the capital of this delusive mummery. For how could the wisdom of your Majesty stoop to participate in such ridiculous beliefs ? Still the people are slow of perception and easily beguiled ; and should they behold your Majesty thus earnestly worshipping at the feet of Buddha, they would cry out, 'See ! the Son of Heaven, the All-Wise, is a fervent believer ; who are we, his people, that we should spare our bodies ?' Then would ensue a scorching of heads and burning of fingers ; crowds would collect together, and, tearing off their clothes and scattering their money, would spend their time from morn to eve in imitation of your Majesty's example. The result would be that by and by young and old, seized with the same enthusiasm, would totally neglect the business of their lives ; and should your Majesty not prohibit it, they would be found flocking to the temples, ready to cut off an arm or slice their bodies as an offering to the god. Thus would our traditions and customs be seriously injured, and ourselves become a laughing-stock on the face of the earth ;—truly, no small matter !

"For Buddha was a barbarian. His language was not the language of China. His clothes were of an alien cut. He did not utter the maxims of our ancient rulers, nor conform to the customs which they have handed down. He did not appreciate the bond between prince and minister, the tie between father and son. Supposing, indeed, this Buddha had come to our capital in the flesh, under an appointment from his own State, then your Majesty might have received him with a few words of admonition, bestowing on him a banquet and a suit of clothes, previous to sending him out of the country with an escort of soldiers, and thereby have avoided any dangerous influence on the minds of the people. But what are the facts? The bone of a man long since dead and decomposed is to be admitted, forsooth, within the precincts of the Imperial Palace! Confucius said, 'Pay all respect to spiritual beings, but keep them at a distance.' And so, when the princes of old paid visits of condolence to one another, it was customary for them to send on a magician in advance, with a peach-wand in his hand, whereby to expel all noxious influences previous to the arrival of his master. Yet now your Majesty is about to causelessly introduce a disgusting object, personally taking part in the proceedings, without the intervention either of the magician or of his peach-wand. Of the officials, not one has raised his voice against it; of the censors, not one has pointed out the enormity of such an act. Therefore your servant, overwhelmed with shame for the censors, implores your Majesty that these bones be handed over for destruction by fire or water, whereby the root of this great evil may be exterminated for all time, and the people know how much the wisdom of your Majesty surpasses that of ordinary men. The glory of such a deed will be beyond all praise. And should the Lord Buddha have power to avenge this insult by the infliction of some misfortune, then let the vials of his wrath be poured out upon the person of your servant, who now calls Heaven to witness that he will not repent him of his oath."

A writer named LI HUA, of whom little is known except that he flourished in the ninth century, has left behind him one very much admired piece entitled " On an Old Battlefield " :—

"Vast, vast,—a limitless extent of flat sand, without a human being in sight, girdled by a stream and dotted with hills, where in the dismal twilight the wind moans at the setting sun. Shrubs gone : grass withered : all chill as the hoar-frost of early morn. The birds of the air fly past : the beasts of the field shun the spot ; for it is, as I was informed by the keeper, the site of an old battlefield. ' Many a time and oft,' said he, ' has an army been overthrown on this spot; and the voices of the dead may frequently be heard weeping and wailing in the darkness of the night.' "

This is how the writer calls up in imagination the ghastly scene of long ago :—

" And now the cruel spear does its work, the startled sand blinds the combatants locked fast in the death-struggle ; while hill and vale and stream groan beneath the flash and crash of arms. By and by, the chill cold shades of night fall upon them, knee-deep in snow, beards stiff with ice. The hardy vulture seeks its nest : the strength of the war-horse is broken. Clothes are of no avail ; hands frost-bitten, flesh cracked. Even nature lends her aid to the Tartars, contributing a deadly blast, the better to complete the work of slaughter begun.

Ambulance waggons block the way: our men succumb to flank attacks. Their officers have surrendered: their general is dead. The river is choked with corpses to its topmost banks: the fosses of the Great Wall are swimming over with blood. All distinctions are obliterated in that heap of rotting bones. . . .

"Faintly and more faintly beats the drum. Strength exhausted, arrows spent, bow-strings snapped, swords shattered, the two armies fall upon one another in the supreme struggle for life or death. To yield is to become the barbarian's slave: to fight is to mingle our bones with the desert sand. . . .

"No sound of bird now breaks from the hushed hillside. All is still save the wind whistling through the long night. Ghosts of the dead wander hither and thither in the gloom: spirits from the nether world collect under the dark clouds. The sun rises and shines coldly over the trampled grass, while the fading moon still twinkles upon the frost flakes scattered around. What sight more horrible than this!"

The havoc wrought by the dreaded Tartars is indeed the theme of many a poem in prose as well as in verse. The following lines by CH'ÊN T'AO, of about this date, record a patriotic oath of indignant volunteers and the mournful issue of fruitless valour:—

> *"They swore the Huns should perish:*
> *they would die if needs they must. . . .*
> *And now five thousand, sable-clad,*
> *have bit the Tartar dust.*
> *Along the river-bank their bones*
> *lie scattered where they may,*
> *But still their forms in dreams arise*
> *to fair ones far away."*

Among their other glories, the T'angs may be said to have witnessed the birth of popular literature, soon to receive, in common with classical scholarship, an impetus the like of which had never yet been felt.

But we must now take leave of this dynasty, the name of which has survived in common parlance to this day. For just as the northerners are proud to call themselves "sons of Han," so do the Chinese of the more southern provinces still delight to be known as the "men of T'ang."

BOOK THE FIFTH

THE SUNG DYNASTY (A.D. 900–1200)

BOOK THE FIFTH

THE SUNG DYNASTY (A.D. 900–1200)

CHAPTER I

THE INVENTION OF BLOCK-PRINTING

THE T'ang dynasty was brought to an end in 907, and during the succeeding fifty years the empire experienced no fewer than five separate dynastic changes. It was not a time favourable to literary effort; still production was not absolutely at a standstill, and some minor names have come down to us.

Of CHANG PI, for instance, of the later Chou dynasty, little is known, except that he once presented a voluminous memorial to his sovereign in the hope of staving off political collapse. The memorial, we are told, was much admired, but the advice contained in it was not acted upon. These few lines of his occur in many a poetical garland :—

> " *After parting, dreams possessed me,*
> *and I wandered you know where,*
> *And we sat in the verandah,*
> *and you sang the sweet old air.*

Then I woke, with no one near me
save the moon, still shining on,
And lighting up dead petals
which like you have passed and gone."

There is, however, at least one name of absorbing interest to the foreign student. FÊNG TAO (881–954) is best known to the Chinese as a versatile politician who served first and last under no less than ten Emperors of four different Houses, and gave himself a sobriquet which finds its best English equivalent in "The Vicar of Bray." He presented himself at the Court of the second Emperor of the Liao dynasty and positively asked for a post. He said he had no home, no money, and very little brains; a statement which appears to have appealed forcibly to the Tartar monarch, who at once appointed him grand tutor to the heir-apparent. By foreigners, on the other hand, he will be chiefly remembered as the inventor of the art of block-printing. It seems probable, indeed, that some crude form of this invention had been already known early in the T'ang dynasty, but until the date of Fêng Tao it was certainly not applied to the production of books. Six years after his death the "fire-led" House of Sung was finally established upon the throne, and thenceforward the printing of books from blocks became a familiar handicraft with the Chinese people.

With the advent of this new line, we pass, as the Chinese fairy-stories say, to "another heaven and earth." The various departments of history, classical scholarship, general literature, lexicography, and poetry were again filled with enthusiastic workers, eagerly encouraged by a succession of enlightened rulers. And although there was a falling-off consequent upon the irruption of the

Golden Tartars in 1125–1127, when the ex-Emperor and his newly appointed successor were carried captive to the north, nevertheless the Sungs managed to create a great epoch, and are justly placed in the very first rank among the builders of Chinese literature.

CHAPTER II

HISTORY—CLASSICAL AND GENERAL
LITERATURE

THE first move made in the department of history was nothing less than to re-write the whole of the chronicles of the T'ang dynasty. The usual scheme had already been carried out by Liu Hsü (897–946), a learned scholar of the later Chin dynasty, but on many grounds the result was pronounced unsatisfactory, and steps were taken to supersede it. The execution of this project was entrusted to Ou-yang Hsiu and Sung C'hi, both of whom were leading men in the world of letters. OU-YANG HSIU (1007–1072) had been brought up in poverty, his mother teaching him to write with a reed. By the time he was fifteen his great abilities began to attract attention, and later on he came out first on the list of candidates for the third or highest degree. His public life was a chequered one, owing to the bold positions he took up in defence of what he believed to be right, regardless of personal interest. Besides the dynastic history, he wrote on all kinds of subjects, grave and gay, including an exposition of the Book of Poetry, a work on ancient inscriptions, anecdotes of the men of his day, an elaborate treatise on the peony, poetry and essays without end. The following is a specimen of his lighter work, greatly admired for the beauty of its style, and diligently read by all students of composition. The theme, as the reader will perceive, is the historian himself :—

"The district of Ch'u is entirely surrounded by hills, and the peaks to the south-west are clothed with a dense and beautiful growth of trees, over which the eye wanders in rapture away to the confines of Shantung. A walk of two or three miles on those hills brings one within earshot of the sound of falling water, which gushes forth from a ravine known as the Wine-Fountain ; while hard by in a nook at a bend of the road stands a kiosque, commonly spoken of as the Old Drunkard's Arbour. It was built by a Buddhist priest, called Deathless Wisdom, who lived among these hills, and who received the above name from the Governor. The latter used to bring his friends hither to take wine ; and as he personally was incapacitated by a very few cups, and was, moreover, well stricken in years, he gave himself the sobriquet of the Old Drunkard. But it was not wine that attracted him to this spot. It was the charming scenery, which wine enabled him to enjoy.

"The sun's rays peeping at dawn through the trees, by and by to be obscured behind gathering clouds, leaving naught but gloom around, give to this spot the alternations of morning and night. The wild-flowers exhaling their perfume from the darkness of some shady dell, the luxuriant foliage of the dense forest of beautiful trees, the clear frosty wind, and the naked boulders of the lessening torrent,—these are the indications of spring, summer, autumn, and winter. Morning is the time to go thither, returning with the shades of night, and although the place presents a different aspect with the changes of the seasons, its charms are subject to no interruption, but continue alway. Burden-carriers sing their way along the road, travellers rest awhile under the trees, shouts from one, responses from another, old people hobbling along, children in arms, children dragged along by hand, backwards and forwards all day long without a break,—these are the people of Ch'u. A cast in the stream and a fine fish taken from some spot where the eddying pools begin to deepen ; a draught of cool wine from the fountain, and a few such dishes of meats and fruits as the hills are able to provide,—these, nicely spread out beforehand, constitute the Governor's feast. And in the revelry of the banquet-hour there is no thought of toil or trouble. Every archer hits his mark, and every player wins his *partie ;* goblets flash from hand to hand, and a buzz of conversation is heard as the guests move unconstrainedly about. Among them is an old man with white hair, bald at the top of his head. This is the drunken Governor, who, when the evening sun kisses the tips of the hills and the falling shadows are drawn out and blurred, bends his steps homewards in company with his friends. Then in the growing darkness are heard sounds above and sounds below ; the beasts of the field and the birds of the air are rejoicing at the departure of man. They, too, can rejoice in hills and in trees, but they cannot rejoice as man rejoices. So also the Governor's friends. They rejoice with him, though they know not at what it is that he rejoices. Drunk, he can rejoice with them, sober, he can discourse with them,—such is the Governor. And should you ask who is the Governor, I reply, 'Ou-yang Hsiu of Lu-ling.'"

Besides dwelling upon the beauty of this piece as vividly portraying the spirit of the age in which it was written, the commentator proudly points out that in it the particle *yeh*, with influences as subtle as those of the Greek γε, occurs no fewer than twenty times.

The next piece is entitled "An Autumn Dirge," and refers to the sudden collapse of summer, so common a phenomenon in the East :—

"One night I had just sat down to my books, when suddenly I heard a sound far away towards the south-west. Listening intently, I wondered what it could be. On it came, at first like the sighing of a gentle zephyr . . . gradually deepening into the plash of waves upon a surf-beat shore . . . the roaring of huge breakers in the startled night, amid howling storm-gusts of wind and rain. It burst upon the hanging bell, and set every one of its pendants tinkling into tune. It seemed like the muffled march of soldiers, hurriedly advancing, bit in mouth, to the attack, when no shouted orders rend the air, but only the tramp of men and horses meet the ear.

"'Boy,' said I, 'what noise is that ? Go forth and see.' 'Sir,' replied the boy on his return, 'the moon and stars are brightly shining : the Silver River spans the sky. No sound of man is heard without : 'tis but the whispering of the trees.'

"'Alas !' I cried, 'autumn is upon us. And is it thus, O boy, that autumn comes ?—autumn, the cruel and the cold ; autumn, the season of rack and mist ; autumn, the season of cloudless skies ; autumn, the season of piercing blasts ; autumn, the season of desolation and blight ! Chill is the sound that heralds its approach, and then it leaps upon us with a shout. All the rich luxuriance of green is changed, all the proud foliage of the forest swept down to earth, withered beneath the icy breath of the destroyer. For autumn is nature's chief executioner, and its symbol is darkness. It has the temper of steel, and its symbol is a sharp sword. It is the avenging angel, riding upon an atmosphere of death. As spring is the epoch of growth, so autumn is the epoch of maturity. And sad is the hour when maturity is passed, for that which passes its prime must die.

"'Still, what is this to plants and trees, which fade away in their due season? . . . But stay; there is man, man the divinest of all things. A hundred cares wreck his heart, countless anxieties trace their wrinkles on his brow, until his inmost self is bowed beneath the burden of life. And swifter still he hurries to decay when vainly striving to attain the unattainable, or grieving over his ignorance of that which can never be known. Then comes the whitening hair—and why not? Has man an adamantine frame, that he should outlast the trees of the field? Yet, after all, who is it, save himself, that steals his strength away? Tell me, O boy, what right has man to accuse his autumn blast?'

"My boy made no answer. He was fast asleep. No sound reached me save that of the cricket chirping its response to my dirge."

The other leading historian of this period was SUNG CH'I (998–1061), who began his career by beating his elder brother at the graduates' examination. He was, however, placed tenth, instead of first, by Imperial command, and in accordance with the precedence of brothers. He rose to high office, and was also a voluminous writer. A great favourite at Court, it is related that he was once at some Imperial festivity when he began to feel cold. The Emperor bade one of the ladies of the seraglio lend him a tippet, whereupon about a dozen of the girls each offered hers. But

Sung Ch'i did not like to seem to favour any one, and rather than offend the rest, continued to sit and shiver. The so-called New History of the T'ang Dynasty, which he produced in co-operation with Ou-yang Hsiu, is generally regarded as a distinct improvement upon the work of Liu Hsü. It has not, however, actually superseded the latter work, which is still included among the recognised dynastic histories, and stands side by side with its rival.

Meanwhile another star had risen, in magnitude to be compared only with the effulgent genius of Ssŭ-ma Ch'ien. SSŬ-MA KUANG (1019–1086) entered upon an official career and rose to be Minister of State. But he opposed the great reformer, Wang An-shih, and in 1070 was compelled to resign. He devoted the rest of his life to the completion of his famous work known as the *T'ung Chien* or Mirror of History, a title bestowed upon it in 1084 by the Emperor, because "to view antiquity as it were in a mirror is an aid in the administration of government." The Mirror of History covers a period from the fifth century B.C. down to the beginning of the Sung dynasty, A.D. 960, and was supplemented by several important works from the author's own hand, all bearing upon the subject. In his youth the latter had been a devoted student, and used to rest his arm upon a kind of round wooden pillow, which roused him to wakefulness by its movement every time he began to doze over his work. On one occasion, in childhood, a small companion fell into a water-kong, and would have been drowned but for the presence of mind of Ssŭ-ma Kuang. He seized a huge stone, and with it cracked the jar so that the water poured out. As a scholar he had a large library, and was so particular in the handling of his books that even after many years' use they were still as good as new. He would not allow his disciples to turn over leaves by scratching them up with the nails, but made them use the forefinger and second finger of the right hand. In 1085 he determined to return to public life, but he had not been many months in the capital, labouring as usual for his country's good, before he succumbed to an illness and died, universally honoured and regretted by his countrymen, to whom he was affectionately known as the Living Buddha.

The following extract from his writings refers to a new and dangerous development in the Censorate, an institution which still plays a singular part in the administration of China :—

"Of old there was no such office as that of Censor. From the highest statesman down to the artisan and trader, every man was free to admonish the Throne. From the time of the Han dynasty onwards, this prerogative was vested in an office, with the weighty responsibility of discussing the government of the empire, the people within the Four Seas, successes, failures, advantages, and disadvantages, in order of importance and of urgency. The sole object in this arrangement was the benefit of the State, not that of the Censor, from whom all ideas of fame or gain were indeed far removed. In 1017 an edict was issued appointing six officers to undertake these Censorial duties, and in 1045 their names were for the first time written out on boards ; and then, in 1062, apparently for better preservation, the names were cut on stone. Thus posterity can point to such an one and say, 'There was a loyal man ;' to another, 'There was a traitor ;' to a third, 'There was an upright man ;' to a fourth, 'There was a scoundrel.' Does not this give cause for fear ?"

Contemporaneously with Ssŭ-ma Kuang lived CHOU TUN-I (1017–1073), who combined the duties of a small military command with prolonged and arduous study. He made himself ill by overwork and strict attention to the interests of the people at all hazards to himself. His chief works were written to elucidate the mysteries of the Book of Changes, and were published after his death by his disciples, with commentaries by Chu Hsi. The following short satire, veiled under the symbolism of flowers, being in a style which the educated Chinaman most appreciates, is very widely known :—

"Lovers of flowering plants and shrubs we have had by scores, but T'ao Ch'ien alone devoted himself to the chrysanthemum. Since the opening days of the T'ang dynasty, it has been fashionable to admire the peony; but my favourite is the water-lily. How stainless it rises from its slimy bed! How modestly it reposes on the clear pool—an emblem of purity and truth! Symmetrically perfect, its subtle perfume is wafted far and wide, while there it rests in spotless state, something to be regarded reverently from a distance, and not to be profaned by familiar approach.

"In my opinion the chrysanthemum is the flower of retirement and culture; the peony the flower of rank and wealth; the water-lily, the Lady Virtue *sans pareille*.

"Alas! few have loved the chrysanthemum since T'ao Ch'ien, and none now love the water-lily like myself, whereas the peony is a general favourite with all mankind."

Ch'êng Hao (1032–1085) and Ch'êng I (1033–1107) were two brothers famed for their scholarship, especially the younger of the two, who published a valuable commentary upon the Book of Changes. The elder attracted some attention by boldly suppressing a stone image in a Buddhist temple which was said to emit rays from its head, and had been the cause of disorderly gatherings of men and women. A specimen of his verse will be given in the next chapter. Ch'êng I wrote some interesting chapters on the art of poetry. In one of these he says, "Asked if a man can make himself a poet by taking pains, I reply that only by taking pains can any one hope to be ranked as such, though on the other hand the very fact of taking pains is likely to be inimical to success. The old couplet reminds us—

> ' E'er one pentameter be spoken
> How many a human heart is broken !'

There is also another old couplet—

> ''Twere sad to take this heart of mine
> And break it o'er a five-foot line.'

Both of these are very much to the point. Confucius himself did not make verses, but he did not advise others to abstain from doing so."

The great reformer and political economist Wang An-shih (1021–1086), who lived to see all his policy reversed, was a hard worker as a youth, and in composition his pen was said to "fly over the paper." As a man he was distinguished by his frugality and his obstinacy. He wore dirty clothes and did not even wash his face, for which Su Hsün denounced him as a beast. He was so cocksure of all his own views that he would never admit the possibility of being wrong, which gained for him the sobriquet of the Obstinate Minister. He attempted to reform the examination system, requiring from the candidate not so much graces of style as a wide acquaintance with practical subjects. "Accordingly," says one Chinese writer, "even the pupils at village schools threw away their text-books of rhetoric, and began to study primers of history, geography, and political economy." He was the author of a work on the written characters, with special reference to those which are formed by the combination of two or more, the meanings of which, taken together, determine the meaning of the compound character. The following is a letter which he wrote to a friend on the study of false doctrines:—

"I have been debarred by illness from writing to you now for some time, though my thoughts have been with you all the while.

"In reply to my last letter, wherein I expressed a fear that you were not progressing with your study of the Canon, I have received several from you, in all of which you seem to think I meant the Canon of Buddha, and you are astonished at my recommendation of such pernicious works. But how could I possibly have intended any other than the Canon of the sages of China? And for you to have thus missed the point of my letter is a good illustration of what I meant when I said I feared you were not progressing with your study of the Canon.

"Now a thorough knowledge of our Canon has not been attained by any one for a very long period. Study of the Canon alone does not suffice for a thorough knowledge of the Canon. Consequently, I have been myself an omnivorous reader of books of all kinds, even, for example, of ancient medical and botanical works. I have, moreover, dipped into treatises on agriculture and on needlework, all of which I have found very profitable in aiding me to seize the great scheme of the Canon itself. For learning in these days is a totally different pursuit from what it was in the olden times; and it is now impossible otherwise to get at the real meaning of our ancient sages.

"There was Yang Hsiung. He hated all books that were not orthodox. Yet he made a wide study of heterodox writers. By force of education he was enabled to take what of good and to reject what of bad he found in each. Their pernicious influence was altogether lost on him; while on the other hand he was prepared the more effectively to elucidate what we know to be the truth. Now, do you consider that I have been corrupted by these pernicious influences? If so, you know me not.

"No! the pernicious influences of the age are not to be sought for in the Canon of Buddha. They are to be found in the corruption and vice of those in high places; in the false and shameless conduct which is now rife among us. Do you not agree with me?"

Su Shih (1036–1101), better known by his fancy name as Su Tung-p'o, whose early education was superintended by his mother, produced such excellent compositions at the examination for his final degree that the examiner, Ou-yang Hsiu, suspected them to be the work of a qualified substitute. Ultimately he came out first on the list. He rose to be a statesman, who made more enemies than friends, and was perpetually struggling against the machinations of unscrupulous opponents, which on one occasion resulted in his banishment to the island of Hainan, then a barbarous and almost unknown region. He was also a brilliant essayist and poet, and his writings are still the delight of the Chinese. The following is an account of a midnight picnic to a spot on the banks of a river at which a great battle had taken place nearly nine hundred years before, and where one of the opposing fleets was burnt to the water's edge, reddening a wall, probably the cliff alongside :—

"In the year 1081, the seventh moon just on the wane, I went with a friend on a boat excursion to the Red Wall. A clear breeze was gently blowing, scarce enough to ruffle the river, as I filled my friend's cup and bade him troll a lay to the bright moon, singing the song of the 'Modest Maid.'

"By and by up rose the moon over the eastern hills, wandering between the Wain and the Goat, shedding forth her silver beams, and linking the water with the sky. On a skiff we took our seats, and shot over the liquid plain, lightly as though travelling through space, riding on the wind without knowing whither we were bound. We seemed to be moving in another sphere, sailing through air like the gods. So I poured out a bumper for joy, and, beating time on the skiff's side, sang the following verse :—

> *'With laughing oars, our joyous prow*
> *Shoots swiftly through the glittering wave—*
> *My heart within grows sadly grave—*
> *Great heroes dead, where are ye now ?'*

"My friend accompanied these words upon his flageolet, delicately adjusting its notes to express the varied emotions of pity and regret, without the slightest break in the thread of sound which seemed to wind around us like a silken skein. The very monsters of the deep yielded to the influence of his strains, while the boat-woman, who had lost her husband, burst into a flood of tears. Overpowered by my own feelings, I settled myself into a serious mood, and asked my friend for some explanation of his art. To this he replied, 'Did not Ts'ao Ts'ao say—

> ' The stars are few, the moon is bright,
> The raven southward wings his flight?'

"'Westwards to Hsia-k'ou, eastwards to Wu-ch'ang, where hill and stream in wild luxuriance blend,—was it not there that Ts'ao Ts'ao was routed by Chou Yü? Ching-chou was at his feet: he was pushing down stream towards the east. His war-vessels stretched stem to stern for a thousand *li:* his banners darkened the sky. He poured out a libation as he neared Chiang-ling; and, sitting in the saddle armed *cap-à-pie*, he uttered those words, did that hero of his age. Yet where is he to-day?

"'Now you and I have fished and gathered fuel to-gether on the river eyots. We have fraternised with the crayfish; we have made friends with the deer. We have embarked together in our frail canoe; we have drawn inspiration together from the wine-flask—a couple of ephemerides launched on the ocean in a rice-husk! Alas! life is but an instant of Time. I long to be like the Great River which rolls on its way without end. Ah, that I might cling to some angel's wing and roam with him for ever! Ah, that I might clasp the bright moon in my arms and dwell with her for aye! Alas! it only remains to me to enwrap these regrets in the tender melody of sound.'

"'But do you forsooth comprehend,' I inquired, 'the mystery of this river and of this moon? The water passes by but is never gone: the moon wanes only to wax once more. Relatively speaking, Time itself is but an instant of time; absolutely speaking, you and I, in common with all matter, shall exist to all eternity. Wherefore, then, the longing of which you speak?

"'The objects we see around us are one and all the property of individuals. If a thing does not belong to me, not a particle of it may be enjoyed by me. But the clear breeze blowing across this stream, the bright moon streaming over yon hills,—these are sounds and sights to be enjoyed without let or hindrance by all. They are the eternal gifts of God to all mankind, and their enjoyment is inexhaustible. Hence it is that you and I are enjoying them now.'

"My friend smiled as he threw away the dregs from his wine-cup and filled it once more to the brim. And then, when our feast was over, amid the litter of cups and plates, we lay down to rest in the boat: for streaks of light from the east had stolen upon us unawares."

The completion of a pavilion which Su Shih had been building, "as a refuge from the business of life," coinciding with a fall of rain which put an end to a severe drought, elicited a grateful record of this divine manifestation towards a suffering people. "The pavilion was named after rain, to commemorate joy." His record concludes with these lines :—

" Should Heaven rain pearls, the cold cannot wear them as clothes;
Should Heaven rain jade, the hungry cannot use it as food.
It has rained without cease for three days—
Whose was the influence at work?
Should you say it was that of your Governor,
The Governor himself refers it to the Son of Heaven.

> *But the Son of Heaven says ' No ! it was God:*
> *And God says ' No ! it was Nature.'*
> *And as Nature lies beyond the ken of man,*
> *I christen this arbour instead."*

Another piece refers to a recluse who—

"Kept a couple of cranes, which he had carefully trained; and every morning he would release them westwards through the gap, to fly away and alight in the marsh below or soar aloft among the clouds as the birds' own fancy might direct. At nightfall they would return with the utmost regularity."

This piece is also finished off with a few poetical lines :—

> *" Away ! away ! my birds, fly westwards now,*
> *To wheel on high and gaze on all below ;*
> *To swoop together, pinions closed, to earth ;*
> *To soar aloft once more among the clouds ;*
> *To wander all day long in sedgy vale ;*
> *To gather duckweed in the stony marsh.*
> *Come back ! come back ! beneath the lengthening shades,*
> *Your serge-clad master stands, guitar in hand.*
> *'Tis he that feeds you from his slender store :*
> *Come back ! come back ! nor linger in the west."*

His account of Sleep-Land is based upon the Drunk-Land of Wang Chi :—

"A pure administration and admirable morals prevail there, the whole being one vast level tract, with no north, south, east, or west. The inhabitants are quiet and affable ; they suffer from no diseases of any kind, neither are they subject to the influences of the seven passions. They have no concern with the ordinary affairs of life ; they do not distinguish heaven, earth, the sun, and the moon ; they toil not, neither do they spin ; but simply lie down and enjoy themselves. They have no ships and no carriages ; their wanderings, however, are the boundless flights of the imagination."

His younger brother, SU CHÊ (1039–1112), poet and official, is chiefly known for his devotion to Taoism. He published an edition, with commentary, of the *Tao-Tê-Ching*.

One of the Four Scholars of his century is HUANG T'ING-CHIEN (1050–1110), who was distinguished as a poet and a calligraphist. He has also been placed among the twenty-four examples of filial piety, for when his mother was ill he watched by her bedside for a whole year without ever taking off his clothes. The following is a specimen of his epistolary style :—

"Hsi K'ang's verses are at once vigorous and purely beautiful, without a vestige of commonplace about them. Every student of the poetic art should know them thoroughly, and thus bring the author into his mind's eye.

"Those who are sunk in the cares and anxieties of this world's strife, even by a passing glance would gain therefrom enough to clear away some pecks of the cobwebs of mortality. How much more they who penetrate further and seize each hidden meaning and enjoy its flavour to the full ? Therefore, my nephew, I send you these poems for family reading, that you may cleanse your heart and solace a weary hour by their perusal.

"As I recently observed to my own young people, the true hero should be many-sided, but he must not be commonplace: It is impossible to cure that. Upon which one of them asked by what characteristics this absence of the commonplace was distinguished. 'It is hard to say,' I replied. 'A man who is not commonplace is, under ordinary circumstances, much like other people. But he who at moments of great trial does not flinch, he is not commonplace.'"

CHÊNG CH'IAO (1108-1166) began his literary career in studious seclusion, cut off from all human intercourse. Then he spent some time in visiting various places of interest, devoting himself to searching out marvels, investigating antiquities, and reading (and remembering) every book that came in his way. In 1149 he was summoned to an audience, and received an honorary post. He was then sent home to copy out his History of China, which covered a period from about B.C. 2800 to A.D. 600. A fine edition of this work, in forty-six large volumes, was published in 1749 by Imperial command, with a preface by the Emperor Ch'ien Lung. He also wrote essays and poetry, besides a treatise in which he showed that the inscriptions on the Stone Drums, now in Peking, belong rather to the latter half of the third century B.C. than to the tenth or eleventh century B.C., as usually accepted.

The name of CHU HSI (1130-1200) is a household word throughout the length and breadth of literary China. He graduated at nineteen, and entered upon a highly successful official career. He apparently had a strong leaning towards Buddhism—some say that he actually became a Buddhist priest ; at any rate, he soon saw the error of his ways, and gave himself up completely to a study of the orthodox doctrine. He was a most voluminous writer. In addition to his revision of the history of Ssŭ-ma Kuang, which, under the title of *T'ung Chien Kang Mu*, is still regarded as the standard history of China, he placed himself first in the first rank of all commentators on the Confucian Canon. He introduced interpretations either wholly or partly at variance with those which had been put forth by the scholars of the Han dynasty and hitherto received as infallible, thus modifying to a certain extent the prevailing standard of political and social morality. His principle was simply one of consistency. He refused to interpret words in a given passage in one sense, and the same words occurring elsewhere in another sense. The result, as a whole, was undoubtedly to quicken with intelligibility many paragraphs the meaning of which had been obscured rather than elucidated by the earlier scholars of the Han dynasty. Occasionally, however, the great commentator o'erleapt himself. Here are two versions of one passage in the Analects, as interpreted by the rival schools, of which the older seems unquestionably to be preferred :—

Han.	*Chu Hsi.*
Mêng Wu asked Confucius concerning filial piety. The Master said, " It consists in giving your parents no cause for anxiety save from your natural ailments."	Mêng Wu asked Confucius concerning filial piety. The Master said, " Parents have the sorrow of thinking anxiously about their children's ailments."

The latter of these interpretations being obviously incomplete, Chu Hsi adds a gloss to the effect that children are therefore in duty bound to take great care of themselves.

In the preface to his work on the Four Books as explained by Chu Hsi, published in 1745, Wang Pu-ch'ing (born 1671) has the following passage :—" Shao Yung tried to explain the Canon of Changes by numbers, and Ch'êng I by the eternal fitness of things; but Chu Hsi alone was able to pierce through the meaning, and appropriate the thought of the prophets who composed it." The other best known works of Chu Hsi are a metaphysical treatise containing the essence of his later speculations, and the Little Learning, a handbook for the young. It has been contended by some that the word "little" in the last title refers not to youthful learners, but to the lower plane on which the book is written, as compared with the Great Learning. The following extract, however, seems to point more towards Learning for the Young as the correct rendering of the title :—

"When mounting the wall of a city, do not point with the finger ; when on the top, do not call out.

"When at a friend's house, do not persist in asking for anything you may wish to have. When going upstairs, utter a loud 'Ahem !' If you see two pairs of shoes outside and hear voices, you may go in ; but if you hear nothing, remain outside. Do not trample on the shoes of other guests, nor step on the mat spread for food ; but pick up your skirts and pass quickly to your allotted place. Do not be in a hurry to arrive, nor in haste to get away.

"Do not bother the gods with too many prayers. Do not make allowances for your own shortcomings. Do not seek to know what has not yet come to pass."

Chu Hsi was lucky enough to fall in with a clever portrait painter, a *rara avis* in China at the present day according to Mr. J. B. Coughtrie, late of Hongkong, who declares that "the style and taste peculiar to the Chinese combine to render a lifelike resemblance impossible, and the completed picture unattractive. The artist lays upon his paper a flat wash of colour to match the complexion of his sitter, and upon this draws a mere map of the features, making no attempt to obtain roundness or relief by depicting light and shadows, and never by any chance conveying the slightest suggestion of animation or expression." Chu Hsi gave the artist a glowing testimonial, in which he states that the latter not merely portrays the features, but "catches the very expression, and reproduces, as it were, the inmost mind of his model." He then adds the following personal tit-bit :—

" I myself sat for two portraits, one large and the other small ; and it was quite a joke to see how accurately he reproduced my coarse ugly face and my vulgar rustic turn of mind, so that even those who had only heard of, but had never seen me, knew at once for whom the portraits were intended." It would be interesting to know if either of these pictures still survives among the Chu family heirlooms.

At the death of Chu Hsi, his coffin is said to have taken up a position, suspended in the air, about three feet from the ground. Whereupon his son-in-law, falling on his knees beside the bier, reminded the departed spirit of the great principles of which he had been such a brilliant exponent in life,—and the coffin descended gently to the ground.

CHAPTER III

POETRY

THE poetry of the Sungs has not attracted so much attention as that of the T'angs. This is chiefly due to the fact that although all the literary men of the Sung dynasty may roughly be said to have contributed their quota of verse, still there were few, if any, who could be ranked as professional poets, that is, as writers of verse and of nothing else, like Li Po, Tu Fu, and many others under the T'ang dynasty. Poetry now began to be, what it has remained in a marked degree until the present day, a department of polite education, irrespective of the particle of the divine gale. More regard was paid to form, and the license which had been accorded to earlier masters was sacrificed to conventionality. The Odes collected by Confucius are, as we have seen, rude ballads of love, and war, and tilth, borne by their very simplicity direct to the human heart. The poetry of the T'ang dynasty shows a masterly combination, in which art, unseen, is employed to enhance, not to fetter and degrade, thoughts drawn from a veritable communion with nature. With the fall of the T'ang dynasty the poetic art suffered a lapse from which it has never recovered ; and now, in modern times, although every student "can turn a verse" because he has been "duly taught," the poems produced disclose a naked artificiality which leaves the reader disappointed and cold.

The poet CH'ÊN T'UAN (d. A.D. 989) began life under favourable auspices. He was suckled by a mysterious lady in a green robe, who found him playing as a tiny child on the bank of a river. He became, in consequence of this supernatural nourishment, exceedingly clever and possessed of a prodigious memory, with a happy knack for verse. Yet he failed to get a degree, and gave himself up "to the joys of hill and stream." While on the mountains some spiritual beings are said to have taught him the art of hibernating like an animal, so that he would go off to sleep for a hundred days at a time. He wrote a treatise on the elixir of life, and was generally inclined to Taoist notions. At death his body remained warm for seven days, and for a whole month a "glory" played around his tomb. He was summoned several times to Court, but to judge by the following poem, officialdom seems to have had few charms for him :—

> " *For ten long years I plodded through*
> *the vale of lust and strife,*
> *Then through my dreams there flashed a ray*
> *of the old sweet peaceful life. . . .*
> *No scarlet-tasselled hat of state*
> *can vie with soft repose;*
> *Grand mansions do not taste the joys*
> *that the poor man's cabin knows.*
> *I hate the threatening clash of arms*
> *when fierce retainers throng,*
> *I loathe the drunkard's revels and*
> *the sound of fife and song;*
> *But I love to seek a quiet nook, and*
> *some old volume bring*
> *Where I can see the wild flowers bloom*
> *and hear the birds in spring.*"

Another poet, YANG I (974–1030), was unable to speak as a child, until one day, being taken to the top of a pagoda, he suddenly burst out with the following lines:—

> " *Upon this tall pagoda's peak*
> *My hand can nigh the stars enclose;*
> *I dare not raise my voice to speak,*
> *For fear of startling God's repose.*"

Mention has already been made of SHAO YUNG (1011–1077) in connection with Chu Hsi and classical scholarship. He was a great traveller, and an enthusiast in the cause of learning. He denied himself a stove in winter and a fan in summer. For thirty years he did not use a pillow, nor had he even a mat to sleep on. The following specimen of his verse seems, however, to belie his character as an ascetic:—

> " *Fair flowers from above in my goblet are shining,*
> *And add by reflection an infinite zest;*
> *Through two generations I've lived unrepining,*
> *While four mighty rulers have sunk to their rest.*
>
> " *My body in health has done nothing to spite me,*
> *And sweet are the moments which pass o'er my head;*
> *But now, with this wine and these flowers to delight me,*
> *How shall I keep sober and get home to bed?*"

Shao Yung was a great authority on natural phenomena, the explanation of which he deduced from principles found in the Book of Changes. On one occasion he was strolling about with some friends when he heard the goatsucker's cry. He immediately became depressed, and said, "When good government is about to prevail, the magnetic current flows from north to south; when bad government is about to prevail, it flows from south to north, and birds feel its influence first of all things. Now hitherto this bird has not been seen at Lo-yang;

from which I infer that the magnetic current is flowing from south to north, and that some southerner is coming into power, with manifold consequences to the State." The subsequent appearance of Wang An-shih was regarded as a verification of his skill.

The great reformer here mentioned found time, amid the cares of his economic revolution, to indulge in poetical composition. Here is his account of a *nuit blanche*, an excellent example of the difficult "stop-short:"—

> " *The incense-stick is burnt to ash,*
> *the water-clock is stilled,*
> *The midnight breeze blows sharply by,*
> *and all around is chilled.*
>
> " *Yet I am kept from slumber*
> *by the beauty of the spring . . .*
> *Sweet shapes of flowers across the blind*
> *the quivering moonbeams fling !*"

Here, too, is a short poem by the classical scholar, Huang T'ing-chien, written on the annual visit for worship at the tombs of ancestors, in full view of the hillside cemetery :—

> " *The peach and plum trees smile with flowers*
> *this famous day of spring,*
> *And country graveyards round about*
> *with lamentations ring.*
> *Thunder has startled insect life*
> *and roused the gnats and bees,*
> *A gentle rain has urged the crops*
> *and soothed the flowers and trees. . . .*
> *Perhaps on this side lie the bones*
> *of a wretch whom no one knows ;*
> *On that, the sacred ashes*
> *of a patriot repose.*

> But who across the centuries
>   can hope to mark each spot
> Where fool and hero, joined in death,
>   beneath the brambles rot?"

The grave student Ch'êng Hao wrote verses like the rest. Sometimes he even condescended to jest:—

> "I wander north, I wander south,
>   I rest me where I please. . . .
> See how the river-banks are nipped
>   beneath the autumn breeze!
> Yet what care I if autumn blasts
>   the river-banks lay bare?
> The loss of hue to river-banks
>   is the river-banks' affair."

In the eleventh and twelfth centuries HUNG CHÜEH-FAN made a name for himself as a poet and calligraphist, but he finally yielded to the fascination of Buddhism and took orders as a priest. This is no trifling ordeal. From three to nine pastilles are placed upon the shaven scalp of the candidate, and are allowed to burn down into the flesh, leaving an indelible scar. Here is a poem by him, written probably before monasticism had damped his natural ardour:—

> "Two green silk ropes, with painted stand,
>   from heights aërial swing,
> And there outside the house a maid
>   disports herself in spring.
> Along the ground her blood-red skirts
>   all swiftly swishing fly,
> As though to bear her off to be
>   an angel in the sky.
> Strewed thick with fluttering almond-blooms
>   the painted stand is seen;
> The embroidered ropes flit to and fro
>   amid the willow green.

> *Then when she stops and out she springs*
> *to stand with downcast eyes,*
> *You think she is some angel*
> *just now banished from the skies."*

Better known as a statesman than as a poet is YEH
SHIH (1150–1223). The following "stop-short," however, referring to the entrance-gate to a beautiful park,
is ranked among the best of its kind :—

> *"'Tis closed !—lest trampling footsteps mar*
> *the glory of the green.*
> *Time after time we knock and knock ;*
> *no janitor is seen.*
> *Yet bolts and bars can't quite shut in*
> *the spring-time's beauteous pall :*
> *A pink-flowered almond-spray peeps out*
> *athwart the envious wall !"*

Of KAO CHÜ-NIEN nothing seems to be known.
His poem on the annual spring worship at the tombs
of ancestors is to be found in all collections :—

> *" The northern and the southern hills*
> *are one large burying-ground,*
> *And all is life and bustle there*
> *when the sacred day comes round.*
> *Burnt paper cash, like butterflies,*
> *fly fluttering far and wide,*
> *While mourners' robes with tears of blood*
> *a crimson hue are dyed.*
> *The sun sets, and the red fox crouches*
> *down beside the tomb ;*
> *Night comes, and youths and maidens laugh*
> *where lamps light up the gloom.*
> *Let him whose fortune brings him wine,*
> *get tipsy while he may,*
> *For no man, when the long night comes,*
> *can take one drop away !"*

CHAPTER IV

DICTIONARIES—ENCYCLOPÆDIAS—MEDICAL JURISPRUDENCE

SEVERAL dictionaries of importance were issued by various scholars during the Sung dynasty, not to mention many philological works of more or less value. The Chinese have always been students of their own language, partly, no doubt, because they have so far never condescended to look at any other. They delight in going back to days when correspondence was carried on by pictures pure and simple; and the fact that there is little evidence forthcoming that such a system ever prevailed has only resulted in stimulating invention and forgery.

A clever courtier, popularly known as "the nine-tailed fox," was CH'ÊN P'ÊNG-NIEN (A.D. 961–1017), who rose to be a Minister of State. He was employed to revise the *Kuang Yün*, a phonetic dictionary by some unknown author, which contained over 26,000 separate characters. This work was to a great extent superseded by the *Chi Yün*, on a similar plan, but containing over 53,000 characters. The latter was produced by Sung Ch'i, mentioned in chap. iii., in conjunction with several eminent scholars.

TAI T'UNG graduated in 1237 and rose to be Governor of T'ai-chou in Chehkiang. Then the Mongols prevailed, and Tai T'ung, unwilling to serve them, pleaded ill-health, and in 1275 retired into private life. There he occupied himself with the composition of the *Liu Shu Ku* or Six Scripts, an examination into the origin and development of writing, which, according to some, was published about A.D. 1250, but according to others, not until so late as the year 1319.

From the rise of the Sung dynasty may be dated the first appearance of the encyclopædia, destined to occupy later so much space in Chinese literature. WU SHU (A.D. 947–1002), whose life was a good instance of "worth by poverty depressed," may fairly be credited with the production of the earliest work of the kind. His *Shih Lei Fu* dealt with celestial and terrestrial phenomena, mineralogy, botany, and natural history, arranged, for want of an alphabet, under categories. It is curiously written in the poetical-prose style, and forms the foundation of a similar book of reference in use at the present day. Wu Shu was placed upon the commission which produced a much more extensive work known as the *T'ai P'ing Yü Lan*. At the head of that commission was LI FANG (A.D. 924–995), a Minister of State and a great favourite with the Emperor. In the last year of his life he was invited to witness the Feast of Lanterns from the palace. On that occasion the Emperor placed Li beside him, and after pouring out for him a goblet of wine and supplying him with various delicacies, he turned to his courtiers and said, "Li Fang has twice served us as Minister of State, yet has he never in any way injured a single fellow-creature. Truly this must be a virtuous man." The *T'ai P'ing Yü Lan* was reprinted in 1812, and is bound up in thirty-two large volumes. It was so named because the Emperor himself went through all the manuscript, a task which occupied him nearly a year. A list of about eight hundred authorities is given, and the Index fills four hundred pages.

As a pendant to this work Li Fang designed the *T'ai P'ing Kuang Chi*, an encyclopædia of biographical and other information drawn from general literature. A list of about three hundred and sixty authorities is given, and the Index fills two hundred and eighty pages. The edition of 1566—a rare work—bound up in twelve thick volumes, stands upon the shelves of the Cambridge University Library.

Another encyclopædist was MA TUAN-LIN, the son of a high official, in whose steps he prepared to follow. The dates of his birth and death are not known, but he flourished in the thirteenth century. Upon the collapse of the Sung dynasty he disappeared from public life, and taking refuge in his native place, he gave himself up to teaching, attracting many disciples from far and near, and fascinating all by his untiring dialectic skill. He left behind him the *Wên Hsien T'ung K'ao*, a large encyclopædia based upon the *T'ung Tien* of Tu Yu, but much enlarged and supplemented by five additional sections, namely, Bibliography, Imperial Lineage, Appointments, Uranography, and Natural Phenomena. This work, which cost its author twenty years of unremitting labour, has long been known to Europeans, who have drawn largely upon its ample stores of antiquarian research.

At the close of the Sung dynasty there was published a curious book on Medical Jurisprudence, which is interesting, in spite of its manifold absurdities, as being the recognised handbook for official use at the present day. No magistrate ever thinks of proceeding to discharge the duties of coroner without taking a copy of these instructions along with him. The present work was compiled by a judge named Sung Tz̆ŭ, from pre-existing works of a similar kind, and we are told in the preface of a fine edition, dated 1842, that "being subjected for many generations to practical tests by the officers of the Board of Punishments, it became daily more and more exact." A few extracts will be sufficient to determine its real value :—

(1.) "Man has three hundred and sixty-five bones, corresponding to the number of days it takes the heavens to revolve.

"The skull of a male, from the nape of the neck to the top of the head, consists of eight pieces—of a Ts'ai-chou man, nine. There is a horizontal suture across the back of the skull, and a perpendicular one down the middle. Female skulls are of six pieces, and have the horizontal but not the perpendicular suture.

"Teeth are twenty-four, twenty-eight, thirty-two, or thirty-six in number. There are three long-shaped breast-bones.

"There is one bone belonging to the heart of the shape and size of a *cash*.

"There is one 'shoulder-well' bone and one 'rice-spoon' bone on each side.

"Males have twelve ribs on each side, eight long and four short. Females have fourteen on each side."

(2.) "Wounds inflicted on the bone leave a red mark and a slight appearance of saturation, and where the bone is broken there will be at each end a halo-like trace of blood. Take a bone on which there are marks of a wound, and hold it up to the light; if these are of a fresh-looking red, the wound was inflicted before death and penetrated to the bone; but if there is no trace of saturation from blood, although there is a wound, it was inflicted after death."

(3.) "The bones of parents may be identified by their children in the following manner. Let the experimenter cut himself or herself with a knife, and cause the blood to drip on to the bones; then if the relationship is an actual fact, the blood will sink into the bone, otherwise it will not. *N.B.*—Should the bones have been washed with salt water, even though the relationship exists, yet the blood will not soak in. This is a trick to be guarded against beforehand.

"It is also said that if parent and child, or husband and wife, each cut themselves and let the blood drip into a basin of water, the two bloods will mix, whereas that of two people not thus related will not mix.

"Where two brothers, who may have been separated since childhood, are desirous of establishing their identity as such, but are unable to do so by ordinary means, bid each one cut himself and let the blood drip into a basin. If they are really brothers, the two bloods will coagulate into one; otherwise not. But because fresh blood will always coagulate with the aid of a little salt or vinegar, people often smear the basin over with these to attain their own ends and deceive others; therefore always wash out the basin you are going to use, or buy a new one from a shop. Thus the trick will be defeated."

(4.) "There are some atrocious villains who, when they have murdered any one, burn the body and throw the ashes away, so that there are no bones to examine.

In such cases you must carefully find out at what time the murder was committed, and where the body was burnt. Then, when you know the place, all witnesses agreeing on this point, you may proceed without further delay to examine the wounds. The mode of procedure is this. Put up your shed near where the body was burnt, and make the accused and witnesses point out themselves the exact spot. Then cut down the grass and weeds growing on this spot, and burn large quantities of fuel till the place is extremely hot, throwing on several pecks of hemp-seed. By and by brush the place clean; then, if the body was actually burnt on this spot, the oil from the seed will be found to have sunk into the ground in the form of a human figure, and wherever there were wounds on the dead man, there on this figure the oil will be found to have collected together, large or small, square, round, long, short, oblique, or straight, exactly as they were inflicted. The parts where there were no wounds will be free from any such appearances."

BOOK THE SIXTH

THE MONGOL DYNASTY (A.D. 1200–1368)

BOOK THE SIXTH

THE MONGOL DYNASTY (A.D. 1200–1368)

CHAPTER I

MISCELLANEOUS LITERATURE—POETRY

THE thirteenth and fourteenth centuries witnessed a remarkable political revolution. China was conquered by the Mongols, and for the first time in history the empire passed under the rule of an alien sovereign. No exact date can be assigned for the transference of the Imperial power. In 1264 Kublai Khan fixed his capital at Peking, and in 1271 he adopted Yüan as his dynastic style. It was not, however, until 1279 that the patriot statesman, Chao Ping, had his retreat cut off, and despairing of his country, took upon his back the boy-Emperor, the last of the Sungs, and jumped from his doomed vessel into the river, thus bringing the great fire-led dynasty to an end.

Kublai Khan, who was a confirmed Buddhist, paid great honour to Confucius, and was a steady patron of literature. In 1269 he caused Bashpa, a Tibetan priest, to construct an alphabet for the Mongol language ; in 1280 the calendar was revised ; and in 1287 the Impe-

rial Academy was opened. But he could not forgive
WÊN T'IEN-HSIANG (1236–1283), the renowned patriot and
scholar, who had fought so bravely but unsuccessfully
against him. In 1279 the latter was conveyed to Peking,
on which journey he passed eight days without eating.
Every effort was made to induce him to own allegiance
to the Mongol Emperor, but without success. He was
kept in prison for three years. At length he was summoned into the presence of Kublai Khan, who said to
him, "What is it you want?" "By the grace of the
Sung Emperor," Wên T'ien-hsiang replied, "I became his
Majesty's Minister. I cannot serve two masters. I only
ask to die." Accordingly he was executed, meeting his
death with composure, and making a final obeisance
southwards, as though his own sovereign was still reigning in his own capital. The following poem was written
by Wên T'ien-hsiang while in captivity :—

"There is in the universe an Aura which permeates all
things and makes them what they are. Below, it shapes
forth land and water ; above, the sun and the stars. In
man it is called spirit ; and there is nowhere where it is
not.

"In times of national tranquillity this spirit lies *perdu* in
the harmony which prevails ; only at some great crisis
is it manifested widely abroad."

[Here follow ten historical instances of devotion and
heroism.]

"Such is this grand and glorious spirit which endureth
for all generations, and which, linked with the sun and
the moon, knows neither beginning nor end. The foundation of all that is great and good in heaven and earth,
it is itself born from the everlasting obligations which
are due by man to man.

"Alas! the fates were against me. I was without resource. Bound with fetters, hurried away towards the north, death would have been sweet indeed; but that boon was refused.

"My dungeon is lighted by the will-o'-the-wisp alone; no breath of spring cheers the murky solitude in which I dwell. The ox and the barb herd together in one stall, the rooster and the phœnix feed together from one dish. Exposed to mist and dew, I had many times thought to die; and yet, through the seasons of two revolving years, disease hovered round me in vain. The dank, unhealthy soil to me became paradise itself. For there was that within me which misfortune could not steal away. And so I remained firm, gazing at the white clouds floating over my head, and bearing in my heart a sorrow boundless as the sky.

"The sun of those dead heroes has long since set, but their record is before me still. And, while the wind whistles under the eaves, I open my books and read; and lo! in their presence my heart glows with a borrowed fire."

"I myself," adds the famous commentator, Lin Hsi-chung, of the seventeenth century, "in consequence of the rebellion in Fuhkien, lay in prison for two years, while deadly disease raged around. Daily I recited this poem several times over, and happily escaped; from which it is clear that the supremest efforts in literature move even the gods, and that it is not the verses of Tu Fu alone which can prevail against malarial fever."

At the final examination for his degree in 1256, Wên T'ien-hsiang had been placed seventh on the list. However, the then Emperor, on looking over the papers of the candidates before the result was announced, was immensely struck by his work, and sent for the grand examiner to reconsider the order of merit. "This essay," said his Majesty, "shows us the moral code of the ancients as in a mirror; it betokens a loyalty enduring as iron and stone." The grand examiner readily admitted the justice of the Emperor's criticism, and when the list was published, the name of Wên T'ienhsiang stood first. The fame of that examiner, WANG YING-LIN (1223–1296), is likely to last for a long time to come. Not because of his association with one of China's greatest patriots, nor because of his voluminous contributions to classical literature, including an extensive encyclopædia, a rare copy of which is to be seen in the University of Leyden, but because of a small primer for schoolboys, which, by almost universal consent, is attributed to his pen. For six hundred years this primer has been, and is still at this moment, the first book put into the hand of every child throughout the empire. It is an epitome of all knowledge, dealing with philosophy, classical literature, history, biography, and common objects. It has been called a sleeve edition of the Mirror of History. Written in lines of three characters to each, and being in doggerel rhyme, it is easily committed to memory, and is known by heart by every Chinaman who has learnt to read. This Three Character Classic, as it is called, has been imitated by Christian missionaries, Protestant and Catholic; and even the T'ai-p'ing rebels, alive to its far-reaching influence, published an imitation of their own. Here are a few specimen lines, rhymed to match the original:—

> "*Men, one and all, in infancy*
> *Are virtuous at heart;*
> *Their moral tendencies the same,*
> *Their practice wide apart.*

Without instruction's kindly aid
Man's nature grows less fair ;
In teaching, thoroughness should be
A never-ceasing care."

It may be added that the meaning of the Three
Character Classic is not explained to the child at the
time. All that the latter has to do is to learn the sounds
and formation of the 560 different characters of which
the book is composed.

A clever boy, who attracted much attention by
the filial piety which he displayed towards his step-
father, was LIU YIN (1241–1293). He obtained office,
but resigned in order to tend his sick mother ; and
when again appointed, his health broke down and he
went into seclusion. The following extract is from his
pen :—

"When God made man, He gave him powers to cope
with the exigencies of his environment, and resources
within himself, so that he need not be dependent upon
external circumstances.

"Thus, in districts where poisons abound, antidotes
abound also ; and in others, where malaria prevails, we
find such correctives as ginger, nutmegs, and dogwood.
Again, fish, terrapins, and clams are the most whole-
some articles of diet in excessively damp climates,
though themselves denizens of the water ; and musk
and deer-horns are excellent prophylactics in earthy
climates, where in fact they are produced. For if these
things were unable to prevail against their surroundings,
they could not possibly thrive where they do, while the
fact that they do so thrive is proof positive that they
were ordained as specifics against those surroundings.

"Chu Hsi said, 'When God is about to send down calamities upon us, He first raises up the hero whose genius shall finally prevail against those calamities.' From this point of view there can be no living man without his appointed use, nor any state of society which man should be unable to put right."

The theory that every man plays his allotted part in the cosmos is a favourite one with the Chinese ; and the process by which the tares are separated from the wheat, exemplifying the use of adversity, has been curiously stated by a Buddhist priest of this date :—

"If one is a man, the mills of heaven and earth grind him to perfection ; if not, to destruction."

A considerable amount of poetry was produced under the Mongol sway, though not so much proportionately, nor of such a high order, as under the great native dynasties. The Emperor Ch'ien Lung published in 1787 a collection of specimens of the poetry of this Yüan dynasty. They fill eight large volumes, but are not much read.

One of the best known poets of this period is LIU CHI (A.D. 1311–1375), who was also deeply read in the Classics and also a student of astrology. He lived into the Ming dynasty, which he helped to establish, and was for some years the trusted adviser of its first ruler. He lost favour, however, and was poisoned by a rival, it is said, with the Emperor's connivance. The following lines, referring to an early visit to a mountain monastery, reveal a certain sympathy with Buddhism :—

> "I mounted when the cock had just begun,
> And reached the convent ere the bells were done ;
> A gentle zephyr whispered o'er the lawn ;
> Behind the wood the moon gave way to dawn.

> *And in this pure sweet solitude I lay,*
> *Stretching my limbs out to await the day,*
> *No sound along the willow pathway dim*
> *Save the soft echo of the bonzes' hymn."*

Here too is an oft-quoted stanza, to be found in any poetry primer :—

> " *A centenarian 'mongst men*
> *Is rare ; and if one comes, what then ?*
> *The mightiest heroes of the past*
> *Upon the hillside sleep at last."*

The prose writings of Liu Chi are much admired for their pure style, which has been said to "smell of antiquity." One piece tells how a certain noble who had lost all by the fall of the Ch'in dynasty, B.C. 206, and was forced to grow melons for a living, had recourse to divination, and went to consult a famous augur on his prospects.

"Alas !" cried the augur, "what is there that Heaven can bestow save that which virtue can obtain ? Where is the efficacy of spiritual beings beyond that with which man has endowed them ? The divining plant is but a dead stalk ; the tortoise-shell a dry bone. They are but matter like ourselves. And man, the divinest of all things, why does he not seek wisdom from within, rather than from these grosser stuffs ?

" Besides, sir, why not reflect upon the past—that past which gave birth to this present ? Your cracked roof and crumbling walls of to-day are but the complement of yesterday's lofty towers and spacious halls. The straggling bramble is but the complement of the shapely garden tree. The grasshopper and the cicada are but the complement of organs and flutes ; the will-o'-the-wisp and firefly, of gilded lamps and painted candles.

Your endive and watercresses are but the complement of the elephant-sinews and camel's hump of days by-gone; the maple-leaf and the rush, of your once rich robes and fine attire. Do not repine that those who had not such luxuries then enjoy them now. Do not be dissatisfied that you, who enjoyed them then, have them now no more. In the space of a day and night the flower blooms and dies. Between spring and autumn things perish and are renewed. Beneath the roaring cascade a deep pool is found; dark valleys lie at the foot of high hills. These things you know; what more can divination teach you?"

Another piece is entitled "Outsides," and is a light satire on the corruption of his day :—

"At Hangchow there lived a costermonger who understood how to keep oranges a whole year without letting them spoil. His fruit was always fresh-looking, firm as jade, and of a beautiful golden hue; but inside —dry as an old cocoon.

"One day I asked him, saying, 'Are your oranges for altar or sacrificial purposes, or for show at banquets? Or do you make this outside display merely to cheat the foolish? as cheat them you most outrageously do.' 'Sir,' replied the orangeman, 'I have carried on this trade now for many years. It is my source of livelihood. I sell; the world buys. And I have yet to learn that you are the only honest man about, and that I am the only cheat. Perhaps it never struck you in this light. The bâton-bearers of to-day, seated on their tiger skins, pose as the martial guardians of the State; but what are they compared with the captains of old? The broad-brimmed, long-robed Ministers of to-day pose as pillars of the constitution; but have they the wisdom of our ancient counsellors ? Evil-doers arise, and none can subdue them. The people are in misery, and none can relieve them. Clerks are corrupt, and none can restrain them. Laws decay, and none can renew them. Our officials eat the bread of the State and know no shame. They sit in lofty halls, ride fine steeds, drink themselves drunk with wine, and batten on the richest fare. Which of them but puts on an awe-inspiring look, a dignified mien ?—all gold and gems without, but dry cocoons within. You pay, sir, no heed to these things, while you are very particular about my oranges.'

" I had no answer to make. Was he really out of conceit with the age, or only quizzing me in defence of his fruit ?"

CHAPTER II

THE DRAMA

IF the Mongol dynasty added little of permanent value to the already vast masses of poetry, of general literature, and of classical exegesis, it will ever be remembered in connection with two important departures in the literary history of the nation. Within the century covered by Mongol rule the Drama and the Novel may be said to have come into existence. Going back to pre-Confucian or legendary days, we find that from time immemorial the Chinese have danced set dances in time to music on solemn or festive occasions of sacrifice or ceremony. Thus we read in the Odes :—

> " *Lightly, sprightly,*
> *To the dance I go,*
> *The sun shining brightly*
> *In the court below.*"

The movements of the dancers were methodical, slow, and dignified. Long feathers and flutes were held in the hand and were waved to and fro as the performers moved right or left. Words to be sung were added, and then gradually the music and singing prevailed over the dance, gesture being substituted. The result was rather an operatic than a dramatic performance, and the words sung were more of the nature of songs than of musical plays. In the *Tso Chuan*, under B.C. 545, we read of an amateur attempt of the kind, organised by stable-boys, which frightened their horses and caused a stampede. Confucius, too, mentions the arrogance of a noble who employed in his ancestral temple the number of singers reserved for the Son of Heaven alone. It is hardly necessary to allude to the exorcism of evil spirits, carried out three times a year by officials dressed up in bearskins and armed with spear and shield, who made a house to house visitation surrounded by a shouting and excited populace. It is only mentioned here because some writers have associated this practice with the origin of the drama in China. All we really know is that in very early ages music and song and dance formed an ordinary accompaniment to religious and other ceremonies, and that this continued for many centuries.

Towards the middle of the eighth century, A.D., the Emperor Ming Huang of the T'ang dynasty, being exceedingly fond of music, established a College, known as the Pear-Garden, for training some three hundred young people of both sexes. There is a legend that this College was the outcome of a visit paid by his Majesty to the moon, where he was much impressed by a troup of skilled performers attached to the Palace of Jade which he found there. It was apparently an institution to provide instrumentalists, vocalists, and possibly dancers, for Court entertainments, although some have held that the "youths of the Pear-Garden" were really actors, and the term is still applied to the dramatic fraternity. Nothing, however, which can be truly identified with the actor's art seems to have been known until the thirteenth century, when suddenly the Drama, as seen in the modern Chinese stage-play, sprang into being. In the present limited state of our knowledge on the subject, it is impossible to say how or why this came about. We cannot trace step by step the development of the drama in China from a purely choral performance, as in Greece. We are simply confronted with the accomplished fact.

At the same time we hear of dramatic performances among the Tartars at a somewhat earlier date. In 1031 K'ung Tao-fu, a descendant of Confucius in the forty-fifth degree, was sent as envoy to the Kitans, and was received at a banquet with much honour. But at a theatrical entertainment which followed, a piece was played in which his sacred ancestor, Confucius, was introduced as the low-comedy man ; and this so disgusted him that he got up and withdrew, the Kitans being forced to apologise. Altogether, it would seem that the drama is not indigenous to China, but may well have been introduced from Tartar sources. However this may be, it is certain that the drama as known under the Mongols is to all intents and purposes the drama of to-day, and a few general remarks may not be out of place.

Plays are acted in the large cities of China at public theatres all the year round, except during one month at the New Year, and during the period of mourning for a deceased Emperor. There is no charge for admission, but all visitors must take some refreshment. The various Trade-Guilds have raised stages upon their premises, and give periodical performances free to all who will stand in an open-air courtyard to watch them. Mandarins and wealthy persons often engage actors to perform in their private houses, generally while a dinner-party is going on. In the country, performances are provided by public subscription, and take place at temples or on temporary stages put up in the roadway.

These stages are always essentially the same. There is no curtain, there are no wings, and no flies. At the back of the stage are two doors, one for entrance and one for exit. The actors who are to perform the first piece come in by the entrance door all together. When the piece is over, and as they are filing out through the exit door, those who are cast for the second piece pass in through the other door. There is no interval, and the musicians, who sit on the stage, make no pause; hence many persons have stated that Chinese plays are ridiculously long, the fact being that half-an-hour to an hour would be about an average length for the plays usually performed, though much longer specimens, such as would last from three to five hours, are to be found in books. Eight or ten plays are often performed at an ordinary dinner-party, a list of perhaps forty being handed round for the chief guests to choose from.

The actors undergo a very severe physical training, usually between the ages of nine and fourteen. They have to learn all kinds of acrobatic feats, these being introduced freely into "military" plays. They also have to practise walking on feet bound up in imitation of women's feet, no woman having been allowed on the stage since the days of the Emperor Ch'ien Lung (A.D. 1736-1796), whose mother had been an actress. They have further to walk about in the open air for an hour or so every day, the head thrown back and the mouth wide open in order to strengthen the voice; and finally, their diet is carefully regulated according to a fixed system of training. Fifty-six actors make up a full company, each of whom must know perfectly from 100 to 200 plays, there being no prompter. These do not include the four- or five-act plays as found in books, but either acting editions of these, cut down to suit the requirements of the stage, or short farces specially written. The actors are ranged under five classes according to their capabilities, and consequently every one knows what part he is expected to take in any given play. Far from being an important personage, as in ancient Greece, the actor is under a social ban; and for three generations his descendants may not compete at the public examinations. Yet he must possess considerable ability in a certain line; for inasmuch as there are no properties and no realism, he is wholly dependent for success upon his own powers of idealisation. There he is indeed supreme. He will gallop across the stage on horseback, dismount, and pass his horse on to a groom. He will wander down a street, and stop at an open shop-window to flirt with a pretty girl. He will hide in a forest, or fight from behind a battlemented wall. He conjures up by histrionic skill the whole paraphernalia of a scene which in Western countries is grossly laid out by supers before the curtain goes up. The general absence of properties is made up to some extent by the dresses of the actors, which are of the most gorgeous character, robes for Emperors and grandees running into figures which would stagger even a West-end manager.

It is obvious that the actor must be a good contortionist, and excel in gesture. He must have a good voice, his part consisting of song and "spoken" in about equal proportions. To show how utterly the Chinese disregard realism, it need only be stated that dead men get up and walk off the stage; sometimes they will even act the part of bearers and make movements as though carrying themselves away. Or a servant will step across to a leading performer and hand him a cup of tea to clear his voice.

The merit of the plays performed is not on a level with the skill of the performer. A Chinese audience does not go to hear the play, but to see the actor. In 1678, at a certain market-town, there was a play performed which represented the execution of the patriot, General Yo Fei (A.D. 1141), brought about by the treachery of a rival, Ch'in Kuei, who forged an order for that purpose. The actor who played Ch'in Kuei (a term since used contemptuously for a spittoon) produced a profound sensation; so much so, that one of the spectators, losing all self-control, leapt upon the stage and stabbed the unfortunate man to death.

Most Chinese plays are simple in construction and weak in plot. They are divided into "military" and "civil," which terms have often been wrongly taken in the senses of tragedy and comedy, tragedy proper being quite unknown in China. The former usually deal with historical episodes and heroic or filial acts by historical characters; and Emperors and Generals and small armies rush wildly about the stage, sometimes engaged in single combat, sometimes in turning head over heels. Battles are fought and rivals or traitors executed before the very eyes of the audience. The "civil" plays are concerned with the entanglements of every-day life, and are usually of a farcical character. As they stand in classical collections or in acting editions, Chinese plays are as unobjectionable as Chinese poetry and general literature. On the stage, however, actors are allowed great license in gagging, and the direction which their gag takes is chiefly the reason which keeps respectable women away from the public play-house.

It must therefore always be remembered that there is the play as it can be read in the library, and again as it appears in the acting edition to be learnt, and finally as it is interpreted by the actor. These three are often very different one from the other.

The following abstract will give a fair idea of the pieces to be found on the play-bill of any Chinese theatre :—

THE THREE SUSPICIONS.

At the close of the Ming dynasty, a certain well-known General was occupied day and night in camp with preparations for resisting the advance of the rebel army which ultimately captured Peking. While thus temporarily absent from home, the tutor engaged for his son fell ill with severe shivering fits, and the boy, anxious to do something to relieve the sufferer, went to his mother's room and borrowed a thick quilt. Late that night, the General unexpectedly returned home, and heard from a slave-girl in attendance of the tutor's illness and of the loan of the quilt. Thereupon, he proceeded straight to the sick-room, to see how the tutor was getting on, but found him fast asleep. As he was about to retire, he espied on the ground a pair of women's slippers, which had been accidentally brought in with the quilt, and at once recognised to whom they belonged. Hastily quitting the still sleeping tutor, and arming himself with a sharp scimitar, he burst into his wife's apartment. He seized the terrified woman by the hair, and told her that she must die ; producing, in reply to her protestations, the fatal pair of slippers. He yielded, however, to the entreaties of the assembled slave-girls, and deferred his vengeance until he had put the following test. He sent a slave-girl to the tutor's room, himself following close behind with his naked weapon ready for use, bearing a message from her mistress to say she was awaiting him in her own room ; in response to which invitation the voice of the tutor was heard from within, saying, " What ! at this hour of the night ? Go away, you bad girl, or I will tell the master when he comes back ! " Still unconvinced, the jealous General bade his trembling wife go herself and summon her paramour ; resolving that if the latter but put foot over the threshold, his life should pay the penalty. But there was no occasion for murderous violence. The tutor again answered from within the bolted door, " Madam, I may not be a saint, but I would at least seek to emulate the virtuous Chao Wên-hua (the Joseph of China). Go, and leave me in peace." The General now changes his tone ; and the injured wife, she too changes hers. She attempts to commit suicide, and is only dissuaded by an abject apology on the part of her husband ; in the middle of which, as the latter is on his knees, a slave-girl creates roars of laughter by bringing her master, in mistake for wine, a brimming goblet of vinegar, the Chinese emblem of connubial jealousy.

The following is a translation of the acting edition of a short play, as commonly performed, illustrating, but not to exaggeration, the slender and insufficient literary art which satisfies the Chinese public, the verses of the original being quite as much doggerel as those of the English version : —

THE FLOWERY BALL.

DRAMATIS PERSONÆ:

Su T'ai-ch'in,	*a Suitor.*
Hu Mao-yüan,	*a Suitor.*
P'ing Kuei,	*a Beggar.*
P'u-sa,	*the Beggar's Guardian Angel.*
Lady Wang,	*daughter of a high Mandarin.*
Gatekeeper.	

Suitors, Servants, &c.

SCENE—*Outside the city of Ch'ang-an.*

Su T'ai-ch'in. *At Ch'ang-an city I reside:*
My father is a Mandarin;
Oh! if I get the Flowery Ball,
My cup of joy will overflow.
My humble name is Su T'ai-ch'in.
To-day the Lady Wang will throw
A Flowery Ball to get a spouse;
And if perchance this ball strikes me,
I am a lucky man indeed.
But now I must go on my way.

[*Walks on towards the city*

Enter Hu Mao-yüan.

Hu Mao-yüan. *My father is a nobleman,*
And I'm a jolly roving blade;
To-day the Lady Wang will throw
A Flowery Ball to get a spouse.
It all depends on destiny
Whether or not this Ball strikes me.
My humble name is Hu Mao-yüan;
But as the Ball is thrown to-day
I must be moving on my way.
Why, that looks very like friend Su!
I'll call: " Friend Su, don't go so fast."

Su. *It's Hu Mao-yüan : now where go you?*

Hu. *To the Governor's palace to get me a wife.*

Su. *To the Flowery Ball? Well, I'm going too.*

[Sings.] *The Lady Wang the Flowery Ball will throw,*

> *That all the world her chosen spouse might see,*
> *Among the noble suitors down below—*
> *But who knows who the lucky man will be?*

Hu [sings.] *I think your luck is sure to take you through.*

Su [sings.] *Your handsome face should bring the Ball to you.*

Hu [sings.] *At any rate it lies between us two.*

Su [sings.] *There's hardly anybody else who'd do.*

Hu [sings.] *Then come let us go, let us make haste and run.*

Su [sings.] *Away let us go, but don't be so slow,*
> *Or we shan't be in time for the fun.*

> [Exeunt.

Enter P'ing Kuei.

P'ing [sings.] *Ah! that day within the garden*
> *When my lady-love divine,*
> *Daughter of a wealthy noble,*
> *Promised that she would be mine.*
> *At the garden gate she pledged me,*
> *Bidding me come here to-day;*
> *From my miserable garret*
> *I have just now crept away.*
> *And as I pass the city gates*
> *I ope my eyes and see*
> *A crowd of noble youths as thick*
> *As leaves upon a tree.*
> *Forward they press, but who knows which*
> *The lucky man will be?*
> *In vain I strain my eager eyes—*
> *Alas! 'twill break my heart—*
> *Among the well-dressed butterflies*
> *I find no counterpart.*
> *Let her be faithless or be true*
> *I lose the Ball as sure as fate;*
> *Though, if she spoke me idle words,*
> *Why trifle at the garden gate?*
> *Nevertheless, I'm bound to go*
> *Whether I get the Ball or no:*
> *My bowl and my staff in my hands—just so.*
> *Rank and fortune often come*
> > *From matrimonial affairs;*
> *I'll think of it all as I walk along—*
> > *And perhaps I'd better say my prayers.*

    Why, here I am at the very spot!
    I'll just walk in.
Gatekeeper. *I say you'll not!*
P'ing [sings.] *Oh! dear, he's stopped me! why, Heaven knows!*
    It must be my hat and tattered clothes.
    I'll stay here and raise an infernal din
    Until they consent to let me in.
Gatekeeper. *I haven't anything to spare,*
    So come again another day.
P'ing. *Oh! let me just go in to look.*
Gatekeeper. *Among the sons of noblemen*
    What can there be for you to see?
    Begone at once, or I'll soon make you.
P'ing. *Alas! alas! what can I do?*
    If I don't get within the court,
    The Lady Wang will tire of waiting.

Enter P'u-sa.

P'u-sa [sings.] *By heaven's supreme command I have flown*
    Through the blue expanse of sky and air;
    For a suffering soul has cried out in woe,
    And Heaven has heard his prayer.
    For the Lady Wang he's nearly broken-hearted,
    But cruel fate still keeps the lovers parted.
    "Hebbery gibbery snobbery snay!"
    On the wings of the wind I'll ride,
    And make the old porter clear out of the way
    Till I get my poor beggar inside.
    The Lady Wang is still within the hall
    Waiting till the Emperor sends the Flowery Ball.
            [*Raises the wind.*

Gatekeeper. *Oh dear! how cold the wind is blowing.*
    I do not see the lady coming,
    And so I think I'll step inside.

Enter Lady Wang.

Lady Wang [sings.] *In gala dress I leave my boudoir,*
    Thinking all the time of thee—
    O Heaven, fulfil a mortal's longings,
    And link my love to me.

My gorgeous cap is broidered o'er
With flocks of glittering birds :
Here shine the seven stars, and there
A boy is muttering holy words.
My bodice dazzles with its lustrous sheen :
My skirts are worked with many a gaudy scene.
　　　　　　　　　　　[Showing Ball.
His Majesty on me bestowed this Ball,
And from a balcony he bid me let it fall,
Then take as husband whomsoe'er it struck,
Prince, merchant, beggar, as might be my luck.
And having left my parents and my home,
Hither to the Painted Tower I've come.
As I slowly mount the stairs,
I ope my eyes and see
A crowd of noble youths as thick
As leaves upon a tree.
But ah! amongst the many forms,
Which meet my eager eye,
The figure of my own true love
I cannot yet descry.
The pledge I gave him at the garden gate
Can he forget?　The hour is waxing late.
　　　And the crowds down below
　　　Bewilder me so
That I am in a most desperate state.
Oh! P'ing Kuei, if you really love me,
Hasten quickly to my side :
If the words you spoke were idle,
Why ask me to be your bride?
He perhaps his ease is taking,
While my foolish heart is breaking.
I can't return till I have done
This work in misery begun,
And so I take the Flowery Ball
And with a sigh I let it fall.
　　　　　　　　　　[Throws down the ball.

P'u-sa. *'Tis thus I seize the envied prize,*
　　　　And give it to my protégé ;
　　　　I'll throw it in his earthen bowl.
　　　　　　　　　　[Throws the ball to P'ing Kuei.

Lady Wang [sings.] *Stay! I hear the people shouting—*
    What, the Ball some beggar struck?
    It must be my own true P'ing Kuei—
    I'll go home and tell my luck!
    Maidens! through the temple kindle
    Incense for my lucky fate;
    Now my true love will discover
    That I can discriminate.

            [Exeunt omnes.

    Enter Hu Mao-yüan *and* Su T'ai-ch'in.

Hu. *The second of the second moon*
    The Dragon wakes to life and power;
    To-day the Lady Wang has thrown
    The Ball from out the Painted Tower.
    No well-born youth was singled out,
    It struck a dirty vagrant lout.
    Friend Su, I'm off: we're done for, as you saw,
    Though for the little paltry wench I do not care a straw.

            [Exeunt.

    Enter Gatekeeper *and* Beggar.

Gatekeeper. *Only one poor beggar now remains within the hall,*
    Who'd have thought that this poor vagrant would have got
      the Ball?
[To P'ing Kuei.] *Sir, you've come off well this morning:*
    You must be a lucky man.
    Come with me to claim your bride, and
    Make the greatest haste you can.

            [Exeunt.

Even the longer and more elaborate plays are proportionately wanting in all that makes the drama piquant to a European, and are very seldom, if ever, produced as they stand in print. Many collections of these have been published, not to mention the acting editions of each play, which can be bought at any bookstall for something like three a penny. One of the best of such collections is the *Yüan ch'ü hsiian tsa chi*, or Miscellaneous Selection of Mongol Plays, bound up in eight thick volumes. It contains one hundred plays in all, with an illustration to each, according to the edition of 1615. A large proportion of these cannot be assigned to any author, and are therefore marked "anonymous." Even when the authors' names are given, they represent men altogether unknown in what the Chinese call literature, from which the drama is rigorously excluded.

The following is a brief outline of a very well known play in five acts by CHI CHÜN-HSIANG, entitled "The Orphan of the Chao family," and founded closely upon fact. It is the nearest approach which the Chinese have made to genuine tragedy :—

A wicked Minister of the sixth century B.C. plotted the destruction of a rival named Chao Tun, and of all his family. He tells in the prologue how he had vainly trained a fierce dog to kill his rival, by keeping it for days without food and then setting it at a dummy, dressed to represent his intended victim, and stuffed with the heart and lights of a sheep. Ultimately, however, he had managed to get rid of all the male members of the family, to the number of three hundred, when he hears —and at this point the play proper begins—that the wife of the last representative has given birth to a son. He promptly sends to find the child, which had meanwhile been carried away to a place of safety. Then a faithful servant of the family hid himself on the hills with another child, while an accomplice informed the Minister where the supposed orphan of the house of Chao was lying hidden. The child was accordingly slain, and by the hand of the Minister himself ; the servant committed suicide. But the real heir escaped, and when he grew up he avenged the wrongs of his family by killing the cruel Minister and utterly exterminating his race.

From beginning to end of this and similar plays there is apparently no attempt whatever at passion or pathos in the language—at any rate, not in the sense in which those terms are understood by us. Nor are there even rhetorical flowers to disguise the expression of commonplace thought. The Chinese actor can do a great deal with such a text; the translator, nothing. There is much, too, of a primitive character in the setting of the play. Explanatory prologues are common, and actors usually begin by announcing their own names and further clearing the way for the benefit of the audience. The following story will give a faint idea of the license conceded to the play-actor.

My attention was attracted on one occasion at Amoy by an unusually large crowd of Chinamen engaged in watching the progress of an open-air theatrical performance. Roars of laughter resounded on all sides, and on looking to see what was the moving cause of this extraordinary explosion of merriment, I beheld to my astonishment a couple of rather seedy-looking foreigners occupying the stage, and apparently acting with such spirit as to bring the house down at every other word. A moment more and it was clear that these men of the West were not foreigners at all, but Chinamen dressed up for the purposes of the piece. The get-up, nevertheless, was remarkably good, if somewhat exaggerated, though doubtless the intention was to caricature or burlesque rather than to reproduce an exact imitation. There was the billy-cock hat, and below it a florid face well supplied with red moustaches and whiskers, the short cut-away coat and light trousers, a blue neck-tie, and last, but not least, the ever-characteristic walking-stick. Half the fun, in fact, was got out of this last accessory ; for with it each one of the two was continually threatening the other, and both united in violent gesticulations directed either against their brother-actors or sometimes against the audience at their feet.

Before going any further it may be as well to give a short outline of the play itself, which happens to be not uninteresting and is widely known from one end of China to the other. It is called "Slaying a Son at the Yamên Gate," and the plot, or rather story, runs as follows :—

A certain general of the Sung dynasty named Yang, being in charge of one of the frontier passes, sent his son to obtain a certain wooden staff from an outlying barbarian tribe. In this expedition the son not only failed signally, but was further taken prisoner by a barbarian lady, who insisted upon his immediately leading her to the altar. Shortly after these nuptials he returns to his father's camp, and the latter, in a violent fit of anger, orders him to be taken outside the Yamên gate and be there executed forthwith. As the soldiers are leading him away, the young man's mother comes and throws herself at the general's feet, and implores him to spare her son. This request the stern father steadily refuses to grant, even though his wife's prayers are backed up by those of his own mother, of a prince of the Imperial blood, and finally by the entreaties of the Emperor himself. At this juncture in rushes the barbarian wife of the general's condemned son, and as on a previous occasion the general himself had been taken prisoner by this very lady, and only ransomed on payment of a heavy sum of money, he is so alarmed that he sits motionless and unable to utter a word while with a dagger she severs the cords that bind her husband, sets him free before the assembled party, and dares any one to lay a hand on him at his peril. The Emperor now loses his temper, and is enraged to think that General Yang should have been awed into granting to a barbarian woman a life that he had just before refused to the entreaties of the Son of Heaven. His Majesty, therefore, at once deprives the father of his command and bestows it upon the son, and the play is brought to a conclusion with the departure of young General Yang and his barbarian wife to subdue the wild tribes that are then harassing the frontier of China. The two foreigners are the pages or attendants of the barbarian wife, and accompany her in that capacity when she follows her husband to his father's camp.

The trick of dressing these pages up to caricature the foreigner of the nineteenth century, on the occasion when I saw the piece, was a mere piece of stage gag, but one which amused the people immensely, and elicited rounds of applause. But when the barbarian wife had succeeded in rescuing her husband from the jaws of death, there was considerable dissatisfaction in the minds of several of the personages on the stage. The Emperor was angry at the slight that had been passed upon his Imperial dignity, the wife and mother of the general, not to mention the prince of the blood, felt themselves similarly slighted, though in a lesser degree, and the enraged father was still more excited at having had his commands set aside, and seeing himself bearded in his own Yamên by a mere barbarian woman. It was consequently felt by all parties that something in the way of slaughter was wanting to relieve their own feelings, and to satisfy the unities of the drama and the cravings of the audience for a sensational finale ; and this desirable end was attained by an order from the Emperor that at any rate the two foreign attendants might be sacrificed for the benefit of all concerned. The two wretched foreigners were accordingly made to kneel on the stage, and their heads were promptly lopped off by the executioner amid the deafening plaudits of the surrounding spectators.

In 1885 a play was performed in a Shanghai theatre which had for its special attraction a rude imitation of a paddle-steamer crowded with foreign men and women. It was wheeled across the back of the stage, and the foreigners and their women, who were supposed to have come with designs upon the Middle Kingdom, were all taken prisoners and executed.

Of all plays of the Mongol dynasty, the one which will best repay reading is undoubtedly the *Hsi Hsiang Chi*, or Story of the Western Pavilion, in sixteen scenes. It is by WANG SHIH-FU, of whom nothing seems to be known except that he flourished in the thirteenth century, and wrote thirteen plays, all of which are included in the collection mentioned above. " The dialogue of this play," says a Chinese critic, "deals largely with wind, flowers, snow, and moonlight," which is simply a euphemistic way of stating that the story is one of passion and intrigue. It is popular with the educated classes, by whom it is regarded more as a novel than as a play.

A lady and her daughter are staying at a temple, where, in accordance with common custom, rooms are let by the priests to ordinary travellers or to visitors who may wish to perform devotional exercises. A young and handsome student, who also happens to be living at the temple, is lucky enough to succeed in saving the two ladies from the clutches of brigands, for which service he has previously been promised the hand of the daughter in marriage. The mother, however, soon repents of her engagement, and the scholar is left disconsolate. At this juncture the lady's-maid of the daughter manages by a series of skilful manœuvres to bring the story to a happy issue.

Just as there have always been poetesses in China, so women are to be found in the ranks of Chinese play-wrights. A four-act drama, entitled " Joining the 'Shirt," was written by one CHANG KUO-PIN, an educated cour-tesan of the day, the chief interest of which play lies perhaps in the sex of the writer.

A father and mother, with son and daughter-in-law, are living happily together, when a poverty-stricken young stranger is first of all assisted by them, and then, without further inquiry, is actually adopted into the family. Soon afterwards the new son persuades the elder brother and his wife secretly to leave home, taking all the property they can lay their hands on, and to journey to a distant part of the country, where there is a potent god from whom the wife is to pray for and obtain a son after what has been already an eighteen months' gestation. On the way, the new brother pushes the husband overboard into the Yang-tsze and disap-pears with the wife, who shortly gives birth to a boy. Eighteen years pass. The old couple have sunk into poverty, and set out, begging their way, to seek for their lost son. Chance—playwright's chance—throws them into the company of their grandson, who has graduated as Senior Classic, and has also, prompted by his mother, been on the look-out for them. Recognition is effected by means of the two halves of a shirt, one of which had always been kept by the old man and the other by the missing son, and after his death by his wife. At this juncture the missing son reappears. He had been rescued from drowning by a boatman, and had become a Buddhist priest. He now reverts to lay life, and the play is brought to an end by the execution of the villain

It is a curious fact that all the best troupes of actors not only come from Peking, but perform in their own dialect, which is practically unintelligible to the masses in many parts of China. These actors are, of course, very well paid, in order to make it worth their while to travel so far from home and take the risks to life and property.

CHAPTER III

THE NOVEL

TURNING now to the second literary achievement of the Mongols, the introduction of the Novel, we find ourselves face to face with the same mystery as that which shrouds the birth of the Drama. The origin of the Chinese novel is unknown. It probably came from Central Asia, the paradise of story-tellers, in the wake of the Mongol conquest. Three centuries had then to elapse before the highest point of development was reached. Fables, anecdotes, and even short stories had already been familiar to the Chinese for many centuries, but between these and the novel proper there is a wide gulf which so far had not been satisfactorily bridged. Some, indeed, have maintained that the novel was developed from the play, pointing in corroboration of their theory to the *Hsi Hsiang Chi*, or Story of the Western Pavilion, described in the preceding chapter. This, however, simply means that the *Hsi Hsiang Chi* is more suited for private reading than for public representation, as is the case with many Western plays.

The Chinese range their novels under four heads, as dealing (1) with usurpation and plotting, (2) with love and intrigue, (3) with superstition, and (4) with brigandage or lawless characters generally. Examples of each class will be given.

The *San kuo chih yen i*, attributed to one LO KUAN-CHUNG, is an historical novel based upon the wars of the Three Kingdoms which fought for supremacy at the beginning of the third century A.D. It consists mainly of stirring scenes of warfare, of cunning plans by skilful generals, and of doughty deeds by blood - stained warriors. Armies and fleets of countless myriads are from time to time annihilated by one side or another,— all this in an easy and fascinating style, which makes the book an endless joy to old and young alike. If a vote were taken among the people of China as to the greatest among their countless novels, the Story of the Three Kingdoms would indubitably come out first.

This is how the great commander Chu-ko Liang is said to have replenished his failing stock of arrows. He sent a force of some twenty or more ships to feign an attack on the fleet of his powerful rival, Ts'ao Ts'ao. The decks of the ships were apparently covered with large numbers of fighting men, but these were in reality nothing more than straw figures dressed up in soldiers' clothes. On each ship there were only a few sailors and some real soldiers with gongs and other noisy instruments. Reaching their destination, as had been carefully calculated beforehand, in the middle of a dense fog, the soldiers at once began to beat on their gongs as if about to go into action ; whereupon Ts'ao Ts'ao, who could just make out the outlines of vessels densely packed with fighting men bearing down upon him, gave orders to his archers to begin shooting. The latter did so, and kept on for an hour and more, until Chu-ko Liang was satisfied with what he had got, and passed the order to retreat.

Elsewhere we read of an archery competition which

recalls the Homeric games. A target is set up, and the prize, a robe, is hung upon a twig just above. From a distance of one hundred paces the heroes begin to shoot. Of course each competitor hits the bull's-eye, one, Parthian-like, with his back to the target, another shooting over his own head; and equally of course the favoured hero shoots at the twig, severs it, and carries off the robe.

The following extract will perhaps be interesting, dealing as it does with the use of anæsthetics long before they were dreamt of in this country. Ts'ao Ts'ao had been struck on the head with a sword by the spirit of a pear-tree which he had attempted to cut down. He suffered such agony that one of his staff recommended a certain doctor who was then very much in vogue :—

"'Dr. Hua,' explained the officer, 'is a mighty skilful physician, and such a one as is not often to be found. His administration of drugs, and his use of acupuncture and counter-irritants are always followed by the speedy recovery of the patient. If the sick man is suffering from some internal complaint and medicines produce no satisfactory result, then Dr. Hua will administer a dose of hashish, under the influence of which the patient becomes as it were intoxicated with wine. He now takes a sharp knife and opens the abdomen, proceeding to wash the patient's viscera with medicinal liquids, but without causing him the slightest pain. The washing finished, he sews up the wound with medicated thread and puts over it a plaster, and by the end of a month or twenty days the place has healed up. Such is his extraordinary skill. One day, for instance, as he was walking along a road, he heard some one groaning deeply, and at once declared that the cause was indigestion. On inquiry, this turned out to be the case; and accordingly, Dr. Hua ordered the sufferer to drink three pints of a decoction of garlic and leeks, which he did, and vomited forth a snake between two and three feet in length, after which he could digest food as before. On another occasion, the Governor of Kuang-ling was very much depressed in his mind, besides being troubled with a flushing of the face and total loss of appetite. He consulted Dr. Hua, and the effect of some medicine administered by him was to cause the invalid to throw up a quantity of red-headed wriggling tadpoles, which the doctor told him had been generated in his system by too great indulgence in fish, and which, although temporarily expelled, would re-appear after an interval of three years, when nothing could save him. And sure enough, he died three years afterwards. In a further instance, a man had a tumour growing between his eyebrows, the itching of which was insupportable. When Dr. Hua saw it, he said, 'There is a bird inside,' at which everybody laughed. However, he took a knife and opened the tumour, and out flew a canary, the patient beginning to recover from that hour. Again, another man had had his toes bitten by a dog, the consequence being that two lumps of flesh grew up from the wound, one of which was very painful while the other itched unbearably. 'There are ten needles,' said Dr. Hua, 'in the sore lump, and two black and white *wei-ch'i* pips in the other.' No one believed this until Dr. Hua opened them with a knife and showed that it was so. Truly he is of the same strain as Pien Ch'iao and Ts'ang Kung of old; and as he is now living not very far from this, I wonder your Highness does not summon him.'

"At this, Ts'ao Ts'ao sent away messengers who were

to travel day and night until they had brought Dr. Hua before him ; and when he arrived, Ts'ao Ts'ao held out his pulse and desired him to diagnose his case.

"'The pain in your Highness's head,' said Dr. Hua, 'arises from wind, and the seat of the disease is the brain, where the wind is collected, unable to get out. Drugs are of no avail in your present condition, for which there is but one remedy. You must first swallow a dose of hashish, and then with a sharp axe I will split open the back of your head and let the wind out. Thus the disease will be exterminated.'

"Ts'ao Ts'ao here flew into a great rage, and declared that it was a plot aimed at his life ; to which Dr. Hua replied, 'Has not your Highness heard of Kuan Yü's wound in the right shoulder ? I scraped the bone and removed the poison for him without a single sign of fear on his part. Your Highness's disease is but a trifling affair ; why, then, so much suspicion ?'

"'You may scrape a sore shoulder-bone,' said Ts'ao Ts'ao, 'without much risk ; but to split open my skull is quite another matter. It strikes me now that you are here simply to avenge your friend Kuan Yü upon this opportunity.' He thereupon gave orders that the doctor should be seized and cast into prison."

There the unfortunate doctor soon afterwards died, and before very long Ts'ao Ts'ao himself succumbed.

The *Shui Hu Chuan* is said to have been written by SHIH NAI-AN of the thirteenth century ; but this name does not appear in any biographical collection, and nothing seems to be known either of the man or of his authorship. The story is based upon the doings of an historical band of brigands, who had actually terrorised a couple of provinces, until they were finally put down, early in the twelfth century. Some of it is very laughable, and all of it valuable for the insight given into Chinese manners and customs. There is a ludicrous episode of a huge swashbuckler who took refuge in a Buddhist temple and became a priest. After a while he reverted to less ascetic habits of life, and returned one day to the temple, in Chinese phraseology, as drunk as a clod, making a great riot and causing much scandal. He did this on a second occasion; and when shut out by the gatekeeper, he tried to burst in, and in his drunken fury knocked to pieces a huge idol at the entrance for not stepping down to his assistance. Then, when he succeeded by a threat of fire in getting the monks to open the gate, "through which no wine or meat may pass," he fell down in the courtyard, and out of his robe tumbled a half-eaten dog's leg, which he had carried away with him from the restaurant where he had drunk himself tipsy. This he amused himself by tearing to pieces and forcing into the mouth of one of his fellow-priests.

The graphic and picturesque style in which this book is written, though approaching the colloquial, has secured for it a position rather beyond its real merits.

The *Hsi Yu Chi*, or Record of Travels in the West, is a favourite novel written in a popular and easy style. It is based upon the journey of Hsüan Tsang to India in search of books, images, and relics to illustrate the Buddhist religion; but beyond the fact that the chief personage is called by Hsüan Tsang's posthumous title, and that he travels in search of Buddhist books, the journey and the novel have positively nothing in common. The latter is a good sample of the fiction in which the Chinese people delight, and may be allowed to detain us awhile.

A stone monkey is born on a mysterious mountain from a stone egg, and is soon elected to be king of the monkeys. He then determines to travel in search of wisdom, and accordingly sets forth. His first step is to gain a knowledge of the black art from a magician, after which he becomes Master of the Horse to God, that is, to the supreme deity in the Taoist Pantheon. Throwing up his post in disgust, he carries on a series of disturbances in the world generally, until at length God is obliged to interfere, and sends various heavenly generals to coerce him. These he easily puts to flight, only returning to his allegiance on being appointed the Great Holy One of All the Heavens. He is soon at his old tricks again, stealing the peaches of immortality from a legendary being known as the Royal Mother in the West, and also some elixir of life, both of which he consumes.

All the minor deities now complain to God of his many misdeeds, and heavenly armies are despatched against him, but in vain. Even God's nephew cannot prevail against him until Lao Tzŭ throws a magic ring at him and knocks him down. He is then carried captive to heaven, but as he is immortal, no harm can be inflicted on him.

At this juncture God places the matter in the hands of Buddha, who is presently informed by the monkey that God must be deposed and that he, the monkey, must for the future reign in his stead. The text now runs as follows :—

"When Buddha heard these words, he smiled scorn-

fully and said, 'What! a devil-monkey like you to seize
the throne of God, who from his earliest years has been
trained to rule, and has lived 1750 æons, each of 129,600
years' duration! Think what ages of apprenticeship he
had to serve before he could reach this state of perfect
wisdom. You are only a brute beast; what mean these
boastful words? Be off, and utter no more such, lest
evil befall, and your very existence be imperilled.'

"'Although he is older than I am,' cried the monkey,
'that is no reason why he should always have the post.
Tell him to get out and give up his place to me, or I will
know the reason why.'

"'What abilities have you,' asked Buddha, 'that
you should claim the divine palace?'

"'Plenty,' replied the monkey. 'I can change myself
into seventy-two shapes; I am immortal; and I can turn
a somersault to a distance of 18,000 *li* (= 6000 miles).
Am I not fit to occupy the throne of heaven?'

"'Well,' aswered Buddha, 'I will make a wager with
you. If you can jump out of my hand, I will request
God to depart to the West and leave heaven to you;
but if you fail, you will go down again to earth and be a
devil for another few æons to come.'

"The monkey readily agreed to this, pointing out that
he could easily jump 18,000 *li*, and that Buddha's hand
was not even a foot long. So after making Buddha promise to carry out the agreement, he grasped his sceptre
and diminished in size until he could stand in the hand,
which was stretched out for him like a lotus-leaf. 'I'm
off!' he cried, and in a moment he was gone. But
Buddha's enlightened gaze was ever upon him, though
he turned with the speed of a whirligig.

"In a brief space the monkey had reached a place

where there were five red pillars, and there he decided to stop. Reflecting, however, that he had better leave some trace as a proof of his visit, he plucked out a hair, and changing it into a pencil, wrote with it on the middle pillar in large characters, *The Great Holy One of All the Heavens reached this point.* The next moment he was back again in Buddha's hand, describing his jump, and claiming his reward.

"'Ah!' said Buddha, 'I knew you couldn't do it.'

"'Why,' said the monkey, 'I have been to the very confines of the universe, and have left a mark there which I challenge you to inspect.'

"'There is no need to go so far,' replied Buddha. 'Just bend your head and look here.'

"The monkey bent down his head, and there, on Buddha's middle finger, he read the following inscription : *The Great Holy One of All the Heavens reached this point.*"

Ultimately, the monkey is converted to the true faith, and undertakes to escort Hsüan Tsang on his journey to the West. In his turn he helps to convert a pig-bogey, whom he first vanquishes by changing himself into a pill, which the pig-bogey unwittingly swallows, thereby giving its adversary a chance of attacking it from inside. These two are joined by a colourless individual, said to represent the passive side of man's nature, as the monkey and pig represent the active and animal sides respectively. The three of them conduct Hsüan Tsang through manifold dangers and hairbreadth escapes safe, until at length they receive final directions from an Immortal as to the position of the palace of Buddha, from which they hope to obtain the coveted books. The scene which follows almost recalls *The Pilgrim's Progress* :—

"Hsüan Tsang accordingly bade him farewell and proceeded on his way. But he had not gone more than a mile or two before he came to a stream of rushing water about a league in breadth, with not a trace of any living being in sight. At this he was somewhat startled, and turning to Wu-k'ung (the name of the monkey) said, 'Our guide must surely have misdirected us. Look at that broad and boiling river; how shall we ever get across without a boat?' 'There is a bridge over there,' cried Wu-k'ung, 'which you must cross over in order to complete your salvation.' At this Hsüan Tsang and the others advanced in the direction indicated, and saw by the side of the bridge a notice-board on which was written, 'The Heavenly Ford.' Now the bridge itself consisted of a simple plank; on which Hsüan Tsang remarked, 'I am not going to trust myself to that frail and slippery plank to cross that wide and rapid stream. Let us try somewhere else.' 'But this is the true path,' said Wu-k'ung; 'just wait a moment and see me go across.' Thereupon he jumped on to the bridge, and ran along the shaky vibrating plank until he reached the other side, where he stood shouting out to the rest to come on. But Hsüan Tsang waved his hand in the negative, while his companions stood by biting their fingers and crying out, 'We can't! we can't! we can't!' So Wu-k'ung ran back, and seizing Pa-chieh (the pig) by the arm, began dragging him to the bridge, all the time calling him a fool for his pains. Pa-chieh then threw himself on the ground, roaring out, 'It's too slippery—it's too slippery. I can't do it. Spare me! spare me!' 'You must cross by this bridge,' replied Wu-k'ung, 'if you want to become a Buddha;' at which Pa-chieh said, 'Then I can't be a Buddha, sir,

I have done with it : I shall never get across that bridge.'

"While these two were in the middle of their dispute, lo and behold a boat appeared in sight, with a man punting it along, and calling out, 'The ferry ! the ferry !' At this Hsüan Tsang was overjoyed, and shouted to his disciples that they would now be able to get across. By his fiery pupil and golden iris, Wu-k'ung knew that the ferryman was no other than Namo Pao-chang-kuang-wang Buddha; but he kept his knowledge to himself, and hailed the boat to take them on board. In a moment it was alongside the bank, when, to his un-utterable horror, Hsüan Tsang discovered that the boat had no bottom, and at once asked the ferryman how he proposed to take them across. 'My boat,' replied the ferryman, 'has been famed since the resolution of chaos into order, and under my charge has known no change. Steady though storms may rage and seas may roll, there is no fear so long as the passenger is light. Free from the dust of mortality, the passage is easy enough. Ten thousand kalpas of human beings pass over in peace. A bottomless ship can hardly cross the great ocean ; yet for ages past I have ferried over countless hosts of passengers.'

"When he heard these words Wu-k'ung cried out, 'Master, make haste on board. This boat, although bottomless, is safe enough, and no wind or sea could overset it.' And while Hsüan Tsang was still hesitating, Wu-k'ung pushed him forwards on to the bridge ; but the former could not keep his feet, and fell head over heels into the water, from which he was immediately rescued by the ferryman, who dragged him on board the boat. The rest also managed, with the aid of Wu-k'ung, to scramble on board ; and then, as the ferryman shoved off, lo ! they beheld a dead body floating away down the stream. Hsüan Tsang was greatly alarmed at this ; but Wu-k'ung laughed and said, ' Fear not, Master ; that dead body is your old self !' And all the others joined in the chorus of ' It is you, sir, it is you ; ' and even the ferryman said, ' Yes, it is you ; accept my best congratulations.'

"A few moments more and the stream was crossed, when they all jumped on shore ; but before they could look round the boat and ferryman had disappeared."

The story ends with a list of the Buddhist *sûtras* and liturgies which the travellers were allowed to carry back with them to their own country.

BOOK THE SEVENTH

THE MING DYNASTY (A.D. 1368–1644)

BOOK THE SEVENTH

THE MING DYNASTY (A.D. 1368–1644)

CHAPTER I

MISCELLANEOUS LITERATURE—MATERIA MEDICA—ENCYCLOPÆDIA OF AGRICULTURE

THE first Emperor of the Ming dynasty, popularly known as the Beggar King, in allusion to the poverty of his early days, so soon as he had extinguished the last hopes of the Mongols and had consolidated his power, turned his attention to literature and education. He organised the great system of competitive examinations which prevails at the present day. He also published a Penal Code, abolishing such punishments as mutilation, and drew up a kind of Domesday Book, under which taxation was regulated. In 1369 he appointed SUNG LIEN (A.D. 1310–1381), in conjunction with other scholars, to produce the History of the Mongol Dynasty. Sung Lien had previously been tutor to the heir apparent. He had declined office, and was leading the life of a simple student. He rose to be President of the Han-lin College, and for many years enjoyed his master's confidence. A grandson, however, became mixed up in a conspiracy, and only the Empress's entreaties saved the old man's life. His sentence was commuted to banishment, and he died on the journey. Apart from the history above mentioned, and a pronouncing dictionary on which he was employed, his literary remains fill only three volumes. The following piece is a satire on the neglect of men of ability, which, according to him, was a marked feature of the administration of the Mongols:—

"Têng Pi, whose cognomen was Po-i, was a man of Ch'in. He was seven feet high. Both his eyes had crimson corners, and they blinked like lightning flashes. In feats of strength he was cock of the walk; and once when his neighbour's bulls were locked in fight, with a blow of his fist he broke the back of one of them and sent it rolling on the ground. The stone drums of the town, which ten men could not lift, he could carry about in his two hands. He was, however, very fond of liquor, and given to quarrelling in his cups; so that when people saw him in this mood, they would keep out of his way, saying that it was safer to be at a distance from such a wild fellow.

"One day he was drinking by himself in a tea-house when two literati happened to pass by. Têng Pi tried to make them join him; but they, having rather a low opinion of the giant, would not accept his invitation. 'Gentlemen,' cried he in a rage, 'if you do not see fit to do as I ask, I will make an end of the pair of you, and then seek safety in flight. I could not brook this treatment at your hands.'

"So the two had no alternative but to walk in. Têng Pi took the place of honour himself, and put his guests on each side of him. He called for more liquor, and began to sing and make a noise. And at last, when he was well tipsy, he threw off his clothes and began to attitudinise. He drew a knife, and flung it down with a bang on the table ; at which the two literati, who were aware of his weakness, rose to take leave.

"'Stop !' shouted Têng Pi, detaining them. 'I too know something about your books. What do you mean by treating me as the spittle of your mouth ? If you don't hurry up and drink, I fear my temper will get the better of me. Meanwhile, you shall ask me anything you like in the whole range of classical literature, and if I can't answer, I will imbrue this blade in my blood.'

"To this the two literati agreed, and forthwith gave him a number of the most difficult allusions they could think of, taken from the Classics ; but Têng Pi was equal to the occasion, and repeated the full quotation in each case without missing a word. Then they tried him on history, covering a period of three thousand years ; but here again his answers were distinguished by accuracy and precision.

"'Ha ! ha !' laughed Têng Pi, 'do you give in now ?' At which his guests looked blankly at each other, and hadn't a word to say. So Têng Pi shouted for wine, and loosed his hair, and jumped about, crying, 'I have floored you, gentlemen, to-day ! Of old, learning made a man of you ; but to-day, all you have to do is to don a scholar's dress and look consumptive. You care only to excel with pen and ink, and despise the real heroes of the age. Shall this be so indeed ?'

"Now these two literati were men of some reputation, and on hearing Têng Pi's words they were greatly shamed, and left the tea-house, hardly knowing how to put one foot before the other. On arriving home they made further inquiries, but no one had ever seen Têng Pi at any time with a book in his hand."

FANG HSIAO-JU (A.D. 1357–1402) is another scholar, co-worker with Sung Lien, who adorned this same period. As a child he was precocious, and by his skill in composition earned for himself the nickname of Little Han Yü. He became tutor to one of the Imperial princes, and was loaded with honours by the second Emperor, who through the death of his father succeeded in 1398 to his grandfather. Then came the rebellion of the fourth son of the first Emperor ; and when Nanking opened its gates to the conqueror, the defeated nephew vanished. It is supposed that he fled to Yünnan, in the garb of a monk, left to him, so the story runs, with full directions by his grandfather. After nearly forty years' wandering, he is said to have gone to Peking, and lived in seclusion in the palace until his death. He was recognised by a eunuch from a mole on his left foot, but the eunuch was afraid to reveal his identity. Fang Hsiao-ju absolutely refused to place his services at the disposal of the new Emperor, who ruled under the year-title of Yung Lo. For this refusal he was cut to pieces in the market-place, his family being as far as possible exterminated and his philosophical writings burned. A small collection of his miscellanies was preserved by a faithful disciple, and afterwards republished. The following is an extract from an essay on taking too much thought for the morrow :—

"Statesmen who forecast the destinies of an empire ofttimes concentrate their genius upon the difficult and neglect the easy. They provide against likely evils, and disregard combinations which yield no ground for suspicion. Yet calamity often issues from neglected quarters, and sedition springs out of circumstances which have been set aside as trivial. Must this be regarded as due to an absence of care?—No. It results because the things that man can provide against are human, while those that elude his vigilance and overpower his strength are divine."

After giving several striking examples from history, the writer continues:—

"All the instances above cited include gifted men whose wisdom and genius overshadowed their generation. They took counsel and provided against disruption of the empire with the utmost possible care. Yet misfortune fell upon every one of them, always issuing from some source where its existence was least suspected. This, because human wisdom reaches only to human affairs and cannot touch the divine. Thus, too, will sickness carry off the children even of the best doctors, and devils play their pranks in the family of an exorcist. How is it that these professors, who succeed in grappling with the cases of others, yet fail in treating their own? It is because in those they confine themselves to the human; in these they would meddle with the divine.

"The men of old knew that it was impossible to provide infallibly against the convulsions of ages to come. There was no plan, no device, by which they could hope to prevail, and they refrained accordingly from vain scheming. They simply strove by the force of Truth and Virtue to win for themselves the approbation of God; that He, in reward for their virtuous conduct, might watch over them, as a fond mother watches over her babes, for ever. Thus, although fools were not wanting to their posterity—fools able to drag an empire to the dust—still, the evil day was deferred. This was indeed foresight of a far-reaching kind.

"But he who, regardless of the favour of Heaven,

may hope by the light of his own petty understanding to establish that which shall endure through all time—he shall be confounded indeed."

The third Emperor of this dynasty, whose nephew, the reigning Emperor, disappeared so mysteriously, mounted the throne in 1403. A worthy son of his father as regarded his military and political abilities, he was a still more enthusiastic patron of literature. He caused to be compiled what is probably the most gigantic encyclopædia ever known, the *Yung Lo Ta Tien*, to produce which 2169 scholars laboured for about three years under the guidance of five chief directors and twenty sub-directors. Judging from the account published in 1795, it must have run to over 500,000 pages. It was never printed because of the cost of the block-cutting; but under a subsequent reign two extra copies were taken, and one of these, imperfect to the extent of about 20,000 pages, is still in the Han-lin College at Peking.[1] The others perished by fire at the fall of the Ming dynasty. Not only did this encyclopædia embrace and illustrate the whole range of Chinese literature, but it included many complete works which would otherwise have been lost. Of these, no fewer than 66 on the Confucian Canon, 41 on history, 103 on philosophy, and 175 on poetry were copied out and inserted in the Imperial Library.

Many names of illustrious scholars must here, as

[1] On the 23rd June 1900, almost while these words were being written, the Han-lin College was burnt to the ground. The writer's youngest son, Mr. Lancelot Giles, who went through the siege of Peking, writes as follows:— "An attempt was made to save the famous *Yung Lo Ta Tien*, but heaps of volumes had been destroyed, so the attempt was given up. I secured vol. 13,345 for myself."

indeed throughout this volume, be passed over in silence. Such writers are more than compensated by the honour they receive from their own countrymen, who place classical scholarship at the very summit of human ambitions, and rank the playwright and the novelist as mere parasites of literature. Between these two extremes there is always to be found a great deal of general writing, which, while it satisfies the fastidious claim of the Chinese critic for form in preference even to matter, is also of sufficient interest for the European reader.

YANG CHI-SHÊNG (1515–1556) was a statesman and a patriot, who had been a cowherd in his youth. He first got himself into trouble by opposing the establishment of a horse-market on the frontier, between China and Tartary, as menacing the safety of his country. Restored to favour after temporary degradation, he impeached a colleague, now known as the worst of the Six Traitorous Ministers of the Ming dynasty. His adversary was too strong for him. Yang was sent to prison, and three years later his head fell. His name has no place in literature ; nor would it be mentioned here except as an introduction to an impassioned memorial which his wife addressed to the Emperor on her husband's behalf :—

" May it please your Majesty,—My husband was chief Minister in the Cavalry Department of the Board of War. Because he advised your Majesty against the establishment of a tradal mart, hoping to prevent Ch'ou Luan from carrying out his design, he was condemned only to a mild punishment; and then, when the latter suffered defeat, he was restored to favour and to his former honours.

"Thereafter, my husband was for ever seeking to make some return for the Imperial clemency. He would deprive himself of sleep. He would abstain from food. All this I saw with my own eyes. By and by, however, he gave ear to some idle rumour of the market-place, and the old habit came strong upon him. He lost his mental balance. He uttered wild statements, and again incurred the displeasure of the Throne. Yet he was not slain forthwith. His punishment was referred to the Board. He was beaten; he was thrown into prison. Several times he nearly died. His flesh was hollowed out beneath the scourge; the sinews of his legs were severed. Blood flowed from him in bowlfuls, splashing him from head to foot. Confined day and night in a cage, he endured the utmost misery.

"Then our crops failed, and daily food was wanting in our poverty-stricken home. I strove to earn money by spinning, and worked hard for the space of three years, during which period the Board twice addressed the Throne, receiving on each occasion an Imperial rescript that my husband was to await his fate in gaol. But now I hear your Majesty has determined that my husband shall die, in accordance with the statutes of the Empire. Die as he may, his eyes will close in peace with your Majesty, while his soul seeks the realms below.

"Yet I know that your Majesty has a humane and kindly heart; and when the creeping things of the earth, —nay, the very trees and shrubs,—share in the national tranquillity, it is hard to think that your Majesty would grudge a pitying glance upon our fallen estate. And should we be fortunate enough to attract the Imperial favour to our lowly affairs, that would be joy indeed. But if my husband's crime is of too deep a dye, I humbly beg that my head may pay the penalty, and that I be permitted to die for him. Then, from the far-off land of spirits, myself brandishing spear and shield, I will lead forth an army of fierce hobgoblins to do battle in your Majesty's behalf, and thus make some return for this act of Imperial grace."

"The force of language," says the commentator, "can no farther go." Yet this memorial, "the plaintive tones of which," he adds, "appeal direct to the heart," was never allowed to reach the Emperor. Twelve years later, the Minister impeached by Yang Chi-shêng was dismissed for scandalous abuse of power, and had all his property confiscated. Being reduced to beggary, he received from the Emperor a handsome silver bowl in which to collect alms ; but so universally hated was he that no one would either give him anything or venture to buy the bowl, and he died of starvation while still in the possession of wealth.

A curiously similar case, with a happier ending, was that of SHÊN SU, who, in the discharge of his duties as Censor, also denounced the same Minister, before whose name the word "traitorous" is now always inserted. Shên Su was thrown into prison, and remained there for fifteen years. He was released in consequence of the following memorial by his wife, of which the commentator says, "for every drop of ink a drop of blood" :—

"May it please your Majesty,—My husband was a Censor attached to the Board of Rites. For his folly in recklessly advising your Majesty, he deserved indeed a thousand deaths ; yet under the Imperial clemency he was doomed only to await his sentence in prison.

"Since then fourteen years have passed away. His aged parents are still alive, but there are no children in his hall, and the wretched man has none on whom he can rely. I alone remain—a lodger at an inn, working day and night at my needle to provide the necessaries of life ; encompassed on all sides by difficulties ; to whom every day seems a year.

"My father-in-law is eighty-seven years of age. He trembles on the brink of the grave. He is like a candle in the wind. I have naught wherewith to nourish him alive or to honour him when dead. I am a lone woman. If I tend the one, I lose the other. If I return to my father-in-law, my husband will die of starvation. If I remain to feed him, my father-in-law may die at any hour. My husband is a criminal bound in gaol. He dares give no thought to his home. Yet can it be that when all living things are rejoicing in life under the wise and generous rule of to-day, we alone should taste the cup of poverty and distress, and find ourselves beyond the pale of universal peace ?

"Oft, as I think of these things, the desire to die comes upon me ; but I swallow my grief and live on, trusting in Providence for some happy termination, some moistening with the dew of Imperial grace. And now that my father-in-law is face to face with death ; now that my husband can hardly expect to live—I venture to offer this body as a hostage, to be bound in prison, while my husband returns to watch over the last hours of his father. Then, when all is over, he will resume his place and await your Majesty's pleasure. Thus my husband will greet his father once again, and the feelings of father and child will be in some measure relieved. Thus I shall give to my father-in-law the comfort of his son, and the duty of a wife towards her husband will be fulfilled."

TSUNG CH'ÊN gained some distinction during this six-teenth century; in youth, by his great beauty, and especi-ally by his eyes, which were said to flash fire even at the sides; later on, by subscribing to the funeral expenses of the above-mentioned Yang Chi-shêng; and finally, by his successful defence of Foochow against the Japanese, whose forces he enticed into the city by a feint of surrender, and then annihilated from the walls. The following piece, which, in the opinion of the com-mentator, "verges upon trifling," is from his corre-spondence. Several sentences of it have quite a Juvenalian ring:—

"I was very glad at this distance to receive your letter, which quite set my mind at rest, together with the present you were so kind as to add. I thank you very much for your good wishes, and especially for your thoughtful allusion to my father.

"As to what you are pleased to say in reference to official popularity and fitness for office, I am much obliged by your remarks. Of my unfitness I am only too well aware; while as to popularity with my supe-riors, I am utterly unqualified to secure that boon.

"How indeed does an official find favour in the present day with his chief? Morning and evening he must whip up his horse and go dance attendance at the great man's door. If the porter refuses to admit him, then honeyed words, a coaxing air, and money drawn from the sleeve, may prevail. The porter takes in his card; but the great man does not come out. So he waits in the stable among grooms, until his clothes are charged with the smell, in spite of hunger, in spite of cold, in spite of a blazing heat. At nightfall, the porter who has pocketed the money comes forth and says his master is tired and begs to be excused, and will he call again next day. So he is forced to come once more as requested. He sits all night in his clothes. At cockcrow he jumps up, performs his toilette, and gallops off and knocks at the entrance gate. 'Who's there?' shouts the porter angrily; and when he explains, the porter gets still more angry and begins to abuse him, saying, 'You are in a fine hurry, you are! Do you think my master sees people at this hour?' Then is the visitor shamed, but has to swallow his wrath and try to persuade the porter to let him in. And the porter, another fee to the good, gets up and lets him in; and then he waits again in the stable as before, until perhaps the great man comes out and summons him to an audience.

"Now, with many an obeisance, he cringes timidly towards the foot of the daïs steps; and when the great man says 'Come!' he prostrates himself twice and remains long without rising. At length he goes up to offer his present, which the great man refuses. He entreats acceptance; but in vain. He implores, with many instances; whereupon the great man bids a servant take it. Then two more prostrations, long drawn out; after which he arises, and with five or six salutations he takes his leave.

"On going forth, he bows to the porter, saying, 'It's all right with your master. Next time I come you need make no delay.' The porter returns the bow, well pleased with his share in the business. Meanwhile, our friend springs on his horse, and when he meets an acquaintance flourishes his whip and cries out, 'I have just been with His Excellency. He treated me very kindly, very kindly indeed.' And then he goes into detail, upon which his friends begin to be more respectful to him as a *protégé* of His Excellency. The great man himself says, 'So-and-so is a good fellow, a very good fellow indeed;' upon which the bystanders of course declare that they think so too.

"Such is popularity with one's superiors in the present day. Do you think that I could be as one of these? No! Beyond sending in a complimentary card at the summer and winter festivals, I do not go near the great from one year's end to another. Even when I pass their doors I stuff my ears and cover my eyes, and gallop quickly by, as if some one was after me. In consequence of this want of breadth, I am of course no favourite with the authorities; but what care I? There is a destiny that shapes our ends, and it has shaped mine towards the path of duty alone. For which, no doubt, you think me an ass."

WANG TAO-K'UN took his third degree in 1547. His instincts seemed to be all for a soldier's life, and he rose to be a successful commander. He found ample time, however, for books, and came to occupy an honourable place among contemporary writers. His works, which, according to one critic, are "polished in style and lofty in tone," have been published in a uniform edition, and are still read. The following is a cynical skit upon the corruption of his day :—

"A retainer was complaining to Po Tzŭ that no one in the district knew how to get on.

"'You gentlemen,' said he, 'are like square handles

which you would thrust into the round sockets of your generation. Consequently, there is not one of you which fits.'

" ' You speak truth,' replied Po Tzŭ ; 'kindly explain how this is so.'

" ' There are five reasons,' said the retainer, ' why you are at loggerheads with the age, as follows :—

" ' (1) The path to popularity lies straight before you, but you will not follow it.

" ' (2) Other men's tongues reach the soft places in the hearts of their superiors, but your tongues are too short.

" ' (3) Others eschew fur robes, and approach with bent backs as if their very clothes were too heavy for them ; but you remain as stiff-necked as planks.

" ' (4) Others respond even before they are called, and seek to anticipate the wishes of their superiors ; whose enemies, were they the saints above, would not escape abuse ; whose friends, were they highwaymen and thieves, would be larded over with praise. But you— you stick at facts and express opinions adverse to those of your superiors, whom it is your special interest to conciliate.

" ' (5) Others make for gain as though bent upon shooting a pheasant, watching in secret and letting fly with care, so that nothing escapes their aim. But you— you hardly bend your bow, or bend it only to miss the quarry that lies within your reach.

" ' One of these five failings is like a tumour hanging to you and impeding your progress in life. How much more all of them !'

" ' It is indeed as you state,' answered Po Tzŭ. 'But would you bid me cut these tumours away ? A man may have a tumour and live. To cut it off is to die. And life with a tumour is better than death without. Besides, beauty is a natural gift ; and the woman who tried to look like Hsi Shih only succeeded in frightening people out of their wits by her ugliness. Now it is my misfortune to have these tumours, which make me more loathsome even than that woman. Still, I can always, so to speak, stick to my needle and my cooking-pots, and strive to make my good man happy. There is no occasion for me to proclaim my ugliness in the market-place.'

"'Ah, sir,' said the retainer, 'now I know why there are so many ugly people about, and so little beauty in the land.'"

Hsü Hsieh graduated as Senior Classic in 1601, and received an appointment in the Han-lin College, where all kinds of State documents are prepared under the superintendence of eminent scholars. Dying young, he left behind him the reputation of a cross-grained man, with whom it was difficult to get along, ardently devoted to study. He swore that if it were granted to him to acquire a brilliant style, he would jump into the sea to circulate his writings. The following piece is much admired. " It is completed," says a commentator, "with the breath of a yawn (with a single effort), and is like a heavenly robe, without seam. The reader looks in vain for paragraphing in this truly inspired piece " :—

" For some years I had possessed an old inkstand, left at my house by a friend. It came into ordinary use as such, I being unaware that it was an antique. However, one day a connoisseur told me it was at least a thousand years old, and urged me to preserve it carefully as a valuable relic. This I did, but never took any further trouble to ascertain whether such was actually the case or not. For supposing that this inkstand really dated from the period assigned, its then owner must have regarded it simply as an inkstand. He could not have known that it was destined to survive the wreck of time and to come to be cherished as an antique. And while we prize it now, because it has descended to us from a distant past, we forget that then, when antiques were relics of a still earlier period, it could not have been of any value to antiquarians, themselves the moderns of what is antiquity to us ! The surging crowd around us thinks of naught but the acquisition of wealth and material enjoyment, occupied only with the struggle for place and power. Men lift their skirts and hurry through the mire ; they suffer indignity and feel no sense of shame. And if from out this mass there arises one spirit purer and simpler than the rest, striving to tread a nobler path than they, and amusing his leisure, for his own gratification, with guitars, and books, and pictures, and other relics of olden times,—such a man is indeed a genuine lover of the antique. He can never be one of the common herd, though the common herd always affect to admire whatever is admittedly admirable. In the same way, persons who aim at advancement in their career will spare no endeavour to collect the choicest rarities, in order, by such gifts, to curry favour with their superiors, who in their turn will take pleasure in ostentatious display of their collections of antiquities. Such is but a specious hankering after antiques, arising simply from a desire to eclipse one's neighbours. Such men are not genuine lovers of the antique. Their tastes are those of the common herd after all, though they make a great show and filch the reputation of true antiquarians, in the hope of thus distinguishing themselves from their fellows, ignorant as they are that what they secure is the name alone without the reality. The man whom I call a genuine antiquarian is he who studies the writings of the ancients, and strives to form himself upon their model, though unable to greet them in the flesh ; who ever and anon, in his wanderings up and down the long avenue of the past, lights upon some choice fragment which brings him in an instant face to face with the immortal dead. Of such enjoyment there is no satiety. Those who truly love antiquity, love not the things, but the men of old, since a relic in the present is much what it was in the past,—a mere thing. And so if it is not to things, but rather to men, that devotion is due, then even I may aspire to be some day an antique. Who shall say that centuries hence an antiquarian of the day may not look up to me as I have looked up to my predecessors ? Should I then neglect myself, and foolishly devote my energies to trifling with things ?

"Such is popular enthusiasm in these matters. It is shadow without substance. But the theme is endless, and I shall therefore content myself with a passing record of my old inkstand."

This chapter may close with the names of two remarkable men. LI SHIH-CHÊN completed in 1578, after twenty-six years of unremitting labour, his great Materia Medica. In 1596 the manuscript was laid before the Emperor, who ordered it to be printed forthwith. It deals (1) with Inanimate substances ; (2) with Plants ; and (3) with Animals, and is illustrated by over 1100 woodcuts. The introductory chapter passes in review forty-two previous works of importance on the same subject, enumerating no fewer than 950 miscellaneous publications on a variety of subjects. The famous "doctrine of signatures," which supposes that the uses of plants and substances are indicated to man by certain appearances peculiar to them, figures largely in this work.

HSÜ KUANG-CH'I (1562–1634) is generally regarded as the only influential member of the mandarinate who has ever become a convert to Christianity. After graduating first among the candidates for the second degree in 1597 and taking his final degree in 1604, he enrolled himself as a pupil of Matteo Ricci, and studied under his guidance to such purpose that he was able to produce works on the new system of astronomy as introduced by the Jesuit Fathers, besides various treatises on mathematical science. He was also author of an encyclopædia of agriculture of considerable value, first published in 1640. This work is illustrated with numerous woodcuts, and treats of the processes and implements of husbandry, of rearing silkworms, of breeding animals, of the manufacture of food, and even of precautions to be taken against famine. The Jesuit Fathers themselves scattered broadcast over China a large number of propagandist publications, written in polished book-style, some few of which are still occasionally to be found in old bookshops.

CHAPTER II

NOVELS AND PLAYS

NOVELS were produced in considerable numbers under the Ming dynasty, but the names of their writers, except in a very few cases, have not been handed down. The marvellous work known as the *Chin P'ing Mei*, from the names of three of the chief female characters, has been attributed to the grave scholar and statesman, Wang Shih-chêng (1526–1593); but this is more a guess than anything else. So also is the opinion that it was produced in the seventeenth century, as a covert satire upon the morals of the Court of the great Emperor K'ang Hsi. The story itself refers to the early part of the twelfth century, and is written in a simple, easy style, closely approaching the Peking colloquial. It possesses one extraordinary characteristic. Many words and phrases are capable of two interpretations, one of which is of a class which renders such passages unfit for ears polite. Altogether the book is objectionable, and would require a translator with the nerve of a Burton.

The *Yü Chiao Li* is a tale of the fifteenth century which has found much favour in the eyes of foreigners, partly because it is of an unusually moderate length. The ordinary Chinaman likes his novels long, and does not mind plenty of repetitions after the style of Homer, which latter feature seems to point in the direction of stories told by word of mouth and written down later on, and may be taken in connection with the opinion already expressed, that the Chinese novel came originally from Central Asia. Here, however, in four small volumes, we have a charming story of a young graduate who falls in love first with a beautiful and accomplished poetess, and then with the fascinating sister of a fascinating friend whose acquaintance — the brother's — he makes casually by the roadside. The friend and the sister turn out to be one and the same person, a very lively girl, who appears in male or female dress as occasion may require ; and what is more, the latter young lady turns out to be the much-loved orphan cousin of the first and still cherished young lady, and also her intellectual equal. The graduate is madly in love with the two girls, and they are irrevocably in love with him. This is a far simpler matter than it would be in Western countries. The hero marries both, and all three live happily ever afterwards.

The *Lieh Kuo Chuan*, anonymous as usual, is a historical novel dealing with the exciting times of the Feudal States, and covering the period between the eighth century B.C. and the union of China under the First Emperor. It is introduced to the reader in these words :—

"The *Lieh Kuo* is not like an ordinary novel, which consists mainly of what is not true. Thus the *Fêng Shên* (a tale of the twelfth century B.C.), the *Shui Hu*, the *Hsi Yu Chi*, and others, are pure fabrications. Even the *San Kuo Chih*, which is very near to truth, contains much that is without foundation. Not so the

Lieh Kuo. There every incident is a real incident, every speech a real speech. Besides, as there is far more to tell than could possibly be told, it is not likely that the writer would go out of his way to invent. Wherefore the reader must look upon the *Lieh Kuo* as a genuine history, and not as a mere novel."

The following extract refers to a bogus exhibition, planned by the scheming State of Ch'in, nominally to make a collection of valuables and hand them over as respectful tribute to the sovereign House of Chou, but really with a view to a general massacre of the rival nobles who stood in the way between the Ch'ins and their treasonable designs :—

"Duke Ai of Ch'in now proceeded with his various officers of State to prepare a place for the proposed exhibition, at the same time setting a number of armed men in ambuscade, with a view to carry out his ambitious designs ; and when he heard that the other nobles had arrived, he went out and invited them to come in. The usual ceremonies over, and the nobles having taken their seats according to precedence, Duke Ai addressed the meeting as follows :—

" ' I, having reverently received the commission of the Son of Heaven, do hereby open this assembly for the exhibition of such valuables as may be brought together from all parts of the empire, the same to be subsequently packed together, and forwarded as tribute to our Imperial master. And since you nobles are now all collected here in this place, it is fitting that our several exhibits be forthwith produced and submitted for adjudication.'

"Sounds of assent from the nobles were heard at the conclusion of this speech, but the Prime Minister of the Ch'i State, conscious that the atmosphere was heavily laden with the vapour of death, as if from treacherous ambush, stepped forward and said :—

"'Of old, when the nobles were wont to assemble, it was customary to appoint one just and upright member to act as arbiter or judge of the meeting; and now that we have thus met for the purposes of this exhibition, I propose, in the interest of public harmony, that some one of us be nominated arbiter in a similar way.'

"Duke Ai readily agreed to the above proposition, and immediately demanded of the assembled nobles who among them would venture to accept the office indicated. These words were scarcely out of his mouth when up rose Pien Chuang, generalissimo of the forces of Chêng, and declared that he was ready to undertake the post. Duke Ai then asked him upon what grounds, as to personal ability, he based his claim; to which Pien Chuang replied, 'Of ability I have little indeed, but I have slain a tiger with one blow of my fist, and in martial prowess I am second to none. Upon this I base my claim.'

"Accordingly, Duke Ai called for a golden tablet, and was on the point of investing him as arbiter of the exhibition, when a voice was heard from among the retainers of the Wu State, loudly urging, 'The slayer of a tiger need be possessed only of physical courage; but how is that a sufficient recommendation for this office? Delay awhile, I pray, until I come and take the tablet myself.'

"By this time Duke Ai had seen that the speaker was K'uai Hui, son of the Duke of Wei, and forthwith inquired of him what his particular claim to the post might be. 'I cut the head off a deadly dragon, and for that feat I claim this post.' Duke Ai thereupon ordered Pien Chuang to transfer to him the golden tablet; but this he refused to do, arguing that the slaughter of a dragon was simply a magician's trick, and not at all to the present purpose. He added that if the tablet was to be taken from him, it would necessitate an appeal to force between himself and his rival. The contest continued thus for some time, until at length the Prime Minister of Ch'i rose again, and solved the difficulty in the following terms:—

"'The slaughter of a tiger involves physical courage, and the slaughter of a dragon is a magician's trick; hence, neither of these acts embraces that combination of mental and physical power which we desire in the arbiter of this meeting. Now, in front of the palace there stands a sacrificial vessel which weighs about a thousand pounds. Let Duke Ai give out a theme; and then let him who replies thereto with most clearness and accuracy, and who can, moreover, seize the aforesaid vessel, and carry it round the platform on which the eighteen representative nobles are seated, be nominated to the post of arbiter and receive the golden tablet.'

"To this plan Duke Ai assented; and writing down a theme, bade his attendants exhibit it among the heroes of the assembled States. The theme was in rhyme, and contained these eight lines:—

> *Say what supports the sky; say what supports the earth;*
> *What is the mystic number which to the universe gave birth?*
> *Whence come the eddying waves of the river's rolling might?*
> *Where shall we seek the primal germ of the mountain's towering*
> *   height?*
> *By which of the elements five is the work of Nature done?*
> *And of all the ten thousand things that are, say which is the*
> *   wondrous one?*
> *Such are the questions seven which I now propound to you;*
> *And he who can answer them straight and well is the trusty man*
> *   and true.'*

"The theme had hardly been uttered, when up started Chi Nien, generalissimo of the Ch'in State, and cried out, 'This is but a question of natural philosophy; what difficulty is there in it?' He thereupon advanced to the front, and, having obtained permission to compete, seized a stylus and wrote down the following reply:—

> *Nothing supports the sky; nothing supports the earth;*
> *How can we guess at the number which to the universe gave birth?*
> *From the reaches above come the eddying waves of the river's rolling might:*
> *How can we tell where to look for the germ of the mountain's towering height?*
> *By every one of the elements five is the work of Nature done;*
> *And of all the ten thousand things that are there is no particular one.*
> *There you have my replies to the questions set by you;*
> *And the arbiter's post I hereby claim as the trusty man and true.'*

"Chi Nien, having delivered this answer, proceeded to tuck up his robe, and, passing to the front of the palace, seized with both hands the sacrificial vessel, and raised it some two feet from the ground, his whole face becoming suffused with colour under the effort. At the same time there arose a great noise of drums and horns, and all the assembled nobles applauded loudly; whereupon Duke Ai personally invested him with the golden tablet and proclaimed him arbiter of the exhibition, for which Chi Nien was just about to return thanks, when suddenly up jumped Wu Yüan, generalissimo of the Ch'u State, and coming forward, declared in an angry tone that Chi Nien's answer did not dispose of the theme in a proper and final manner; that he had not removed the sacrificial vessel from its place, and that consequently he had not earned the appointment which Wu Yüan now contended should be bestowed upon himself. Duke Ai, in view of his scheme for seizing the persons of the various nobles, was naturally anxious that the post of arbiter should fall to one of his own officers, and was much displeased at this attempt on the part of Wu Yüan; however, he replied that if the latter could dispose of the theme and carry round the sacrificial vessel, the office of arbiter would be his. Wu Yüan thereupon took a stylus and indited the following lines:—

> ' *The earth supports the sky; the sky supports the earth.*
> Five *is the mystic number which to the universe gave birth.*
> *Down from the sky come the eddying waves of the river's rolling might.*
> *In the K'un-lun range we must seek the germ of the mountain's towering height.*
> *By* truth, *of the elements five, can most good work be done;*
> *And of all the ten thousand things that are,* man *is the wondrous one.*
> *There you have my replies to the questions set this day;*
> *The answers are clear and straight to the point, and given without delay.'*

"As soon as he had finished writing, he handed his reply to Duke Ai, who at once saw that he had in every way disposed of the theme with far greater skill than Chi Nien, and accordingly now bade him show his strength upon the sacrificial vessel. Wu Yüan immediately stepped forward, and, holding up his robe with his left hand, seized the vessel with his right, raising it up and bearing it round the platform before the assembled nobles, and finally depositing it in its original place, without so much as changing colour. The nobles gazed at each other in astonishment at this feat, and with one accord declared him to be the hero of the day; so that Duke Ai had no alternative but to invest him with the golden tablet and announce his appointment to the post of arbiter."

The *Ching Hua Yüan* is a less pretentious work than the preceding, but of an infinitely more interesting character. Dealing with the reign of the Empress Wu, who in A.D. 684 set aside the rightful heir and placed herself upon the throne, which she occupied for twenty years, this work describes how a young graduate, named T'ang, disgusted with the establishment of examinations and degrees for women, set out with a small party on a voyage of exploration. Among all the strange places which they visited, the most curious was the Country of Gentlemen, where they landed and proceeded at once to the capital city.

"There, over the city gate, T'ang and his companions read the following legend :—

' Virtue is man's only jewel !'

"They then entered the city, which they found to be a busy and prosperous mart, the inhabitants all talking the Chinese language. Accordingly, T'ang accosted one of the passers-by, and asked him how it was his nation had become so famous for politeness and consideration of others ; but, to his great astonishment, the man did not understand the meaning of his question. T'ang then asked him why this land was called the 'Country of Gentlemen,' to which he likewise replied that he did not know. Several other persons of whom they inquired giving similar answers, the venerable To remarked that the term had undoubtedly been adopted by the inhabitants of adjacent countries, in consequence of the polite manners and considerate behaviour of these people. 'For,' said he, 'the very labourers in the fields and foot-passengers in the streets step aside to make room for one another. High and low, rich and poor, mutually respect each other's feelings without reference to the wealth or social status of either; and this is, after all, the essence of what constitutes the true gentleman.'

"'In that case,' cried T'ang, 'let us not hurry on, but rather improve ourselves by observing the ways and customs of this people.'

"By and by they arrived at the market-place, where they saw an official runner standing at a stall engaged in making purchases. He was holding in his hand the articles he wished to buy, and was saying to the owner of the stall, 'Just reflect a moment, sir, how impossible it would be for me to take these excellent goods at the absurdly low price you are asking. If you will oblige me by doubling the amount, I shall do myself the honour of accepting them; otherwise, I cannot but feel that you are unwilling to do business with me to-day.'

"'How very funny!' whispered T'ang to his friends. 'Here, now, is quite a different custom from ours, where the buyer invariably tries to beat down the seller, and the seller to run up the price of his goods as high as possible. This certainly looks like the 'consideration for others' of which we spoke just now.'

"The man at the stall here replied, 'Your wish, sir, should be law to me, I know; but the fact is, I am already overwhelmed with shame at the high price I have ventured to name. Besides, I do not profess to adhere rigidly to 'marked prices,' which is a mere trick of the trade, and consequently it should be the aim of every purchaser to make me lower my terms to the very smallest figure; you, on the contrary, are trying to raise the price to an exorbitant figure; and although I fully appreciate your kindness in that respect, I must really ask you to seek what you require at some other establishment. It is quite impossible for me to execute your commands.'

"T'ang was again expressing his astonishment at this extraordinary reversal of the platitudes of trade, when the would-be purchaser replied, 'For you, sir, to ask such a low sum for these first-class goods, and then to turn round and accuse me of over-considering your interests, is indeed a sad breach of etiquette. Trade could not be carried on at all if all the advantages were on one side and the losses on the other; neither am I more devoid of brains than the ordinary run of people that I should fail to understand this principle and let you catch me in a trap.'

"So they went on wrangling and jangling, the stall-keeper refusing to charge any more and the runner insisting on paying his own price, until the latter made a show of yielding and put down the full sum demanded on the counter, but took only half the amount of goods. Of course the stall-keeper would not consent to this, and they would both have fallen back upon their original positions had not two old gentlemen who happened to be passing stepped aside and arranged the matter for them, by deciding that the runner was to pay the full price but to receive only four-fifths of the goods.

"T'ang and his companions walked on in silence, meditating upon the strange scene they had just witnessed; but they had not gone many steps when they came across a soldier similarly engaged in buying things at an open shop-window. He was saying, 'When I asked the price of these goods, you, sir, begged me to take them at my own valuation; but now that I am willing to do so, you complain of the large sum I offer, whereas the truth is that it is actually very much below their real value. Do not treat me thus unfairly.'

"'It is not for me, sir,' replied the shopkeeper, 'to demand a price for my own goods; my duty is to leave that entirely to you. But the fact is, that these goods are old stock, and are not even the best of their kind; you would do much better at another shop. However, let us say half what you are good enough to offer; even then I feel I shall be taking a great deal too much. I could not think, sir, of parting with my goods at your price.'

"'What is that you are saying, sir?' cried the soldier. 'Although not in the trade myself, I can tell superior from inferior articles, and am not likely to mistake one for the other. And to pay a low price for a good article is simply another way of taking money out of a man's pocket.'

"'Sir,' retorted the shopkeeper, 'if you are such a stickler for justice as all that, let us say half the price you first mentioned, and the goods are yours. If you object to that, I must ask you to take your custom elsewhere. You will then find that I am not imposing on you.'

"The soldier at first stuck to his text, but seeing that the shopkeeper was not inclined to give way, he laid down the sum named and began to take his goods, picking out the very worst he could find. Here, however, the shopkeeper interposed, saying, 'Excuse me, sir, but you are taking all the bad ones. It is doubtless very kind of you to leave the best for me, but if all men were like you there would be a general collapse of trade.'

"'Sir,' replied the soldier, 'as you insist on accepting only half the value of the goods, there is no course open to me but to choose inferior articles. Besides, as a matter of fact, the best kind will not answer my purpose so well as the second or third best; and although I fully recognise your good intentions, I must really ask to be allowed to please myself.'

"'There is no objection, sir,' said the shopkeeper, 'to your pleasing yourself, but low-class goods are sold at a low price, and do not command the same rates as superior articles.'

"Thus they went on bandying arguments for a long time without coming to any definite agreement, until at last the soldier picked up the things he had chosen and tried to make off with them. The bystanders, however, all cried shame upon him and said he was a downright cheat, so that he was ultimately obliged to take some of the best kind and some of the inferior kind and put an end to the altercation.

"A little farther on our travellers saw a countryman who had just paid the price of some purchases he had succeeded in making, and was hurrying away with them, when the shopkeeper called after him, 'Sir! sir! you have paid me by mistake in finer silver than we are accustomed to use here, and I have to allow you a considerable discount in consequence. Of course this is a mere trifle to a gentleman of your rank and position, but still for my own sake I must ask leave to make it all right with you.'

"'Pray don't mention such a small matter,' replied the countryman, 'but oblige me by putting the amount to my credit for use at a future date when I come again to buy some more of your excellent wares.'

"'No, no,' answered the shopkeeper, 'you don't catch old birds with chaff. That trick was played upon me last year by another gentleman, and to this day I have never set eyes upon him again, though I have made every endeavour to find out his whereabouts. As it is, I can now only look forward to repaying him in the next life ; but if I let you take me in in the same way, why, when the next life comes and I am changed, maybe into a horse or a donkey, I shall have quite enough to do to find him, and your debt will go dragging on till the life after that. No, no, there is no time like the present ; hereafter I might very likely forget what was the exact sum I owed you.'

"They continued to argue the point until the countryman consented to accept a trifle as a set-off against the fineness of his silver, and went away with his goods, the shopkeeper bawling after him as long as he was in sight that he had sold him inferior articles at a high rate, and was positively defrauding him of his money. The countryman, however, got clear away, and the shopkeeper returned to his grumbling at the iniquity of the age. Just then a beggar happened to pass, and so in anger at having been compelled to take more than his due he handed him the difference. 'Who knows,' said he, 'but that the present misery of this poor fellow may be retribution for overcharging people in a former life ?'

"'Ah,' said T'ang, when he had witnessed the finale of this little drama, 'truly this is the behaviour of gentlemen !'

"Our travellers then fell into conversation with two respectable - looking old men who said they were brothers, and accepted their invitation to go and take a cup of tea together. Their hosts talked eagerly about China, and wished to hear many particulars of 'the first nation in the world.' Yet, while expressing their admiration for the high literary culture of its inhabitants and their unqualified successes in the arts and sciences, they did not hesitate to stigmatise as unworthy a great people certain usages which appeared to them deserving of the utmost censure. They laughed at the superstitions of Fêng-Shui, and wondered how intelligent men could be imposed upon year after year by the mountebank professors of such baseless nonsense. 'If it is true,' said one of them, 'that the selection of an auspicious day and a fitting spot for the burial of one's father or mother is certain to bring prosperity to the survivors, how can you account for the fact that the geomancers themselves are always a low, poverty-stricken lot ? Surely they would begin by appropriating the very best positions themselves, and so secure whatever good fortune might happen to be in want of an owner.'

"Then again with regard to bandaging women's feet in order to reduce their size. 'We can see no beauty,' said they, 'in such monstrosities as the feet of your ladies. Small noses are usually considered more attractive than large ones ; but what would be said of a man who sliced a piece off his own nose in order to reduce it within proper limits ?'

"And thus the hours slipped pleasantly away until it was time to bid adieu to their new friends and regain their ship."

The *Chin Ku Ch'i Kuan*, or Marvellous Tales, Ancient and Modern, is a great favourite with the romance-reading Chinaman. It is a collection of forty stories said to have been written towards the close of the Ming dynasty by the members of a society who held meetings for that purpose. Translations of many, if not

all, of these have been published. The style is easy,
very unlike that of the *P'ing Shan Lêng Yen*, a well-
known novel in what would be called a high-class
literary style, being largely made up of stilted dialogue
and over-elaborated verse composed at the slightest
provocation by the various characters in the story.
These were P'ing and Yen, two young students in love
with Shan and Lêng, two young poetesses who charmed
even more by their literary talent than by their fascinating beauty. On one occasion a pretended poet, named
Sung, who was a suitor for the hand of Miss Lêng, had
been entertained by her uncle, and after dinner the
party wandered about in the garden. Miss Lêng was
summoned, and when writing materials had been produced, as usual on such occasions, Mr. Sung was asked
to favour the company with a sonnet. "Excuse me,"
he replied, "but I have taken rather too much wine for
verse-making just now." "Why," rejoined Miss Lêng,
"it was after a gallon of wine that Li Po dashed off a
hundred sonnets, and so gained a name which will
live for a thousand generations." "Of course I could
compose," said Mr. Sung, "even after drinking, but I
might become coarse. It is better to be fasting, and to
feel quite clear in the head. Then the style is more
finished, and the verse more pleasing." "Ts'ao Chih,"
retorted Miss Lêng, "composed a sonnet while taking
only seven steps, and his fame will be remembered for
ever. Surely occasion has nothing to do with the matter."
In the midst of Mr. Sung's confusion, the uncle proposed
that the former should set a theme for Miss Lêng instead,
to which he consented, and on looking about him caught
sight through the open window of a paper kite, which
he forthwith suggested, hoping in his heart to completely

puzzle the sarcastic young lady. However, in the time that it takes to drink a cup of tea, she had thrown off the following lines :—

> *"Cunningly made to look like a bird,*
> *It cheats fools and little children.*
> *It has a body of bamboo, light and thin,*
> *And flowers painted on it, as though something wonderful.*
> *Blown by the wind it swaggers in the sky,*
> *Bound by a string it is unable to move.*
> *Do not laugh at its sham feet,*
> *If it fell, you would see only a dry and empty frame."*

All this was intended in ridicule of Mr. Sung himself and of his personal appearance, and is a fair sample of what the reader may expect throughout.

The *Erh Tou Mei,* or "Twice Flowering Plum-trees," belongs to the sixteenth or seventeenth century, and is by an unknown author. It is a novel with a purpose, being apparently designed to illustrate the beauty of filial piety, the claims of friendship, and duty to one's neighbour in general. Written in a simple style, with no wealth of classical allusion to soothe the feelings of the pedant, it contains several dramatic scenes, and altogether forms a good panorama of Chinese everyday life. Two heroes are each in love with two heroines, and just as in the *Yü Chiao Li,* each hero marries both. There is a slender thread of fact running through the tale, the action of which is placed in the eighth century, and several of the characters are actually historical. One of the four lovely heroines, in order to keep peace between China and the Tartar tribes which are continually harrying the borders, decides to sacrifice herself on the altar of patriotism and become the bride of the Khan.

The parting at the frontier is touchingly described ; but the climax is reached when, on arrival at her destination, she flings herself headlong over a frightful precipice, rather than pass into the power of the hated barbarian, a waiting-maid being dressed up in her clothes and handed over to the unsuspecting Khan. She herself does not die. Caught upon a purple cloud, she is escorted back to her own country by a bevy of admiring angels.

There is also an effective scene, from which the title of the book is derived, when the plum trees, whose flowers had been scattered by a storm of wind and rain, gave themselves up to fervent prayer. "The Garden Spirit heard their earnest supplications, and announced them to the Guardian Angel of the town, who straightway flew up to heaven and laid them at the feet of God." The trees were then suffered to put forth new buds, and soon bloomed again, more beautiful than ever.

The production of plays was well sustained through the Ming dynasty, for the simple reason that the Drama, whether an exotic or a development within the boundaries of the Middle Kingdom, had emphatically come to stay. It had caught on, and henceforth forms the ideal pastime of the cultured, reflective scholar, and of the laughter-loving masses of the Chinese people.

The *P‘i Pa Chi*, or "Story of the Guitar," stands easily at the head of the list, being ranked by some admirers as the very finest of all Chinese plays. It is variously arranged in various editions under twenty-four or forty-two scenes ; and many liberties have been taken with the text, long passages having been interpolated and many other changes made. It was first performed in 1704, and was regarded as a great advance in the dramatic art upon the early plays of the Mongols. The author's name was KAO TSÊ-CH'ÊNG, and his hero is said to have been taken from real life in the person of a friend who actually rose from poverty to rank and affluence. The following is an outline of the plot.

A brilliant young graduate and his beautiful wife are living, as is customary, with the husband's parents. The father urges the son to go to the capital and take his final degree. "At fifteen," says the old man, "study; at thirty, act." The mother, however, is opposed to this plan, and declares that they cannot get along without their son. She tells a pitiful tale of another youth who went to the capital, and after infinite suffering was appointed Master of a Workhouse, only to find that his parents had already preceded him thither in the capacity of paupers. The young man finally decides to do his duty to the Son of Heaven, and forthwith sets off, leaving the family to the kind care of a benevolent friend. He undergoes the examination, which in the play is turned into ridicule, and comes out in the coveted position of Senior Classic. The Emperor then instructs one of his Ministers to take the Senior Classic as a son-in-law; but our hero refuses, on the ground, so it is whispered, that the lady's feet are too large. The Minister is then compelled to put on pressure, and the marriage is solemnised, this part of the play concluding with an effective scene, in which on being asked by his new wife to sing, our hero suggests such songs as "Far from his True Love," and others in a similar style. Even when he agrees to sing "The Wind through the Pines," he drops unwittingly into "Oh for my home once more;" and then when recalled to his senses, he relapses again into a song about a deserted wife.

Meanwhile misfortunes have overtaken the family left behind. There has been a famine, the public granaries have been discovered to be empty instead of full, and the parents and wife have been reduced to starvation. The wife exerts herself to the utmost, selling all her jewels to buy food; and when at length, after her mother-in-law's death, her father-in-law dies too, she cuts off her hair and tries to sell it in order to buy a coffin, being prevented only by the old friend who has throughout lent what assistance he could. The next thing is to raise a tumulus over the grave. This she tries to do with her own hands, but falls asleep from fatigue. The Genius of the Hills sees her in this state, and touched by her filial devotion, summons the white monkey of the south and the black tiger of the north, spirits who, with the aid of their subordinates, complete the tumulus in less than no time. On awaking, she recognises supernatural intervention, and then determines to start for the capital in search of her husband, against whom she entertains very bitter feelings. She first sets to work to paint the portraits of his deceased parents, and then with these for exhibition as a means of obtaining alms, and with her guitar, she takes her departure. Before her arrival the husband has heard by a letter, forged in order to get a reward, that his father and mother are both well, and on their way to rejoin him. He therefore goes to a temple to pray Buddha for a safe conduct, and there picks up the rolled-up pictures of his father and mother which have been dropped by his wife, who has also visited the temple to ask for alms. The picture is sent unopened to his study. And now the wife, in continuing her search, accidentally gains admission to her husband's house, and is kindly received by the second wife. After a few misunderstandings the truth comes out, and the second wife, who is in full sympathy with the first, recommends her to step into the study and leave a note for the husband. This note, in the shape of some uncomplimentary verses, is found by the latter together with the pictures which have been hung up against the wall; the second wife introduces the first; there is an explanation; and the curtain, if there was such a thing in a Chinese theatre, would fall upon the final happiness of the husband and his two wives.

Of course, in the above sketch of a play, which is about as long as one of Shakespeare's, a good many side-touches have been left out. Its chief beauties, according to Chinese critics, are to be found in the glorification of duty to the sovereign, of filial piety to a husband's parents, and of accommodating behaviour on the part of the second wife tending so directly to the preservation of peace under complicated circumstances. The forged letter is looked upon as a weak spot, as the hero would know his father's handwriting, and so with other points which it has been suggested should be cut out. "But because a stork's neck is too long," says an editor, "you can't very well remedy the defect by taking a piece off." On the other hand, the pathetic character of the play gives it a high value with the Chinese; for, as we are told in the prologue, "it is much easier to make people laugh than cry." And if we can believe all that is said on this score, every successive generation has duly paid its tribute of tears to the *P'i Pa Chi*.

CHAPTER III

POETRY

THOUGH the poetry of the Ming dynasty shows little falling off, in point of mere volume, there are far fewer great poets to be found than under the famous Houses of T'ang and Sung. The name, however, which stands first in point of chronological sequence, is one which is widely known. HSIEH CHIN (1369–1415) was born when the dynasty was but a year old, and took his final degree before he had passed the age of twenty. His precocity had already gained for him the reputation of being an Inspired Boy, and, later on, the Emperor took such a fancy to him, that while Hsieh Chin was engaged in writing, his Majesty would often deign to hold the ink-slab. He was President of the Commission which produced the huge encyclopædia already described, but he is now chiefly known as the author of what appears to be a didactic poem of about 150 lines, which may be picked up at any bookstall. It is necessary to say "about 150 lines," since no two editions give identically the same number of lines, or even the same text to each line. It is also very doubtful if Hsieh Chin actually wrote such a poem. In many editions, lines are boldly stolen from the early Han poetry and pitchforked in without rhyme or reason, thus making the transitions even more awkward than they otherwise would be. All editors seem to be agreed upon the four opening lines, which state that the Son of Heaven holds heroes in high esteem, that his Majesty urges all to study diligently, and that everything in this world is second-class, with the sole exception of book-learning. It is in fact the old story that

> *" Learning is better than house or land ;*
> *For when house and land are gone and spent,*
> *Then learning is most excellent."*

Farther on we come to four lines often quoted as enumerating the four greatest happinesses in life, to wit,

> *" A gentle rain after long drought,*
> *Meeting an old friend in a foreign clime,*
> *The joys of the wedding-day,*
> *One's name on the list of successful candidates."*

The above lines occur *à propos* of nothing in particular, and are closely followed in some editions by more precepts on the subject of earnest application. Then after reading that the Classics are the best fields to cultivate, we come upon four lines with a dash of real poetry in them :—

> *" Man in his youth-time's rosy glow,*
> *The pink peach flowering in the glade . . . .*
> *Why, yearly, when spring breezes blow,*
> *Does each one flush a deeper shade ?"*

More injunctions to burn the midnight oil are again strangely followed by a suggestion that three cups of wine induce serenity of mind, and that if a man is but dead drunk, all his cares disappear, which is only another way of saying that

> **"** *The best of life is but intoxication."*

Altogether, this poem is clearly a patchwork, of which some parts may have come from Hsieh Chin's pen. Here is a short poem of his in defence of official venality, about which there is no doubt :—

> " *In vain hands bent on sacrifice*
> *or clasped in prayer we see ;*
> *The ways of God are not exactly*
> *what those ways should be.*
> *The swindler and the ruffian*
> *lead pleasant lives enough,*
> *While judgments overtake the good*
> *and many a sharp rebuff.*
> *The swaggering bully stalks along*
> *as blithely as you please,*
> *While those who never miss their prayers*
> *are martyrs to disease.*
> *And if great God Almighty fails*
> *to keep the balance true,*
> *What can we hope that paltry*
> *mortal magistrates will do ?*"

The writer came to a tragic end. By supporting the claim of the eldest prince to be named heir apparent, he made a lasting enemy of another son, who succeeded in getting him banished on one charge, and then imprisoned on a further charge. After four years' confinement he was made drunk, probably without much difficulty, and was buried under a heap of snow.

The Emperor who reigned between 1522 and 1566 as the eleventh of his line was not a very estimable personage, especially in the latter years of his life, when he spent vast sums over palaces and temples, and wasted most of his time in seeking after the elixir of life. In 1539 he despatched General Mao to put down a rising in Annam, and gave him an autograph poem as a send-off.

The verses are considered spirited by Chinese critics, and are frequently given in collections, which certainly would not be the case if Imperial authorship was their only claim :—

> "Southward, in all the panoply
>   of cruel war arrayed,
> See, our heroic general points
>   and waves his glittering blade!
> Across the hills and streams
>   the lizard-drums terrific roll,
> While glint of myriad banners
>   flashes high from pole to pole. . . .
> Go, scion of the Unicorn,
>   and prove thy heavenly birth,
> And crush to all eternity
>   these insects of the earth;
> And when thou com'st, a conqueror,
>   from those wild barbarian lands,
> WE will unhitch thy war-cloak
>   with our own Imperial hands!"

The courtesans of ancient and mediæval China formed a class which now seems no longer to exist. Like the *hetairæ* of Greece, they were often highly educated, and exercised considerable influence. Biographies of the most famous of these ladies are in existence, extending back to the seventh century A.D. The following is an extract from that of Hsieh Su-su, who flourished in the fourteenth century, and "with whom but few of the beauties of old could compare":—

"Su-su's beauty was of a most refined style, with a captivating sweetness of voice and grace of movement. She was a skilful artist, sweeping the paper with a few rapid touches, which produced such speaking effects that few, even of the first rank, could hope to excel her work. She was a fine horsewoman, and could shoot

from horseback with a cross-bow. She would fire one
pellet, and then a second, which would catch up the first
and smash it to atoms in mid-air. Or she would throw
a pellet on to the ground, and then grasping the cross-
bow in her left hand, with her right hand passed behind
her back, she would let fly and hit it, not missing once
in a hundred times. She was also very particular about
her friends, receiving no one unless by his talents he had
made some mark in the world."

The poetical effusions, and even plays, of many of
these ladies have been carefully preserved, and are
usually published as a supplement to any dynastic collection. Here is a specimen by CHAO TS'AI-CHI (fifteenth
century), of whom no biography is extant :—

> *" The tide in the river beginning to rise,*
> *Near the sad hour of parting, brings tears to our eyes ;*
> *Alas ! that these furlongs of willow-strings gay*
> *Cannot hold fast the boat that will soon be away !"*

Another specimen, by a lady named CHAO LI-HUA
(sixteenth century), contains an attempt at a pun, which
is rather lamely brought out in the translation :—

> *" Your notes on paper, rare to see,*
> *Two flying joy-birds bear ;* [1]
> *Be like the birds and fly to me,*
> *Not like the paper, rare !"*

These examples sufficiently illustrate this small department of literature, which, if deficient in work of real
merit, at any rate contains nothing of an indelicate
character.

A wild harum-scarum young man was FANG SHU-SHAO,

[1] Chinese note-paper is ornamented with all kinds of pictures, which sometimes cover the whole sheet.

who, like many other Chinese poets, often took more wine than was good for him. He was famed for his poetry, and also for his calligraphy, specimens of his art being highly prized by collectors. In 1642, we are told, "he was ill with his teeth;" and at length got into his coffin, which all Chinese like to keep handy, and wrote a farewell to the world, resting his paper on the edge of the coffin as he wrote. On completion of the piece he laid himself down and died. Here are the lines :—

> "An eternal home awaits me;
> > shall I hesitate to go?
> Or struggle for a few more hours
> > of fleeting life below?
> A home wherein the clash of arms
> > I can never hear again!
> And shall I strive to linger
> > in this thorny world of pain?
> The breeze will soon blow cool o'er me,
> > and the bright moon shine o'erhead,
> When blended with the gems of earth
> > I lie in my last bed.
> My pen and ink shall go with me
> > inside my funeral hearse,
> So that if I've leisure ' over there'
> > I may soothe my soul with verse."

BOOK THE EIGHTH

THE MANCHU DYNASTY (A.D. 1644–1900)

BOOK THE EIGHTH

THE MANCHU DYNASTY (A.D. 1644–1900)

CHAPTER I

THE "LIAO CHAI"—THE "HUNG LOU MÊNG"

By 1644 the glories of the great Ming dynasty had departed. Misgovernment, referred by Chinese writers to the ascendency of eunuchs, had resulted in rebellion, and the rebel chief with a large army was pressing upon the capital. On the 9th April Peking fell. During the previous night the Emperor, who had refused to flee, slew the eldest Princess, commanded the Empress to commit suicide, and sent his three sons into hiding. At dawn the bell was struck for the Court to assemble ; but no one came. His Majesty then ascended the Wan Sui Hill in the palace grounds, and wrote on the lapel of his robe a last decree :—" We, poor in virtue and of contemptible personality, have incurred the wrath of God on high. My Ministers have deceived me. I am ashamed to meet my ancestors ; and therefore I myself take off my crown, and, with my hair covering my face, await dismemberment at the hands of the rebels. Do not hurt a single one of my people ! " He then hanged himself, as did one faithful eunuch. At this juncture the Chinese commander-in-chief made overtures to the Manchu Tartars, who had long been consolidating their forces, and were already a serious menace to China. An agreement was hurriedly entered into, and Peking was retaken. The Manchus took possession definitively of the throne, which they had openly claimed since 1635, and imposed the "pigtail" upon the Chinese people.

Here then was the great empire of China, bounded by the Four Seas, and stretching to the confines of the habitable earth, except for a few barbarian islands scattered on its fringe, with its refined and scholarly people, heirs to a glorious literature more than twenty centuries old, in the power of a wild race of herdsmen, whose title had been established by skill in archery and horsemanship. Not much was to be expected on behalf of the "humanities" from a people whose own written language had been composed to order so late as 1599, and whose literary instincts had still to be developed. Yet it may be said without fear of contradiction that no age ever witnessed anything like the extensive encouragement of literature and patronage of literary men exhibited under the reigns of two Emperors of this dynasty. Of this, however, in the next chapter.

The literature of this dynasty may be said to begin with a writer who was after all but a mere storyteller. It has already been stated that novels and plays are not included by the Chinese in the domain of pure literature. Such is the rule, to which there is in practice, if not in theory, one very notable exception.

P'U SUNG-LANG, author of the *Liao Chai Chih I*, which may be conveniently rendered by "Strange Stories," was born in 1622, and took his first degree in 1641. Though an excellent scholar and a most polished writer, he failed, as many other good men have done, to take the higher degrees by which he had hoped to enter upon an official career. It is generally understood that this failure was due to neglect of the beaten track of academic study. At any rate, his disappointment was overwhelming. All else that we have on record of P'u Sung-ling, besides the fact that he lived in close companionship with several eminent scholars of the day, is gathered from his own words, written when, in 1679, he laid down his pen upon the completion of a task which was to raise him within a short period to a foremost rank in the Chinese world of letters. The following are extracts from this record :—

"Clad in wistaria, girdled with ivy,[1]—thus sang Ch'ü Yüan in his *Li Sao*. Of ox-headed devils and serpent gods, he of the long nails[2] never wearied to tell. Each interprets in his own way the music of heaven; and whether it be discord or not, depends upon antecedent causes. As for me, I cannot, with my poor autumn firefly's light, match myself against the hobgoblins of the age.[3] I am but the dust in the sunbeam,

[1] Said of the bogies of the hills, in allusion to their *clothes*. Here quoted with reference to the official classes, in ridicule of the title under which they hold posts which, from a literary point of view, they are totally unfit to occupy.

[2] A poet of the T'ang dynasty, whose eyebrows met, whose nails were very long, and who could write very fast.

[3] This is another hit at the ruling classes. Hsi K'ang, the celebrated poet, musician, and alchemist (A.D. 223–262), was sitting one night alone, playing upon his lute, when suddenly a man with a tiny face walked in, and began to stare hard at him, the stranger's face enlarging all the time. "I'm not going to match myself against a devil!" cried the musician after a few moments, and instantly blew out the light.

a fit laughing-stock for devils.[1] For my talents are not those of Yü Pao,[2] elegant explorer of the records of the gods ; I am rather animated by the spirit of Su Tung-p'o, who loved to hear men speak of the supernatural. I get people to commit what they tell me to writing, and subsequently I dress it up in the form of a story ; and thus in the lapse of time my friends from all quarters have supplied me with quantities of material, which, from my habit of collecting, has grown into a vast pile.

"When the bow[3] was hung at my father's door, he dreamed that a sickly-looking Buddhist priest, but half-covered by his stole, entered the chamber. On one of his breasts was a round piece of plaster like a *cash;* and my father, waking from sleep, found that I, just born, had a similar black patch on my body. As a child, I was thin and constantly ailing, and unable to hold my own in the battle of life. Our home was chill and desolate as a monastery ; and working there for my livelihood with my pen, I was as poor as a priest with his alms-bowl. Often and often I put my hand to my head and exclaimed, 'Surely he who sat with his face to the wall[4] was myself

[1] When Liu Chüan, Governor of Wu-ling, determined to relieve his poverty by trade, he saw a devil standing by his side, laughing and rubbing its hands for glee. "Poverty and wealth are matters of destiny," said Liu Chüan, "but to be laughed at by a devil—," and accordingly he desisted from his intention.

[2] A writer who flourished in the early part of the fourth century, and composed a work in thirty books, entitled "Supernatural Researches."

[3] The birth of a boy was formerly signalled by hanging a bow at the door ; that of a girl, by displaying a small towel—indicative of the parts that each would hereafter play in the drama of life.

[4] Alluding to the priest Dharma-nandi, who came from India to China, and tried to convert the Emperor Wu Ting of the Liang dynasty ; but failing in his attempt, he retired full of mortification to a temple at Sung-shan, where he sat for nine years before a rock, until his own image was imprinted thereon.

in a previous state of existence ; ' and thus I referred my non-success in this life to the influence of a destiny surviving from the last. I have been tossed hither and thither in the direction of the ruling wind, like a flower falling in filthy places ; but the six paths[1] of transmigration are inscrutable indeed, and I have no right to complain. As it is, midnight finds me with an expiring lamp, while the wind whistles mournfully without; and over my cheerless table I piece together my tales, vainly hoping to produce a sequel to the *Infernal Regions*.[2] With a bumper I stimulate my pen, yet I only succeed thereby in ' venting my excited feelings,' and as I thus commit my thoughts to writing, truly I am an object worthy of commiseration. Alas ! I am but the bird that, dreading the winter frost, finds no shelter in the tree, the autumn insect that chirps to the moon and hugs the door for warmth. For where are they who know me ? They are ' in the bosky grove and at the frontier pass '[3]—wrapped in an impenetrable gloom ! "

For many years these "Strange Stories" circulated only in manuscript. P'u Sung-ling, as we are told in a colophon by his grandson to the first edition, was too poor to meet the heavy expense of block-cutting; and it was not until so late as 1740, when the author must have been already for some time a denizen of the dark land

---

[1] The six *gâti* or conditions of existence, viz., angels, men, demons, hungry devils, brute beasts, and tortured sinners.

[2] The work of a well-known writer, named Lin I-ch'ing, who flourished during the Sung dynasty.

[3] The great poet Tu Fu dreamt that his greater predecessor, Li T'ai-po, appeared to him, "coming when the maple-grove was in darkness, and returning while the frontier pass was still obscured,"—that is, at night, when no one could see him ; the meaning being that he never came at all, and that those " who know me (P'u Sung-ling) " are equally non-existent.

he so much loved to describe, that his aforesaid grandson printed and published the collection now so universally famous. Since then many editions have been laid before the Chinese public, the best of which is that by Tan Ming-lun, a Salt Commissioner, who flourished during the reign of Tao Kuang, and who in 1842 produced, at his own expense, an excellent edition in sixteen small octavo volumes of about 160 pages each.

Any reader of these stories as transferred into another language might fairly turn round and ask the why and the wherefore of the profound admiration—to use a mild term—which is universally accorded to them by the literati of China. The answer is to be found in the incomparable style in which even the meanest of them is arrayed. All the elements of form which make for beauty in Chinese composition are there in overwhelming force. Terseness is pushed to its extreme limits; each particle that can be safely dispensed with is scrupulously eliminated, and every here and there some new and original combination invests perhaps a single word with a force it could never have possessed except under the hands of a perfect master of his art. Add to the above copious allusions and adaptations from a course of reading which would seem to have been co-extensive with the whole range of Chinese literature, a wealth of metaphor and an artistic use of figures generally, to which only the writings of Carlyle form an adequate parallel, and the result is a work which for purity and beauty of style is now universally accepted in China as among the best and most perfect models. Sometimes the story runs plainly and smoothly enough, but the next moment we may be plunged into pages of abstruse text, the meaning of which is so involved in quotations from and allusions to the poetry or history of the past three thousand years as to be recoverable only after diligent perusal of the commentary, and much searching in other works of reference.

Premising that, according to one editor, the intention of most of these stories is to " glorify virtue and to censure vice," the following story, entitled " The Talking Pupils," may be taken as a fair illustration of the extent to which this pledge is redeemed :—

"At Ch'ang-an there lived a scholar named Fang Tung, who, though by no means destitute of ability, was a very unprincipled rake, and in the habit of following and speaking to any woman he might chance to meet. The day before the spring festival of Clear Weather he was strolling about outside the city when he saw a small carriage with red curtains and an embroidered awning, followed by a crowd of waiting-maids on horseback, one of whom was exceedingly pretty and riding on a small palfrey. Going closer to get a better view, Mr. Fang noticed that the carriage curtain was partly open, and inside he beheld a beautifully dressed girl of about sixteen, lovely beyond anything he had ever seen. Dazzled by the sight, he could not take his eyes off her, and now before, now behind, he followed the carriage for many a mile. By and by he heard the young lady call out to her maid, and, when the latter came alongside, say to her, 'Let down the screen for me. Who is this rude fellow that keeps on staring so ?' The maid accordingly let down the screen, and looking angrily at Mr. Fang, said to him, 'This is the bride of the Seventh Prince in the City of Immortals going home to see her parents, and no village girl that you should stare at her thus.' Then taking a handful of dust she threw it at him and blinded him. He rubbed his eyes and looked round, but the carriage and horses were gone. This frightened him, and he went off home, feeling very uncomfortable about the eyes. He sent for a doctor to examine them, and on the pupils was found a small film, which had increased by next morning, the eyes watering incessantly all the time. The film went on growing, and in a few days was as thick as a *cash*. On the right pupil there came a kind of spiral, and as no medicine was of any avail, the sufferer gave himself up to grief and wished for death. He then bethought himself of repenting of his misdeeds, and hearing that the *Kuang-ming sûtra* could relieve misery, he got a copy and hired a man to teach it to him. At first it was very tedious work, but by degrees he became more composed, and spent every evening in a posture of devotion, telling his beads. At the end of a year he had arrived at a state of perfect calm, when one day he heard a small voice, about as loud as a fly's, calling out from his left eye, 'It's horridly dark in here.' To this he heard a reply from the right eye, saying, 'Let us go out for a stroll, and cheer ourselves up a bit.' Then he felt a wriggling in his nose which made it itch, just as if something was going out of each of his nostrils, and after a while he felt it again as if going the other way. Afterwards he heard a voice from one eye say, 'I hadn't seen the garden for a long time; the epidendrums are all withered and dead.' Now Mr. Fang was very fond of these epidendrums, of which he had planted a great number, and had been accustomed to water them himself, but since the loss of his sight he had never even alluded to them. Hearing, however, these words, he at once asked his wife why she had let the epidendrums die. She inquired how he knew they were dead, and when he told her, she went out to see, and found them actually withered away. They were both very much astonished at this, and his wife proceeded to conceal herself in the room. She then observed two tiny people, no bigger than a bean, come down from her husband's nose and run out of the door, where she lost sight of them. In a little while they came back and flew up to his face, like bees or beetles seeking their nests. This went on for some days until Mr. Fang heard from the left eye, 'This roundabout road is not at all convenient. It would be as well for us to make a door.' To this the right eye answered, 'My wall is too thick; it wouldn't be at all an easy job.' 'I'll try and open mine,' said the left eye, 'and then it will do for both of us.' Whereupon Mr. Fang felt a pain in his left eye as if something was being split, and in a moment he found he could see the tables and chairs in the room. He was delighted at this, and told his wife, who examined his eye and discovered an opening in the film, through which she could see the black pupil shining out beneath, the eyeball itself looking like a cracked peppercorn. By next morning the film had disappeared, and when his eye was closely examined it was observed to contain two pupils. The spiral on the right eye remained as before, and then they knew that the two pupils had taken up their abode in one eye. Further, although Mr. Fang was still blind of one eye, the sight of the other was better than that of the two together. From this time he was more careful of his behaviour, and acquired in his part of the country the reputation of a virtuous man."

To take another specimen, this time with a dash of

humour in it. A certain man, named Wang (*anglicè* Smith), decided to study Tao—in other words, the black art—at a temple of the Taoist persuasion. The priest, who seems to have had a touch of Squeers in his composition, warned Wang that he would probably not be able to stand the training; but on the latter insisting, the priest allowed him to join the other novices, and then sent him to chop wood. He was kept at this task so long that, although he managed to witness several extraordinary feats of magical skill performed by the priest, he scarcely felt that he was making progress himself.

"After a time he could not stand it any longer; and as the priest taught him no magical arts, he determined not to wait, but went to him and said, 'Sir, I travelled many long miles for the benefit of your instruction. If you will not teach me the secret of immortality, let me, at any rate, learn some trifling trick, and thus soothe my cravings for a knowledge of your art. I have now been here two or three months, doing nothing but chop firewood, out in the morning and back at night, work to which I was never accustomed in my own home.' 'Did I not tell you,' replied the priest, 'that you would never support the fatigue? To-morrow I will start you on your way home.' 'Sir,' said Wang, 'I have worked for you a long time. Teach me some small art, that my coming here may not have been wholly in vain.' 'What art?' asked the priest. 'Well,' answered Wang, 'I have noticed that whenever you walk about anywhere, walls and so on are no obstacle to you. Teach me this, and I'll be satisfied.' The priest laughingly assented, and taught Wang a formula which he bade him recite. When he had done so he told him to walk through the wall; but Wang, seeing the wall in front of him, didn't like to walk at it. As, however, the priest bade him try, he walked quietly up to it and was there stopped. The priest here called out, 'Don't go so slowly. Put your head down and rush at it.' So Wang stepped back a few paces and went at it full speed; and the wall yielding to him as he passed, in a moment he found himself outside. Delighted at this, he went in to thank the priest, who told him to be careful in the use of his power, or otherwise there would be no response, handing him at the same time some money for his expenses on the way. When Wang got home, he went about bragging of his Taoist friends and his contempt for walls in general; but as his wife disbelieved his story, he set about going through the performance as before. Stepping back from the wall, he rushed at it full speed with his head down; but coming in contact with the hard bricks, finished up in a heap on the floor. His wife picked him up and found he had a bump on his forehead as big as a large egg, at which she roared with laughter; but Wang was overwhelmed with rage and shame, and cursed the old priest for his base ingratitude."

Episodes with a familiar ring about them are often to be found embedded in this collection. For instance :—

"She then became a dense column of smoke curling up from the ground, when the priest took an uncorked gourd and threw it right into the midst of the smoke. A sucking noise was heard, and the whole column was drawn into the gourd; after which the priest corked it up closely and put it in his pouch."

Of such points the following story contains another good example :—

"A countryman was one day selling his pears in the market. They were unusually sweet and fine flavoured, and the price he asked was high. A Taoist priest in rags and tatters stopped at the barrow and begged one of them. The countryman told him to go away, but as he did not do so, he began to curse and swear at him. The priest said, 'You have several hundred pears on your barrow; I ask for a single one, the loss of which, sir, you would not feel. Why then get angry?' The lookers-on told the countryman to give him an inferior one and let him go; but this he obstinately refused to do. Thereupon the beadle of the place, finding the commotion too great, purchased a pear and handed it to the priest. The latter received it with a bow, and turning to the crowd said, 'We who have left our homes and given up all that is dear to us, are at a loss to understand selfish, niggardly conduct in others. Now I have some exquisite pears which I shall do myself the honour to put before you.' Here somebody asked, 'Since you have pears yourself why don't you eat those?' 'Because,' replied the priest, 'I wanted one of these pips to grow them from.' So saying he munched up the pear; and when he had finished took a pip in his hand, unstrapped a pick from his back, and proceeded to make a hole in the ground several inches deep, wherein he deposited the pip, filling in the earth as before. He then asked the bystanders for a little hot water to water it with, and one among them who loved a joke fetched him some boiling water from a neighbouring shop. The priest poured this over the place where he had made the hole, and every eye was fixed upon him when sprouts were seen shooting up, and gradually growing larger and larger. By and by there was a tree with branches sparsely covered with leaves; then flowers, and last of all fine, large, sweet-smelling pears hanging in great profusion. These the priest picked and handed round to the assembled crowd until all were gone, when he took his pick and hacked away for a long time at the tree, finally cutting it down. This he shouldered, leaves and all, and sauntered quietly away. Now from the very beginning our friend the countryman had been amongst the crowd, straining his neck to see what was going on, and forgetting all about his business. At the departure of the priest he turned round and discovered that every one of his pears was gone. He then knew that those the old fellow had been giving away so freely were really his own pears. Looking more closely at the barrow, he also found that one of the handles was missing, evidently having been newly cut off. Boiling with rage, he set out in pursuit of the priest, and just as he turned the corner he saw the lost barrow-handle lying under the wall, being, in fact, the very pear-tree that the priest had cut down. But there were no traces of the priest, much to the amusement of the crowd in the market-place."

Here again is a scene, the latter part of which would almost justify the belief that Mr. W. S. Gilbert was a student of Chinese, and had borrowed some of his best points in "Sweethearts" from the author of the *Liao Chai* :—

"Next day Wang strolled into the garden, which was of moderate size, with a well-kept lawn and plenty of trees and flowers. There was also an arbour consisting of three posts with a thatched roof, quite shut in on all sides by the luxuriant vegetation. Pushing his way among the flowers, Wang heard a noise from one of the trees, and looking up saw Ying-ning, who at once burst out laughing and nearly fell down. 'Don't! don't!' cried Wang, 'you'll fall!' Then Ying-ning came down, giggling all the time, until, when she was near the ground, she missed her hold and tumbled down with a run. This stopped her merriment, and Wang picked her up, gently squeezing her hand as he did so. Ying-ning began laughing again, and was obliged to lean against a tree for support, it being some time before she was able to stop. Wang waited till she had finished, and then drew the flower out of his sleeve and handed it to her. 'It's dead,' said she; 'why do you keep it?' 'You dropped it, cousin, at the Feast of Lanterns,' replied Wang, 'and so I kept it.' She then asked him what was his object in keeping it, to which he answered, 'To show my love, and that I have not forgotten you. Since that day when we met I have been very ill from thinking so much of you, and am quite changed from what I was. But now that it is my unexpected good fortune to meet you, I pray you have pity on me.' 'You needn't make such a fuss about a trifle,' replied she, 'and with your own relatives too. I'll give orders to supply you with a whole basketful of flowers when you go away.' Wang told her she did not understand, and when she asked what it was she didn't understand, he said, 'I didn't care for the flower itself; it was the person who picked the flower.' 'Of course,' answered she, 'everybody cares for their relations; you needn't have told me that.' 'I wasn't talking about ordinary relations,' said Wang, 'but about husbands and wives.' 'What's the difference?' asked Ying-ning. 'Why,' replied Wang, 'husband and wife are always together.' 'Just what I shouldn't like,' cried she, 'to be always with anybody.'"

The pair were ultimately united, and lived happily ever afterwards, in spite of the fact that the young lady subsequently confessed that she was the daughter of a fox, and exhibited supernatural powers. On one occasion these powers stood her in good stead. Being very fond of flowers, she went so far as to pick from a neighbour's tree.

"One day the owner saw her, and gazed at her some time in rapt astonishment; however, she didn't move, deigning only to laugh. The gentleman was much smitten with her; and when she smilingly descended the wall on her own side, pointing all the time with her finger to a spot hard by, he thought she was making an assignation. So he presented himself at nightfall at the same place, and sure enough Ying-ning was there. Seizing her hand to tell his passion, he found that he was grasping only a log of wood which stood against the wall; and the next thing he knew was that a scorpion had stung him violently on the finger. There was an end of his romance, except that he died of the wound during the night."

In one of the stories a visitor at a temple is much struck by a fresco painting containing the picture of a lovely girl picking flowers, and stands in rapt admiration before it. Then he feels himself borne gently into the painted wall, *à la* "Alice through the Looking-glass," and in the region beyond plays a part in a domestic drama, finally marrying the heroine of the picture. But the presence of a mortal being suspected by "a man in golden armour with a face as black as jet," he was glad to make his way back again; and when he rejoined a friend who had been waiting for him, they noticed that the girl in the picture now wore her hair done up as a married woman.

There is a Rip van Winkle story, with the pathetic return of the hero to find, as the Chinese poet says—

> "*City and suburb as of old,*
> *But hearts that loved us long since cold.*"

There is a sea-serpent story, and a story of a big bird or rukh; also a story about a Jonah, who, in obedience to an order flashed by lightning on the sky when their junk was about to be swamped in a storm, was transferred by his fellow-passengers to a small boat and cut adrift. So soon as the unfortunate victim had collected his senses and could look about him, he found that the junk had capsized and that every soul had been drowned.

The following is an extract from a story in which a young student named Liu falls in love with a girl named Fêng-hsien, who was the daughter of a fox, and therefore possessed of the miraculous powers which the Chinese associate with that animal:—

"'But if you would really like to have something that has belonged to me,' said she, 'you shall.' Whereupon she took out a mirror and gave it to him, saying, 'Whenever you want to see me, you must look for me in your books; otherwise I shall not be visible;' and in a moment she had vanished. Liu went home very melancholy at heart; but when he looked in the mirror, there was Fêng-hsien standing with her back to him, gazing, as it were, at some one who was going away, and about a hundred paces from her. He then bethought himself of her injunctions, and settled down to his studies, refusing to receive any visitors; and a few days subsequently, when he happened to look in the mirror, there was Fêng-hsien, with her face turned towards him, and smiling in every feature. After this, he was always taking out the mirror to look at her. However, in about a month his good resolutions began to disappear, and he once more went out to enjoy himself and waste his time as before. When he returned home and looked in the mirror, Fêng-hsien seemed to be crying bitterly; and the day after, when he looked at her again, she had her back turned towards him as on the day he received the mirror. He now knew that it was because he had neglected his studies, and forthwith set to work again with all diligence, until in a month's time she had turned round once again. Henceforward, whenever anything interrupted his progress, Fêng-hsien's countenance became sad; but whenever he was getting on well her sadness was changed to smiles. Night and morning Liu would look at the mirror, regarding it quite in the light of a revered preceptor, and in three years' time he took his degree in triumph. 'Now,' cried he, 'I shall be able to look Fêng-hsien in the face.' And there sure enough she was, with her delicately-pencilled arched eyebrows, and her teeth just showing between her lips, as happy-looking as she could be, when, all of a sudden, she seemed to speak, and Liu heard her say, 'A pretty pair we make, I must allow,' and the next moment Fêng-hsien stood by his side."

Here is a story of the nether world, a favourite theme with P'u Sung-ling. It illustrates the popular belief that at death a man's soul is summoned to Purgatory by spiritual lictors, who are even liable to make mistakes. Cataleptic fits or trances give rise to many similar tales about persons visiting the realms below and being afterwards restored to life.

"A man named Chang died suddenly, and was escorted at once by devil-lictors into the presence of the King of Purgatory. His Majesty turned to Chang's record of good and evil, and then, in great anger, told the lictors they had brought the wrong man, and bade them take him back again. As they left the judgment-hall, Chang persuaded his escort to let him have a look at Purgatory, and accordingly the devils conducted him through the nine sections, pointing out to him the Knife Hill, the Sword Tree, and other objects of interest. By and by they reached a place where there was a Buddhist priest hanging suspended in the air, head downwards, by a rope through a hole in his leg. He was shrieking with pain and longing for death ; and when Chang approached, lo ! he saw that it was his own brother. In great distress, he asked his guides the reason of this punishment, and they informed him that the priest was suffering thus for collecting subscriptions on behalf of his order, and then privately squandering the proceeds in gambling and debauchery. 'Nor,' added they, 'will he escape this torment unless he repents him of his misdeeds.' When Chang came round, he thought his brother was already dead, and hurried off to the Hsing-fu monastery, to which the latter belonged. As he went in at the door he heard a loud shrieking, and on proceeding to his brother's room, he found him laid up with a very bad abscess in his leg, the leg itself being tied up above him to the wall, this being, as his brother informed him, the only bearable position in which he could lie. Chang now told him what he had seen in Purgatory, at which the priest was so terrified that he at once gave up taking wine and meat, and devoted himself entirely to religious exercises. In a fortnight he was well, and was known ever afterwards as a most exemplary priest."

Snatches of verse are to be found scattered about the pages of these stories, enough to give a taste of the writer's quality without too much boring the reader. These lines are much admired:—

> " With wine and flowers we chase the hours
>   In one eternal spring ;
>   No moon, no light, to cheer the night—
>   Thyself that ray must bring."

But we have seen perhaps enough of P'u Sung-ling. "If," as Han Yü exclaimed, "there is knowledge after death," the profound and widespread esteem in which this work is held by the literati of China must indeed prove a soothing balm to the wounded spirit of the Last of the Immortals.

The *Hung Lou Mêng*, conveniently but erroneously known as "The Dream of the Red Chamber," is the work referred to already as touching the highest point of development reached by the Chinese novel. It was probably composed during the latter half of the seventeenth century. The name of its author is unknown. It is usually published in 24 vols. octavo, containing 120 chapters, which average at the least 30 pages each, making a grand total of about 4000 pages. No fewer than 400 personages of more or less importance are introduced first and last into the story, the plot of which is worked out with a completeness worthy of Fielding, while the delineation of character—of so many characters —recalls the best efforts of the greatest novelists of the West. As a panorama of Chinese social life, in which almost every imaginable feature is submitted in turn to the reader, the *Hung Lou Mêng* is altogether without a rival. Reduced to its simplest terms, it is an original and effective love story, written for the most part in an easy, almost colloquial, style, full of humorous and pathetic episodes of everyday human life, and interspersed with short poems of high literary finish. The opening chapters, which are intended to form a link between the world of spirits and the world of mortals, belong to the supernatural ; after that the story runs smoothly along upon earthly lines, always, however, overshadowed by the near presence of spiritual influences. Some idea of the novel as a whole may perhaps be gathered from the following abstract.

Four thousand six hundred and twenty-three years ago the heavens were out of repair. So the Goddess of Works set to and prepared 36,501 blocks of precious jade, each 240 feet square by 120 feet in depth. Of these, however, she only used 36,500, and cast aside the single remaining block upon one of the celestial peaks.

This stone, under the process of preparation, had become as it were spiritualised. It could expand or contract. It could move. It was conscious of the existence of an external world, and it was hurt at not having been called upon to accomplish its divine mission.

One day a Buddhist and a Taoist priest, who happened to be passing that way, sat down for a while to rest, and forthwith noticed the disconsolate stone which lay there, no bigger than the pendant of a lady's fan. "Indeed, my friend, you are not wanting in spirituality," said the Buddhist priest to the stone, as he picked it up and laughingly held it forth upon the palm of his hand. "But we cannot be certain that you will ever prove to be of any real use; and, moreover, you lack an inscription, without which your destiny must necessarily remain unfulfilled." Thereupon he put the stone in his sleeve and rose to proceed on his journey.

"And what, if I may ask," inquired his companion, "do you intend to do with the stone you are thus carrying away?"

"I mean," replied the other, "to send it down to earth, to play its allotted part in the fortunes of a certain family now anxiously expecting its arrival. You see, when the Goddess of Works rejected this stone, it used to fill up its time by roaming about the heavens, until chance brought it alongside of a lovely crimson flower. Being struck with the great beauty of this flower, the stone remained there for some time, tending its *protégée* with the most loving care, and daily moistening its roots with the choicest nectar of the sky, until at length, yielding to the influence of disinterested love, the flower changed its form and became a most beautiful girl.

"'Dear stone,' cried the girl, in her new-found ecstasy of life, 'the moisture thou hast bestowed upon me here I will repay thee in our future state with my tears!'"

Ages afterwards, another priest, in search of light, saw this self-same stone lying in its old place, but with a record inscribed upon it—a record of how it had not been used to repair the heavens, and how it subsequently went down into the world of mortals, with a full description of all it did, and saw, and heard while in that state.

"Brother Stone," said the priest, "your record is not

one that deals with the deeds of heroes among men. It does not stir us with stories either of virtuous statesmen or of deathless patriots. It seems to be but a simple tale of the loves of maidens and youths, hardly important enough to attract the attention of the great busy world."

"Sir Priest," replied the stone, "what you say is indeed true; and what is more, my poor story is adorned by no rhetorical flourish nor literary art. Still, the world of mortals being what it is, and its complexion so far determined by the play of human passion, I cannot but think that the tale here inscribed may be of some use, if only to throw a further charm around the banquet hour, or to aid in dispelling those morning clouds which gather over last night's excess."

Thereupon the priest looked once more at the stone, and saw that it bore a plain unvarnished tale of—

> "*Beauty and anguish walking hand in hand*
> *The downward slope to death,*"

telling how a woman's artless love had developed into deep, destroying passion; and how from the thrall of a lost love one soul had been raised to a sublimer, if not a purer conception of man's mission upon earth. He therefore copied it out from beginning to end. Here it is:—

Under a dynasty which the author leaves unnamed, two brothers had greatly distinguished themselves by efficient service to the State. In return, they had been loaded with marks of Imperial favour. They had been created nobles of the highest rank. They had amassed wealth. The palaces assigned to them were near together in Peking, and there their immediate descendants were enjoying the fruits of ancestral success when this story opens. The brothers had each a son and heir; but at the date at which we are now, fathers and sons had all four passed away. The wife of one of the sons only was still alive, a hale and hearty old lady of about eighty years of age. Of her children, one was a daughter. She had married and gone away south, and *her* daughter, Tai-yü, is the heroine of this tale. The son of the old lady's second son and first cousin to Tai-yü is the hero, living with his grandmother. His name is Pao-yü.

The two noble families were now at the very zenith of wealth and power. Their palatial establishments were replete with every luxury. Feasting and theatricals were the order of the day, and, to crown all, Pao-yü's sister had been chosen to be one of the seventy-two wives allotted to the Emperor of China. No one stopped to think that human events are governed by an inevitable law of change. He who is mighty to-day shall be lowly to-morrow : the rich shall be made poor, and the poor rich. Or if any one, more thoughtful than the rest, did pause awhile in knowledge of the appointments of Heaven, he was fain to hope that the crash would not come, at any rate, in his own day.

Things were in this state when Tai-yü's mother died, and her father decided to place his motherless daughter under the care of her grandmother at Peking. Accompanied by her governess, the young lady set out at once for the capital, and reached her destination in safety. It is not necessary to dwell upon her beauty nor upon her genius, though both are minutely described in the original text. Suffice it to say that during the years which have elapsed since she first became known to the public, many brave men are said to have died for love of this entrancing heroine of fiction.

Tai-yü was received most kindly by all. Especially so by her grandmother, who shed bitter tears of sorrow over the premature death of Tai-yü's mother, her lost and favourite child. She was introduced to her aunts and cousins, and cousins and aunts, in such numbers that the poor girl must have wondered how ever she should remember all their names. Then they sat down and talked. They asked her all about her mother, and how she fell ill, and what medicine she took, and how she died and was buried, until the old grandmother wept again. "And what medicine do you take, my dear?" asked the old lady, seeing that Tai-yü herself seemed very delicate, and carried on her clear cheek a suspicious-looking flush.

"Oh, I have done nothing ever since I could eat," replied Tai-yü, "but take medicine of some kind or other. I have also seen all the best doctors, but they have not done me any particular good. When I was only three years of age, a nasty old priest came and wanted my parents to let me be a nun. He said it was the only way to save me."

"Oh, we will soon cure you here," said her grandmother, smiling. "We will make you well in no time."

Tai-yü was then taken to see more of her relatives, including her aunt, the mother of Pao-yü, who warned her against his peculiar temper, which she said was very uncertain and variable. "What! the one with the jade?" asked Tai-yü. "But we shall not be together," she immediately added, somewhat surprised at this rather unusual warning. "Oh yes, you will," said her aunt. "He is dreadfully spoilt by his grandmother, who allows him to have his own way in everything. Instead of being hard at work, as he ought to be by now, he idles away his time with the girls, thinking only how he can enjoy himself, without any idea of making a career or adding fresh lustre to the family name. Beware of him, I tell you."

The dinner-hour had now arrived, and after the meal Tai-yü was questioned as to the progress she had made in her studies. She was already deep in the mysteries of the Four Books, and it was agreed on all sides that she was far ahead of her cousins, when suddenly a noise was heard outside, and in came a most elegantly dressed youth about a year older than Tai-yü, wearing a cap lavishly adorned with pearls. His face was like the full autumn moon. His complexion like morning flowers in spring. Pencilled eyebrows, a well-cut shapely nose, and eyes like rippling waves were among the details which went to make up an unquestionably handsome exterior. Around his neck hung a curious piece of jade; and as soon as Tai-yü became fully conscious of his presence, a thrill passed through her delicate frame. She felt that somewhere or other she had looked upon that face before.

Pao-yü—for it was he—saluted his grandmother with great respect, and then went off to see his mother; and while he is absent it may be as well to say a few words about the young gentleman's early days.

Pao-yü, a name which means Precious Jade, was so called because he was born, to the great astonishment of everybody, with a small tablet of jade in his mouth—a beautifully bright mirror-like tablet, bearing a legend inscribed in the quaint old style of several thousand years ago. A family consultation resulted in a decision that this stone was some divine talisman, the purpose of which was not for the moment clear, but was doubtless to be revealed by and by. One thing was certain. As this tablet had come into the world with the child, so it should accompany him through life; and accordingly Pao-yü was accustomed to wear it suspended around his neck. The news of this singular phenomenon spread far and wide. Even Tai-yü had heard of it long before she came to take up her abode with the family.

And so Pao-yü grew up, a wilful, wayward boy. He was a bright, clever fellow and full of fun, but very averse to books. He declared, in fact, that he could not read at all unless he had as fellow-students a young lady on each side of him, to keep his brain clear! And when his father beat him, as was frequently the case, he would cry out, "Dear girl! dear girl!" all the time, in order, as he afterwards explained to his cousins, to take away the pain. Women, he argued, are made of water, with pellucid mobile minds, while men are mostly made of mud, mere lumps of uninformed clay.

By this time he had returned from seeing his mother and was formally introduced to Tai-yü. "Ha!" cried he, "I have seen her before somewhere. What makes her eyes so red? Indeed, cousin Tai-yü, we shall have to call you Cry-baby if you cry so much." Here some reference was made to his jade tablet, and this put him into an angry mood at once. None of his cousins had any, he said, and he was not going to wear his any more. A family scene ensued, during which Tai-yü went off to bed and cried herself to sleep.

Shortly after this, Pao-yü's mother's sister was compelled by circumstances to seek a residence in the capital. She brought with her a daughter, Pao-ch ai, another cousin to Pao-yü, but about a year older than he was ; and besides receiving a warm welcome, the two were invited to settle themselves comfortably down in the capacious family mansion of their relatives. Thus it was that destiny brought Pao-yü and his two cousins together under the same roof.

The three soon became fast friends. Pao-ch'ai had been carefully educated by her father, and was able to hold her own even against the accomplished Tai-yü. Pao-yü loved the society of either or both. He was always happy so long as he had a pretty girl by his side, and was, moreover, fascinated by the wit of these two young ladies in particular.

He had, however, occasional fits of moody depression, varied by discontent with his superfluous worldly surroundings. " In what am I better," he would say, " than a wallowing hog ? Why was I born and bred amid this splendid magnificence of wealth, instead of in some coldly furnished household where I could have enjoyed the pure communion of friends ? These silks and satins, these rich meats and choice wines, of what avail are they to this perishable body of mine ? O wealth ! O power ! I curse you both, ye cankerworms of my earthly career."

All these morbid thoughts, however, were speedily dispelled by the presence of his fair cousins, with whom, in fact, Pao-yü spent most of the time he ought to have devoted to his books. He was always running across to see either one or other of these young ladies, or meeting both of them in general assembly at his grandmother's. It was at a *tête-à-tête* with Pao-ch'ai that she made him show her his marvellous piece of jade, with the inscription, which she read as follows :—

> " *Lose me not, forget me not,*
> *Eternal life shall be thy lot.*"

The indiscretion of a slave-girl here let Pao-yü become aware that Pao-ch'ai herself possessed a wonderful gold amulet, upon which also were certain words inscribed ; and of course Pao-yü insisted on seeing it at once. On it was written—

> " *Let not this token wander from thy side,*
> *And youth perennial shall with thee abide.*"

In the middle of this interesting scene, Tai-yü walks in, and seeing how intimately the two are engaged, "hopes she doesn't intrude." But even in those early days the ring of her voice betrayed symptoms of that jealousy to which later on she succumbed. Meanwhile she almost monopolises the society of Pao-yü, and he, on his side, finds himself daily more and more attracted by the sprightly mischievous humour of the beautiful Tai-yü, as compared with the quieter and more orthodox loveliness of Pao-ch'ai. Pao-ch'ai does not know what jealousy means. She too loves to bandy words, exchange verses, or puzzle over conundrums with her mercurial cousin ; but she never allows her thoughts to wander towards him otherwise than is consistent with the strictest maidenly reserve.

Not so Tai-yü. She had been already for some time Pao-yü's chief companion when they were joined by Pao-ch'ai. She had come to regard the handsome boy almost as a part of herself, though not conscious of the fact until called upon to share his society with another. And so it was that although Pao-yü showed an open preference for herself, she still grudged the lesser attentions he paid to Pao-ch'ai. As often as not these same

attentions originated in an irresistible impulse to tease.
Pao-yü and Tai-yü were already lovers in so far that
they were always quarrelling; the more so, that their
quarrels invariably ended, as they should end, in the
renewal of love. As a rule, Tai-yü fell back upon the
ultima ratio of all women—tears; and of course Pao-yü,
who was not by any means wanting in chivalry, had no
alternative but to wipe them away. On one particular
occasion, Tai-yü declared that she would die; upon
which Pao-yü said that in that case he would become a
monk and devote his life to Buddha; but in this instance
it was he who shed the tears and she who had to wipe
them away.

All this time Tai-yü and Pao-ch'ai were on terms of
scrupulous courtesy. Tai-yü's father had recently died,
and her fortunes now seemed to be bound up more
closely than ever with those of the family in which she
lived. She had a handsome gold ornament given her to
match Pao-ch'ai's amulet, and the three young people
spent their days together, thinking only how to get most
enjoyment out of every passing hour. Sometimes, however, a shade of serious thought would darken Tai-yü's
moments of enforced solitude; and one day Pao-yü
surprised her in a secluded part of the garden, engaged
in burying flowers which had been blown down by the
wind, while singing the following lines :—

> " *Flowers fade and fly,*
> *and flying fill the sky;*
> *Their bloom departs, their perfume gone,*
> *yet who stands pitying by?*
> *And wandering threads of gossamer*
> *on the summer-house are seen,*
> *And falling catkins lightly dew-steeped*
> *strike the embroidered screen.*

A girl within the inner rooms,
  I mourn that spring is done,
A skein of sorrow binds my heart,
  and solace there is none.
I pass into the garden,
  and I turn to use my hoe,
Treading o'er fallen glories
  as I lightly come and go.
There are willow-sprays and flowers of elm.
  and these have scent enow,
I care not if the peach and plum
  are stripped from every bough.
The peach-tree and the plum-tree too
  next year may bloom again,
But next year, in the inner rooms,
  tell me, shall I remain ?
By the third moon new fragrant nests
  shall see the light of day,
New swallows flit among the beams,
  each on its thoughtless way.
Next year once more they'll seek their food
  among the painted flowers,
But I may go, and beams may go,
  and with them swallow bowers.
Three hundred days and sixty make
  a year, and therein lurk
Daggers of wind and swords of frost
  to do their cruel work.
How long will last the fair fresh flower
  which bright and brighter glows?
One morn its petals float away,
  but whither no one knows.
Gay blooming buds attract the eye,
  faded they're lost to sight;
Oh, let me sadly bury them
  beside these steps to-night!
Alone, unseen, I seize my hoe,
  with many a bitter tear;
They fall upon the naked stem
  and stains of blood appear.

The night-jar now has ceased to mourn,
      the dawn comes on apace,
I seize my hoe and close the gates,
      leaving the burying-place;
But not till sunbeams fleck the wall
      does slumber soothe my care,
The cold rain pattering on the pane
      as I lie shivering there.
You wonder that with flowing tears
      my youthful cheek is wet;
They partly rise from angry thoughts,
      and partly from regret.
Regret—that spring comes suddenly;
      anger—it cannot last,
No sound to herald its approach,
      or warn us that 'tis past.
Last night within the garden
      sad songs were faintly heard,
Sung, as I knew, by spirits,
      spirits of flower and bird.
We cannot keep them here with us,
      these much-loved birds and flowers,
They sing but for a season's space,
      and bloom a few short hours.
Ah! would that I on feathered wing
      might soar aloft and fly,
With flower spirits I would seek
      the confines of the sky.
But high in air
What grave is there?[1]
No, give me an embroidered bag
      wherein to lay their charms,
And Mother Earth, pure Mother Earth,
      shall hide them in her arms.
Thus those sweet forms which spotless came
      shall spotless go again,
Nor pass besmirched with mud and filth
      along some noisome drain.

---

[1] These two lines are short in the original.

> *Farewell, dear flowers, for ever now,*
> *thus buried as 'twas best,*
> *I have not yet divined when I*
> *with you shall sink to rest.*
> *I who can bury flowers like this*
> *a laughing-stock shall be;*
> *I cannot say in days to come*
> *what hands shall bury me.*
> *See how when spring begins to fail*
> *each opening flow'ret fades;*
> *So too there is a time of age*
> *and death for beauteous maids;*
> *And when the fleeting spring is gone,*
> *and days of beauty o'er,*
> *Flowers fall, and lovely maidens die,*
> *and both are known no more."*

Meanwhile, Pao-yü's father had received an appointment which took him away to a distance, the consequence being that life went on at home in a giddier round than usual. Nothing the old grandmother liked better than a picnic or a banquet—feasting, in fact, of some kind, with plenty of wine and mirth. But now, somehow or other, little things were always going wrong. In every pot of ointment the traditional fly was sure to make its appearance; in every sparkling goblet a bitter something would always bubble up. Money was not so plentiful as it had been, and there seemed to be always occurring some unforeseen drain upon the family resources. Various members of one or other of the two grand establishments get into serious trouble with the authorities. Murder, suicide, and robbery happen upon the premises. The climax of prosperity had been reached and the hour of decadence had arrived. Still all went merry as a marriage-bell, and Pao-yü and Tai-yü continued the agreeable pastime of love-making. In this they were further favoured by circumstances. Pao-ch'ai's mother gave up the apartments which had been assigned to her, and went to live in lodgings in the city, of course taking Pao-ch'ai with her. Some time previous to this, a slave-girl had casually remarked to Pao-yü that her young mistress, Tai-yü, was about to leave and go back again to the south. Pao-yü fainted on the spot, and was straightway carried off and put to bed. He bore the departure of Pao-ch'ai with composure. He could not even hear of separation from his beloved Tai-yü.

And she was already deeply in love with him. Long, long ago her faithful slave-girl had whispered into her ear the soft possibility of union with her cousin. Day and night she thought about Pao-yü, and bitterly regretted that she had now neither father nor mother on whom she could rely to effect the object that lay nearest to her heart. One evening, tired out under the ravages of the great passion, she flung herself down, without undressing, upon a couch to sleep. But she had hardly closed her eyes ere her grandmother and a whole bevy of aunts and cousins walked in to offer, as they said, their hearty congratulations. Tai-yü was astonished, and asked what on earth their congratulations meant; upon which it was explained to her that her father had married again, and that her stepmother had arranged for her a most eligible match, in consequence of which she was to leave for home immediately. With floods of tears Tai-yü entreated her grandmother not to send her away. She did not want to marry, and she would rather become a slave-girl at her grandmother's feet than fall in with the scheme proposed. She exhausted every argument, and even invoked the spirit of her dead mother to plead her cause; but the old lady was obdurate, and finally went away, saying that the arrangement would have to be carried out. Then Tai-yü saw no escape but the one last resource of all; when at that moment Pao-yü entered, and with a smile on his face began to offer her *his* congratulations too.

"Thank you, cousin," cried she, starting up and seizing him rudely by the arm. "Now I know you for the false, fickle creature you are!"

"What is the matter, dear girl?" inquired Pao-yü in amazement. "I was only glad for your sake that you had found a lover at last."

"And what lover do you think I could ever care to find now?" rejoined Tai-yü.

"Well," replied Pao-yü, "I should of course wish it to be myself. I consider you indeed mine already; and if you think of the way I have always behaved towards you . . ."

"What!" said Tai-yü, partly misunderstanding his words, "can it be you after all? and do you really wish me to remain with you?"

"You shall see with your own eyes," answered Pao-yü, "even into the inmost recesses of my heart, and then perhaps you will believe."

Thereupon he drew a knife, and plunging it into his body, ripped himself open so as to expose his heart to view. With a shriek Tai-yü tried to stay his hand, and felt herself drenched with the flow of fresh warm blood; when suddenly Pao-yü uttered a loud groan, and crying out, "Great heaven, my heart is gone!" fell senseless to the ground. "Help! help!" screamed Tai-yü; "he is dying! he is dying!" "Wake up! wake up!" said Tai-yü's maid; "whatever has given you nightmare like this?"

So Tai-yü waked up and found that she had had a

bad dream. But she had something worse than that. She had a bad illness to follow; and strange to say, Pao-yü was laid up at the same time. The doctor came and felt her pulse—both pulses, in fact—and shook his head, and drank a cup of tea, and said that Tai-yü's vital principle wanted nourishment, which it would get out of a prescription he then and there wrote down. As to Pao-yü, he was simply suffering from a fit of temporary indigestion.

So Tai-yü got better, and Pao-yü recovered his spirits. His father had returned home, and he was once more obliged to make some show of work, and consequently had fewer hours to spend in the society of his cousin. He was now a young man, and the question of his marriage began to occupy a foremost place in the minds of his parents and grandmother. Several names were proposed, one especially by his father; but it was finally agreed that it was unnecessary to go far afield to secure a fitting bride. It was merely a choice between the two charming young ladies who had already shared so much in his daily life. But the difficulty lay precisely there. Where each was perfection it became invidious to choose. In another famous Chinese novel, already described, a similar difficulty is got over in this way—the hero marries both. Here, however, the family elders were distracted by rival claims. By their gentle, winning manners, Pao-ch'ai and Tai-yü had made themselves equally beloved by all the inmates of these two noble houses, from the venerable grandmother down to the meanest slave-girl. Their beauty was of different styles, but at the bar of man's opinion each would probably have gained an equal number of votes. Tai-yü was undoubtedly the cleverer of the two, but Pao-ch'ai had better health ; and in the judgment of those with whom the decision rested, health carried the day. It was arranged that Pao-yü was to marry Pao-ch'ai.

This momentous arrangement was naturally made in secret. Various preliminaries would have to be gone through before a verbal promise could give place to formal betrothal. And it is a well-ascertained fact that secrets can only be kept by men, while this one was confided to at least a dozen women. Consequently, one night when Tai-yü was ill and alone in her room, yearning for the love that had already been contracted away to another, she heard two slave-girls outside whispering confidences, and fancied she caught Pao-yü's name. She listened again, and this time without doubt, for she heard them say that Pao-yü was engaged to marry a lady of good family and many accomplishments. Just then a parrot called out, "Here's your mistress : pour out the tea !" which frightened the slave-girls horribly ; and they forthwith separated, one of them running inside to attend upon Tai-yü herself. She finds her young mistress in a very agitated state, but Tai-yü is always ailing now.

This time she was seriously ill. She ate nothing. She was racked by a dreadful cough. Even a Chinese doctor could now hardly fail to see that she was far advanced in a decline. But none knew that the sickness of her body had originated in sickness of the heart.

One night she grew rapidly worse and worse, and lay to all appearances dying. A slave-girl ran to summon her grandmother, while several others remained in the room talking about Pao-yü and his intended marriage. "It was all off," said one of them. "His grandmother would not agree to the young lady chosen by his father.

She had already made her own choice—of another young lady who lives in the family, and of whom we are all very fond." The dying girl heard these words, and it then flashed across her that after all she must herself be the bride intended for Pao-yü. "For if not I," argued she, "who can it possibly be?" Thereupon she rallied as it were by a supreme effort of will, and, to the great astonishment of all, called for a drink of tea. Those who had come expecting to see her die were now glad to think that her youth might ultimately prevail.

So Tai-yü got better once more; but only better, not well. For the sickness of the soul is not to be cured by drugs. Meanwhile, an event occurred which for the time being threw everything else into the shade. *Pao-yü lost his jade tablet.* After changing his clothes, he had forgotten to put it on, and had left it lying upon his table. But when he sent to fetch it, it was gone. A search was instituted high and low, without success. The precious talisman was missing. No one dared tell his grandmother and face the old lady's wrath. As to Pao-yü himself, he treated the matter lightly. Gradually, however, a change came over his demeanour. He was often absent-minded. At other times his tongue would run away with him, and he talked nonsense. At length he got so bad that it became imperative to do something. So his grandmother had to be told. Of course she was dreadfully upset, but she made a move in the right direction, and offered an enormous reward for its recovery. The result was that within a few days the reward was claimed. But in the interval the tablet seemed to have lost much of its striking brilliancy; and a closer inspection showed it to be in reality nothing more than a clever imitation. This was a crushing disappointment to all. Pao-yü's illness was increasing day by day. His father had received another appointment in the provinces, and it was eminently desirable that Pao-yü's marriage should take place previous to his departure. The great objection to hurrying on the ceremony was that the family were in mourning. Among other calamities which had befallen of late, the young lady in the palace had died, and her influence at Court was gone. Still, everything considered, it was deemed advisable to solemnise the wedding without delay. Pao-yü's father, little as he cared for the character of his only son, had been greatly shocked at the change which he now saw. A worn, haggard face, with sunken, lack-lustre eyes; rambling, inconsequent talk— this was the heir in whom the family hopes were centred. The old grandmother, finding that doctors were of little avail, had even called in a fortune-teller, who said pretty much what he was wanted to say, viz., that Pao-yü should marry some one with a golden destiny to help him on.

So the chief actors in the tragedy about to be enacted had to be consulted at last. They began with Pao-ch'ai, for various reasons; and she, like a modest, well-bred maiden, received her mother's commands in submissive silence. Further, from that day she ceased to mention Pao-yü's name. With Pao-yü, however, it was a different thing altogether. His love for Tai-yü was a matter of some notoriety, especially with the slave-girls, one of whom even went so far as to tell his mother that his heart was set upon marrying her whom the family had felt obliged to reject. It was therefore hardly doubtful how he would receive the news of his betrothal to Pao-ch'ai; and as in his present state of health the

consequences could not be ignored, it was resolved to
have recourse to stratagem. So the altar was prepared,
and naught remained but to draw the bright death across
the victim's throat.

In the short time which intervened, the news was
broken to Tai-yü in an exceptionally cruel manner.
She heard by accident in conversation with a slave-girl
in the garden that Pao-yü was to marry Pao-ch'ai. The
poor girl felt as if a thunderbolt had pierced her brain.
Her whole frame quivered beneath the shock. She
turned to go back to her room, but half unconsciously
followed the path that led to Pao-yü's apartments.
Hardly noticing the servants in attendance, she almost
forced her way in, and stood in the presence of her
cousin. He was sitting down, and he looked up and
laughed a foolish laugh when he saw her enter; but
he did not rise, and he did not invite her to be seated.
Tai-yü sat down without being asked, and without a
word spoken on either side. And the two sat there, and
stared and leered at each other, until they both broke
out into wild delirious laughter, the senseless crazy
laughter of the madhouse. "What makes you ill,
cousin?" asked Tai-yü, when the first burst of their
dreadful merriment had subsided. "I am in love with
Tai-yü," he replied; and then they both went off into
louder screams of laughter than before.

At this point the slave-girls thought it high time to
interfere, and, after much more laughing and nodding of
heads, Tai-yü was persuaded to go away. She set off to
run back to her own room, and sped along with a newly
acquired strength. But just as she was nearing the door,
she was seen to fall, and the terrified slave-girl who rushed
to pick her up found her with her mouth full of blood.

By this time all formalities have been gone through and the wedding day is fixed. It is not to be a grand wedding, but of course there must be a trousseau. Pao-ch'ai sometimes weeps, she scarcely knows why; but preparations for the great event of her life leave her, fortunately, very little leisure for reflection. Tai-yü is in bed, and, but for a faithful slave-girl, alone. Nobody thinks much about her at this juncture; when the wedding is over she is to receive a double share of attention. One morning she makes the slave-girl bring her all her poems and various other relics of the happy days gone by. She turns them over and over between her thin and wasted fingers until finally she commits them all to the flames. The effort is too much for her, and the slave-girl in despair hurries across to the grandmother's for assistance. She finds the whole place deserted, but a moment's thought reminds her that the old lady is doubtless with Pao-yü. So thither she makes her way as fast as her feet can carry her, only, however, to be still further amazed at finding the rooms shut up, and no one there. Utterly confused, and not knowing what to make of these unlooked-for circumstances, she is about to run back to Tai-yü's room, when to her great relief she espies a fellow-servant in the distance, who straightway informs her that it is Pao-yü's wedding-day, and that he had moved into another suite of apartments. And so it was. Pao-yü had joyfully agreed to the proposition that he should marry his cousin, for he had been skilfully given to understand that the cousin in question was Tai-yü. And now the much wished-for hour had arrived. The veiled bride, accompanied by the very slave-girl who had long ago escorted her from the south, alighted from her sedan-chair at Pao-yü's door. The wedding march was played, and the young couple proceeded to the final ceremony of worship, which made them irrevocably man and wife. Then, as is customary upon such occasions, Pao-yü raised his bride's veil. For a moment he seemed as though suddenly turned into stone, as he stood there speechless and motionless, with fixed eyes gazing upon a face he had little expected to behold. Meanwhile, Pao-ch'ai retired into an inner apartment; and then, for the first time, Pao-yü found his voice.

"Am I dreaming?" cried he, looking round upon his assembled relatives and friends.

"No, you are married," replied several of those nearest to him. "Take care; your father is outside. He arranged it all."

"Who was that?" said Pao-yü, with averted head, pointing in the direction of the door through which Pao-ch'ai had disappeared.

"It was Pao-ch'ai, your wife . . ."

"Tai-yü, you mean; Tai-yü is my wife," shrieked he, interrupting them; "I want Tai-yü! I want Tai-yü! Oh, bring us together, and save us both!" Here he broke down altogether. Thick sobs choked his further utterance, until relief came in a surging flood of tears.

All this time Tai-yü was dying, dying beyond hope of recall. She knew that the hour of release was at hand, and she lay there quietly waiting for death. Every now and again she swallowed a teaspoonful of broth, but gradually the light faded out of her eyes, and the slave-girl, faithful to the last, felt that her young mistress's fingers were rapidly growing cold. At that moment, Tai-yü's lips were seen to move, and she was distinctly heard to say, "O Pao-yü, Pao-yü . . ." Those words were her last.

Just then, breaking in upon the hushed moments which succeed dissolution, sounds of far-off music were borne along upon the breeze. The slave-girl crept stealthily to the door, and strained her ear to listen ; but she could hear nothing save the soughing of the wind as it moaned fitfully through the trees.

But the bridegroom himself had already entered the valley of the dark shadow. Pao-yü was very ill. He raved and raved about Tai-yü, until at length Pao-ch'ai, who had heard the news, took upon herself the painful task of telling him she was already dead. "Dead ?" cried Pao-yü, "dead ?" and with a loud groan he fell back upon the bed insensible. A darkness came before his eyes, and he seemed to be transported into a region which was unfamiliar to him. Looking about, he saw some one advancing towards him, and immediately called out to the stranger to be kind enough to tell him where he was. "You are on the road to the next world," replied the man ; "but your span of life is not yet complete, and you have no business here." Pao-yü explained that he had come in search of Tai-yü, who had lately died ; to which the man replied that Tai-yü's soul had already gone back to its home in the pure serene. "And if you would see her again," added the man, "return to your duties upon earth. Fulfil your destiny there, chasten your understanding, nourish the divinity that is within you, and you may yet hope to meet her once more." The man then flung a stone at him and struck him over the heart, which so frightened Pao-yü that he turned to retrace his steps. At that moment he heard himself loudly called by name ; and opening his eyes, saw his mother and grandmother standing by the side of his bed.

They had thought that he was gone, and were overjoyed at seeing him return to life, even though it was
the same life as before, clouded with the great sorrow of
unreason. For now they could always hope ; and when
they saw him daily grow stronger and stronger in bodily
health, it seemed that ere long even his mental equilibrium might be restored. The more so that he had
ceased to mention Tai-yü's name, and treated Pao-ch'ai
with marked kindness and respect.

All this time the fortunes of the two grand families are
sinking from bad to worse. Pao-yü's uncle is mixed up
in an act of disgraceful oppression ; while his father,
at his new post, makes the foolish endeavour to be an
honest incorrupt official. He tries to put his foot down
upon the system of bribery which prevails, but succeeds
only in getting himself recalled and impeached for maladministration of affairs. The upshot of all this is that
an Imperial decree is issued confiscating the property and
depriving the families of their hereditary rank. Besides
this, the lineal representatives are to be banished ; and
within the walls which have been so long sacred to mirth
and merrymaking, consternation now reigns supreme.
"O high Heaven," cries Pao-yü's father, as his brother
and nephew start for their place of banishment, " that
the fortunes of our family should fall like this ! "

Of all, perhaps the old grandmother felt the blow
most severely. She had lived for eighty-three years in
affluence, accustomed to the devotion of her children
and the adulation of friends. But now money was
scarce, and the voice of flattery unheard. The courtiers
of prosperous days forgot to call, and even the servants
deserted at their posts. And so it came about that the
old lady fell ill, and within a few days was lying upon

her death-bed. She spoke a kind word to all, except to Pao-ch'ai. For her she had only a sigh, that fate had linked her with a husband whose heart was buried in the grave. So she died, and there was a splendid funeral, paid for out of funds raised at the pawnshop. Pao-ch'ai appeared in white; and among the flowers which were gathered around the bier, she was unanimously pronounced to be the fairest blossom of all.

Then other members of the family die, and Pao-yü relapses into a condition as critical as ever. He is in fact at the point of death, when a startling announcement restores him again to consciousness. A Buddhist priest is at the outer gate, and he has brought back Pao-yü's lost tablet of jade. There was, of course, great excitement on all sides; but the priest refused to part with the jade until he had got the promised reward. And where now was it possible to raise such a sum as that, and at a moment's notice? Still it was felt that the tablet must be recovered at all costs. Pao-yü's life depended on it, and he was the sole hope of the family. So the priest was promised his reward, and the jade was conveyed into the sick-room. But when Pao-yü clutched it in his eager hand, he dropped it with a loud cry and fell back gasping upon the bed.

In a few minutes Pao-yü's breathing became more and more distressed, and a servant ran out to call in the priest, in the hope that something might yet be done. The priest, however, had disappeared, and by this time Pao-yü had ceased to breathe.

Immediately upon the disunion of body and soul which mortals call death, the spirit of Pao-yü set off on its journey to the Infinite, led by a Buddhist priest. Just then a voice called out and said that Tai-yü was awaiting him, and at that moment many familiar faces crowded round him, but as he gazed at them in recognition, they changed into grinning goblins. At length he reached a spot where there was a beautiful crimson flower in an enclosure, so carefully tended that neither bees nor butterflies were allowed to settle upon it. It was a flower, he was told, which had been to fulfil a mission upon earth, and had recently returned to the Infinite. He was now taken to see Tai-yü. A bamboo screen which hung before the entrance to a room was raised, and there before him stood his heart's idol, his lost Tai-yü. Stretching forth his hands, he was about to speak to her, when suddenly the screen was hastily dropped. The priest gave him a shove, and he fell backwards, awaking as though from a dream.

Once more he had regained a new hold upon life; once more he had emerged from the very jaws of death. This time he was a changed man. He devoted himself to reading for the great public examination, in the hope of securing the much coveted degree of Master of Arts. Nevertheless, he talks little, and seems to care less, about the honours and glory of this world; and what is stranger than all, he appears to have very much lost his taste for the once fascinating society of women. For a time he seems to be under the spell of a religious craze, and is always arguing with Pao-ch'ai upon the advantages of devoting one's life to the service of Buddha. But shortly before the examination he burned all the books he had collected which treated of immortality and a future state, and concentrated every thought upon the great object before him.

At length the day comes, and Pao-yü, accompanied by a nephew who is also a candidate, prepares to enter the arena. His father was away from home. He had gone southwards to take the remains of the grandmother and of Tai-yü back to their ancestral burying-ground. So Pao-yü first goes to take leave of his mother, and she addresses to him a few parting words, full of encouragement and hope. Then Pao-yü falls upon his knees, and implores her pardon for all the trouble he has caused her. "I can only trust," he added, "that I shall now be successful, and that you, dear mother, will be happy." And then amid tears and good wishes, the two young men set out for the examination-hall, where, with several thousand other candidates, they are to remain for some time immured.

The hours and days speed apace, full of arduous effort to those within, of anxiety to those without. At last the great gates are thrown wide open, and the vast crowd of worn-out, weary students bursts forth, to meet the equally vast crowd of eager, expectant friends. In the crush that ensues, Pao-yü and his nephew lose sight of each other, and the nephew reaches home first. There the feast of welcome is already spread, and the wine-kettles are put to the fire. So every now and again somebody runs out to see if Pao-yü is not yet in sight. But the time passes and he comes not. Fears as to his personal safety begin to be aroused, and messengers are sent out in all directions. Pao-yü is nowhere to be found. The night comes and goes. The next day and the next day, and still no Pao-yü. He has disappeared without leaving behind him the faintest clue to his whereabouts. Meanwhile, the list of successful candidates is published, and Pao-yü's name stands seventh on the list. His nephew has the 130th place. What a triumph for the family, and what rapture would have been theirs, but for the mysterious absence of Pao-yü.

Thus their joy was shaded by sorrow, until hope, springing eternal, was unexpectedly revived. Pao-yü's winning essay had attracted the attention of the Emperor, and his Majesty issued an order for the writer to appear at Court. An Imperial order may not be lightly disregarded; and it was fervently hoped by the family that by these means Pao-yü might be restored to them. This, in fact, was all that was wanting now to secure the renewed prosperity of the two ancient houses. The tide of events had set favourably at last. Those who had been banished to the frontier had greatly distinguished themselves against the banditti who ravaged the country round about. There was Pao-yü's success and his nephew's; and above all, the gracious clemency of the Son of Heaven. Free pardons were granted, confiscated estates were returned. The two families basked again in the glow of Imperial favour. Pao-ch'ai was about to become a mother; the ancestral line might be continued after all. But Pao-yü, where was he? That remained a mystery still, against which even the Emperor's mandate proved to be of no avail.

It was on his return journey that Pao-yü's father heard of the success and disappearance of his son. Torn by conflicting emotions he hurried on, in his haste to reach home and aid in unravelling the secret of Pao-yü's hiding-place. One moonlight night, his boat lay anchored alongside the shore, which a storm of the previous day had wrapped in a mantle of snow. He was sitting writing at a table, when suddenly, through the half-open door, advancing towards him over the bow of the boat, his silhouette sharply defined against the surrounding snow, he saw the figure of a shaven-headed Buddhist priest. The priest knelt down, and struck his head four times upon the ground, and then, without a word, turned back to join two other priests who were awaiting him. The three vanished as imperceptibly as they had come; before, indeed, the astonished father was able to realise that he had been, for the last time, face to face with Pao-yü!

CHAPTER II

THE EMPERORS K'ANG HSI AND CH'IEN LUNG

THE second Emperor of the Manchu dynasty, known to the world by his year-title K'ANG HSI, succeeded to the throne in 1662 when he was only eight years of age, and six years later he took up the reins of government. Fairly tall and well-proportioned, he loved all manly exercises and devoted three months annually to hunting. Large bright eyes lighted up his face, which was pitted with small-pox. Contemporary observers vie in praising his wit, understanding, and liberality of mind. Indefatigable in government, he kept a careful watch on his Ministers, his love for the people leading him to prefer economy to taxation. He was personally frugal, yet on public works he would lavish large sums. He patronised the Jesuits, whom he employed in surveying the empire, in astronomy, and in casting cannon; though latterly he found it necessary to impose restrictions on their propagandism. In spite of war and rebellion, which must have encroached seriously upon his time, he found leisure to initiate and carry out, with the aid of the leading scholars of the day, several of the greatest literary enterprises the world has ever seen. The chief of these are (1) the *K'ang Hsi Tzŭ Tien*, the great standard dictionary of the Chinese language; (2) the *P'ei Wên Yün Fu*, a huge concordance to all literature, bound up in forty-four large closely-printed volumes ; (3) the *P'ien Tzŭ Lei P'ien*, a similar work, with a different arrangement, bound up in thirty-six large volumes ; (4) the *Yüan Chien Lei Han*, an encyclopædia, bound up in forty-four volumes ; and (5) the *T'u Shu Chi Ch'êng*, a profusely illustrated encyclopædia, in 1628 volumes of about 200 pages to each. To the above must be added a considerable collection of literary remains, in prose and verse, which, of course, were actually the Emperor's own work. It cannot be said that any of these remains are of a high order, or are familiar to the public at large, with a single and trifling exception. The so-called Sacred Edict is known from one end of China to the other. It originally consisted of sixteen moral maxims delivered in 1670 under the form of an edict by the Emperor K'ang Hsi. His Majesty himself had just reached the mature age of sixteen. He had then probably discovered that men's morals were no longer what they had been in the days of "ancient kings," and with boyish earnestness he made a kindly effort to do something for the people whose welfare was destined to be for so many years to come his chief and most absorbing care. The maxims are commonplace enough, but for the sake of the great Emperor who loved his "children" more than himself they have been exalted into utterances almost divine. Here are the first, seventh, and eleventh maxims, as specimens :—

"Pay great attention to filial piety and to brotherly obedience, in order to give due weight to human relationships."

"Discard strange doctrines, in order to glorify the orthodox teaching."

"Educate your sons and younger brothers, in order to hinder them from doing what is wrong."

K'ang Hsi died in 1722, after completing a full cycle of sixty years as occupant of the Dragon Throne. His son and successor, Yung Chêng, caused one hundred picked scholars to submit essays enlarging upon the maxims of his father, and of these the sixteen best were chosen, and in 1724 it was enacted that they should be publicly read to the people on the 1st and 15th of each month in every city and town in the empire. This law is still in force. Subsequently, the sixteen essays were paraphrased into easy colloquial; and now the maxims, the essays, and the paraphrase, together make up a volume which may be roughly said to contain the whole duty of man.

In 1735 the Emperor Yung Chêng died, and was succeeded by his fourth son, who reigned as CH'IEN LUNG. An able ruler, with an insatiable thirst for knowledge, and an indefatigable administrator, he rivals his grandfather's fame as a sovereign and a patron of letters. New editions of important historical works and of encyclopædias were issued by Imperial order, and under the superintendence of the Emperor himself. In 1772 there was a general search for all literary works worthy of preservation, and ten years later a voluminous collection of these was published, embracing many rare books taken from the great encyclopædia of the Emperor Yung Lo. A descriptive catalogue of the Imperial Library, containing 3460 works arranged under the four heads of Classics, History, Philosophy, and General Literature, was drawn up in 1772–1790. It gives the history of each work, which is also criticised. The vastness of this catalogue led to the publication of an abridgment, which omits all works not actually preserved in the Library. The personal writings of this Emperor are very voluminous. They consist of a general collection containing a variety of notes on current or ancient topics, prefaces to books, and the like, and also of a collection of poems. Of these last, those produced between 1736 and 1783 were published, and reached the almost incredible total of 33,950 separate pieces. It need hardly be added that nearly all are very short. Even thus the output must be considered a record, apart from the fact that during the reign there was a plentiful supply both of war and rebellion. Burmah and Nepaul were forced to pay tribute; Chinese supremacy was established in Tibet; and Kuldja and Kashgaria were added to the empire. In 1795, on completing a cycle of sixty years of power, the Emperor abdicated in favour of his son, and three years later he died.

His Majesty's poetry, though artificially correct, was mediocre enough. The following stanza, "On Hearing the Cicada," is a good example, conforming as it does to all the rules of versification, but wanting in that one feature which makes the "stop-short" what it is, viz., that "although the words end, the sense still goes on":—

> " *The season is a month behind*
> *in this land of northern breeze,*
> *When first I hear the harsh cicada*
> *shrieking through the trees.*
> *I look, but cannot mark its form*
> *amid the foliage fair,—*
> *Naught but a flash of shadow*
> *which goes flitting here and there.*"

Here, instead of being carried away into some suggested train of thought, the reader is fairly entitled to ask "What then?"

The following is a somewhat more spirited production. It is a song written by Ch'ien Lung, to be inserted and sung in a play entitled " Picking up Gold," by a beggar who is fortunate enough to stumble across a large nugget :—

" *A brimless cap of felt stuck on my head;*
No coat,—a myriad-patchwork quilt instead;
In my hand a bamboo staff;
Hempen sandals on my feet;
As I slouch along the street,
' *Pity the poor beggar,*' *to the passers-by I call,*
Hoping to obtain broken food and dregs of wine.
Then when night's dark shadows fall,
Oh merrily, Oh merrily I laugh,
Drinking myself to sleep, sheltered in some old shrine.

Black, black, the clouds close round on every side;
White, white, the gossamer flakes fly far and wide.
Ai-yah! is't jade that sudden decks the eaves?
With silver tiles meseems the streets are laid.
Oh, in what glorious garb Nature's arrayed,
Displaying fairy features on a lovely face!
But stay! the night is drawing on apace;
Nothing remains my homeward track to guide;
See how the feathered snow weighs down the palm-tree leaves!

I wag my head and clap my hands, ha! ha!
I clap my hands and wag my head, ha! ha!
There in the drift a lump half-sunken lies;
The beggar's luck has turned up trumps at last!
O gold!—for thee dear relatives will part,
Dear friends forget their hours of friendship past,
Husband and wife tear at each other's heart,
Father and son sever life's closest ties;
For thee, the ignoble thief all rule and law defies.

What men of this world most adore is gold;
The devils deep in hell the dross adore;
Where gold is there the gods are in its wake.
Now shall I never more produce the snake;

Stand begging where the cross-roads meet no more;
Or shiver me to sleep in the rush hut, dank and cold;
Or lean against the rich or poor man's door.
Away my yellow bowl, my earthen jar!
See, thus I rend my pouch and hurl my gourd afar!

An official hat and girdle I shall wear,
And this shrunk shank in boots with pipeclayed soles encase;
On fête and holiday how jovial I shall be,
Joining my friends in the tavern or the tea-shop o'er their tea;
Swagger, swagger, swagger, with such an air and grace.
Sometimes a sleek steed my 'Excellence' will bear;
Or in a sedan I shall ride at ease,
One servant with my hat-box close behind the chair,
While another on his shoulders carries my valise."

. . . . . .

CHAPTER III

CLASSICAL AND MISCELLANEOUS LITERATURE
—POETRY

FOREMOST among the scholars of the present dynasty stands the name of KU CHIANG (1612–1681). Remaining faithful to the Mings after their final downfall, he changed his name to Ku Yen-wu, and for a long time wandered about the country in disguise. He declined to serve under the Manchus, and supported himself by farming. A profound student, it is recorded that in his wanderings he always carried about with him several horse-loads of books to consult whenever his memory might be at fault. His writings on the Classics, history, topography, and poetry are still highly esteemed. To foreigners he is best known as the author of the *Jih Chih Lu*, which contains his notes, chiefly on the Classics and history, gathered during a course of reading which extended over thirty years. He also wrote many works upon the ancient sounds and rhymes.

CHU YUNG-SHUN (1617–1689) was delicate as a child, and his mother made him practise the Taoist art of prolonging life indefinitely, which seems to be nothing more than a system of regular breathing with deep inspirations. He was a native of a town in Kiangsu, at the sack of which, by the conquering Tartars, his father perished rather than submit to the new dynasty. In consequence of his father's death he steadily declined to enter upon a public career, and gave up his life to study and teaching. He was the author of commentaries upon the Great Learning and the Doctrine of the Mean, and of other works; but none of these is so famous as his Family Maxims, a little book which, on account of the author's name, has often been attributed to the great commentator Chu Hsi. The piquancy of these maxims disappears in translation, owing as they do much more to literary form than to subject-matter. Here are two specimens :—

"Forget the good deeds you have done ; remember the kindnesses you have received."

"Mind your own business, follow out your destiny, live in accord with the age, and leave the rest to God. He who can do this is near indeed."

His own favourite saying was—

"To know what ought to be known, and to do what ought to be done, that is enough. There is no time for anything else."

Three days before his death he struggled into the ancestral hall, and there before the family tablets called the spirits of his forefathers to witness that he had never injured them by word or deed.

LAN TING-YÜAN (1680–1733), better known as Lan Lu-chou, devoted himself as a youth to poetry, literature, and political economy. He accompanied his brother to Formosa as military secretary, and his account of the expedition attracted public attention. Recommended to the Emperor, he became magistrate of P'u-lin, and distinguished himself as much by his just and incorrupt administration as by his literary abilities. He managed, however, to make enemies among his superior officers, and within three years he was impeached for insubordination and thrown into prison. His case was subsequently laid before the Emperor, who not only set him free, but appointed him to be Prefect at Canton, bestowing upon him at the same time some valuable medicine, an autograph copy of verses, a sable robe, some joss-stick, and other coveted marks of Imperial favour. But all was in vain. He died of a broken heart one month after taking up his post. His complete works have been published in twenty small octavo volumes, of which works perhaps the best known of all is a treatise on the proper training of women, which fills two of the above volumes. This is divided under four heads, namely, Virtue, Speech, Personal Appearance, and Duty, an extended education in the intellectual sense not coming within the writer's purview. The chapters are short, and many of them are introduced by some ancient aphorism, forming a convenient peg upon which to hang a moral lesson, copious extracts being made from the work of the Lady Pan of the Han dynasty. A few lines from his preface may be interesting :—

"Good government of the empire depends upon morals; correctness of morals depends upon right ordering of the family; and right ordering of the family depends upon the wife. . . . If the curtain which divides the men from the women is too thin to keep them apart, misfortune will come to the family and to the State. Purification of morals, from the time of the creation until now, has always come from women. Women are not all alike; some are good and some are bad. For bringing them to a proper uniformity there is nothing like education. In old days both boys and girls were educated . . . but now the books used no longer exist, and we know not the details of the system. . . . The education of a woman is not like that of her husband, which may be said to continue daily all through life. For he can always take up a classic or a history, or familiarise himself with the works of miscellaneous writers ; whereas a woman's education does not extend beyond ten years, after which she takes upon herself the manifold responsibilities of a household. She is then no longer able to give her undivided attention to books, and cannot investigate thoroughly, the result being that her learning is not sufficiently extensive to enable her to grasp principles. She is, as it were, carried away upon a flood, without hope of return, and it is difficult for her to make any use of the knowledge she has acquired. Surely then a work on the education of women is much to be desired."

This is how one phase of female virtue is illustrated by anecdote :—

"A man having been killed in a brawl, two brothers were arrested for the murder and brought to trial. Each one swore that he personally was the murderer, and that the other was innocent. The judge was thus unable to decide the case, and referred it to the Prince. The Prince bade him summon their mother, and ask which of them had done the deed. 'Punish the younger,' she replied through a flood of tears. 'People are usually more fond of the younger,' observed the judge ; 'how is it you wish me to punish him ?' 'He is my own child,' answered the woman ; 'the elder is the son of my husband's first wife. When my husband died he begged me to take care of the boy, and I promised I would. If now I were to let the elder be punished while

the younger escaped, I should be only gratifying my
private feelings and wronging the dead. I have no
alternative.' And she wept on until her clothes were
drenched with tears. Meanwhile the judge reported to
the Prince, and the latter, astonished at her magnanimity,
pardoned both the accused."

Two more of the above twenty volumes are devoted
to the most remarkable of the criminal cases tried by
him during his short magisterial career. An extract
from the preface (1729) to his complete works, penned
by an ardent admirer, will give an idea of the estimation
in which these are held :—

"My master's judicial capacity was of a remarkably
high order, as though the mantle of Pao Hsiao-su [1] had
descended upon him. In very difficult cases he would
investigate dispassionately and calmly, appearing to
possess some unusual method for worming out the
truth ; so that the most crafty lawyers and the most
experienced scoundrels, whom no logic could entangle
and no pains intimidate, upon being brought before
him, found themselves deserted by their former cunning,
and confessed readily without waiting for the application of torture. I, indeed, have often wondered how
it is that torture is brought into requisition so much
in judicial investigations. For, under the influence of
the 'three wooden instruments,' what evidence is there
which cannot be elicited ?—to say nothing of the danger
of a mistake and the unutterable injury thus inflicted
upon the departed spirits in the realms below. Now,
my master, in investigating and deciding cases, was
fearful only lest his people should not obtain a full and
fair hearing; he, therefore, argued each point with them

---

[1] A Solomonic judge under the Sung dynasty.

quietly and kindly until they were thoroughly committed to a certain position, with no possibility of backing out, and then he decided the case upon its merits as thus set forth. By such means, those who were bambooed had no cause for complaint, while those who were condemned to die died without resenting their sentence ; the people were unable to deceive him, and they did not even venture to make the attempt. Thus did he carry out the Confucian doctrine of respecting popular feeling ;[1] and were all judicial officers to decide cases in the same careful and impartial manner, there would not be a single injured suitor under the canopy of heaven."

The following is a specimen case dealing with the evil effects of superstitious doctrines :—

"The people of the Ch'ao-yang district are great on bogies, and love to talk of spirits and Buddhas. The gentry and their wives devote themselves to Ta Tien, but the women generally of the neighbourhood flock in crowds to the temples to burn incense and adore Buddha, forming an unbroken string along the road. Hence, much ghostly and supernatural nonsense gets spread about; and hence it was that the Hou-t'ien sect came to flourish. I know nothing of the origin of this sect. It was started amongst the Ch'ao-yang people by two men, named Yen and Chou respectively, who said that they had been instructed by a white-bearded Immortal, and who, when an attempt to arrest them was made by a predecessor in office, absconded with their families and remained in concealment. By and by, however, they came back, calling themselves the White Lily or the White Aspen sect. I imagine that White

---

[1] " In hearing litigations, I am like any other body. What is necessary is to cause the people to have no litigations " (Legge).

Lily was the real designation, the alteration in name being simply made to deceive. Their 'goddess' was Yen's own wife, and she pretended to be able to summon wind and bring down rain, enslave bogies and exorcise spirits, being assisted in her performances by her paramour, a man named Hu, who called himself the Immortal of Pencil Peak. He used to aid in writing out charms, spirting water, curing diseases, and praying for heirs; and he could enable widows to hold converse with their departed husbands. The whole district was taken in by these people, and went quite mad about them, people travelling from afar to worship them as spiritual guides, and, with many offerings of money, meats, and wines, enrolling themselves as their humble disciples, until one would have said it was market-day in the neighbourhood. I heard of their doings one day as I was returning from the prefectural city. They had already established themselves in a large building to the north of the district; they had opened a preaching-hall, collected several hundred persons together, and for the two previous days had been availing themselves of the services of some play-actors to sing and perform at their banquets. I immediately sent off constables to arrest them; but the constables were afraid of incurring the displeasure of the spirits and being seized by the soldiers of the infernal regions, while so much protection was afforded by various families of wealth and position that the guilty parties succeeded in preventing the arrest of a single one of their number. Therefore I proceeded in person to their establishment, knocked at the door, and seized the goddess, whom I subjected to a searching examination as to the whereabouts of her accomplices; but the interior of the place being, as it was, a perfect maze of

passages ramifying in every direction, when I seized a
torch and made my way along, even if I did stumble up
against any one, they were gone in a moment before I
had time to see where. It was a veritable nest of secret
villany, and one which I felt ought to be searched to the
last corner. Accordingly, from the goddess's bed in a
dark and out-of-the-way chamber I dragged forth some
ten or a dozen men; while out of the Immortal's bed-
room I brought a wooden seal of office belonging to the
Lady of the Moon, also a copy of their magic ritual,
a quantity of soporifics, wigs, clothes, and ornaments,
of the uses of which I was then totally ignorant. I
further made a great effort to secure the person of the
Immortal himself; and when his friends and rich sup-
porters saw the game was up, they surrendered him over
to justice. At his examination he comported himself in
a very singular manner, such being indeed the chief
means upon which he relied, besides the soporifics and
fine dresses, to deceive the eyes and ears of the public.
As to his credulous dupes, male and female, when they
heard the name of the Lady of the Moon they would be
at first somewhat scared; but by and by, seeing that the
goddess was certainly a woman, they would begin to
regain courage, while the Immortal himself, with his
hair dressed out and his face powdered and his skirts
fluttering about, hovered round the goddess, and assum-
ing all the airs and graces of a supernatural beauty,
soon convinced the spectators that he was really the
Lady of the Moon, and quite put them off the scent as
to his real sex. Adjourning now to one of the more
remote apartments, there would follow worship of
Maitrêya Buddha, accompanied by the recital of some
sútra; after which soporific incense would be lighted,

and the victims be thrown into a deep sleep. This soporific, or 'soul confuser,' as it is otherwise called, makes people feel tired and sleepy; they are recovered by means of a charm and a draught of cold water. The promised heirs and the interviews with deceased husbands are all supposed to be brought about during the period of trance—for which scandalous impostures the heads of these villains hung up in the streets were scarcely a sufficient punishment. However, reflecting that it would be a great grievance to the people were any of them to find themselves mixed up in such a case just after a bad harvest, and also that among the large number who had become affiliated to this society there would be found many old and respectable families, I determined on a plan which would put an end to the affair without any troublesome *esclandre*. I burnt all the depositions in which names were given, and took no further steps against the persons named. I ordered the goddess and her paramour to receive their full complement of blows (viz., one hundred), and to be punished with the heavy *cangue;* and, placing them at the yamên gate, I let the people rail and curse at them, tear their flesh and break their heads, until they passed together into their boasted Paradise. The husband and some ten others of the gang were placed in the *cangue*, bambooed, or punished in some way; and as for the rest, they were allowed to escape with this one more chance to turn over a new leaf. I confiscated the building, destroyed its disgraceful hiding-places, changed the whole appearance of the place, and made it into a literary institution to be dedicated to five famous heroes of literature. I cleansed and purified it from all taint, and on the 1st and 15th of each moon I would, when at leisure, indulge with the scholars of the district in literary recreations. I formed, in fact, a literary club; and, leasing a plot of ground for cultivation, devoted the returns therefrom to the annual Confucian demonstrations and to the payment of a regular professor. Thus the true doctrine was caused to flourish, and these supernatural doings to disappear from the scene; the public tone was elevated, and the morality of the place vastly improved.

"When the Brigadier-General and the Lieutenant-Governor heard what had been done, they very much commended my action, saying: 'Had this sect not been rooted out, the evil results would have been dire indeed; and had you reported the case in the usual way, praying for the execution of these criminals, your merit would undoubtedly have been great; but now, without selfish regard to your own interests, you have shown yourself unwilling to hunt down more victims than necessary, or to expose those doings in such a manner as to lead to the suicide of the persons implicated. Such care for the fair fame of so many people is deserving of all praise.'"

Although not yet of the same national importance as at the present day, it was still impossible that the foreign question should have escaped the notice of such an observant man as Lan Ting-yüan. He flourished at a time when the spread of the Roman Catholic religion was giving just grounds for apprehension to thoughtful Chinese statesmen. Accordingly, we find amongst his collected works two short notices devoted to a consideration of trade and general intercourse with the various nations of barbarians. They are interesting as the untrammelled views of the greatest living Chinese scholar of the date at which they were written, namely, in 1732. The following is one of these notices :—

"To allow the barbarians to settle at Canton was a mistake. Ever since Macao was given over, in the reign of Chia Ching (1522–1567) of the Ming dynasty, to the red-haired barbarians, all manner of nations have continued without ceasing to flock thither. They build forts and fortifications and dense settlements of houses. Their descendants will overshadow the land, and all the country beyond Hsiang-shan will become a kingdom of devils. 'Red-haired' is a general term for the barbarians of the western islands. Amongst them there are the Dutch, French, Spaniards, Portuguese, English, and Yü-sŭ-la [? Islam], all of which nations are horribly fierce. Wherever they go they spy around with a view to seize on other people's territory. There was Singapore, which was originally a Malay country ; the red-haired barbarians went there to trade, and by and by seized it for an emporium of their own. So with the Philippines, which were colonised by the Malays ; because the Roman Catholic religion was practised there, the Western foreigners appropriated it in like manner for their own. The Catholic religion is now spreading over China. In Hupeh, Hunan, Honan, Kiangsi, Fuhkien, and Kuangsi, there are very few places whither it has not reached. In the first year of the Emperor Yung Chêng [1736], the Viceroy of Fuhkien, Man Pao, complained that the Western foreigners were preaching their religion and tampering with the people, to the great detriment of the localities in question ; and he petitioned that the Roman Catholic chapels in the various provinces might be turned into lecture-rooms and schools, and that all Western foreigners might be sent to Macao, to wait until an opportunity should present itself of sending them back to their own countries. However, the Viceroy of Kuangtung, out of mistaken kindness, memorialised the Throne that such of the barbarians as were old or sick and unwilling to go away might be permitted to remain in the Roman Catholic establishment at Canton, on the condition that if they proselytised, spread their creed, or chaunted their sacred books, they were at once to be punished and sent away. The scheme was an excellent one, but what were the results of it ? At present more than 10,000 men have joined the Catholic chapel at Canton, and there is also a department for women, where they have similarly got together about 2000. This is a great insult to China, and seriously injures our national traditions, enough to make every man of feeling grind his teeth with rage. The case by no means admits of 'teaching before punishing.'

" Now these traders come this immense distance with the object of making money. What then is their idea in paying away vast sums in order to attract people to their faith ? Thousands upon thousands they get to join them, not being satisfied until they have bought up the whole province. Is it possible to shut one's eyes and stop one's ears, pretending to know nothing about it and making no inquiries whatever ? There is an old saying among the people—'Take things in time. A little stream, if not stopped, may become a great river.' How much more precaution is needed, then, when there is a general inundation and men's hearts are restless and disturbed ? In Canton the converts to Catholicism are very numerous ; those in Macao are in an inexpugnable fortress. There is a constant interchange of arms between the two, and if any trouble like that of the Philippines or Singapore should arise, I cannot say how we should meet it. At the present moment, with a pattern of Imperial virtue on the Throne, whose power and majesty have penetrated into the most distant regions, this foolish design of the barbarians should on no account be tolerated. Wise men will do well to be prepared against the day when it may be necessary for us to retire before them, clearing the country as we go."

The following extract from a letter to a friend was written by Lan Ting-yüan in 1724, and proves that if he objected to Christianity, he was not one whit more inclined to tolerate Buddhism :—

"Of all the eighteen provinces, Chehkiang is the one where Buddhist priests and nuns most abound. In the three prefectures of Hangchow, Chia-hsing, and Huchow there cannot be fewer than several tens of thousands of them, of whom, by the way, not more than one-tenth have willingly taken the vows. The others have been given to the priests when quite little, either because their parents were too poor to keep them, or in return for some act of kindness ; and when the children grow up, they are unable to get free. Buddhist nuns are also in most cases bought up when children as a means of making a more extensive show of religion, and are carefully prevented from running away. They are not given in marriage—the desire for which is more or less implanted in every human breast, and exists even amongst prophets and sages. And thus to condemn thousands and ten thousands of human beings to the dull monotony of the cloister, granting that they strictly keep their religious vows, is more than sufficient to seriously interfere with the equilibrium of the universe. Hence floods, famines, and the like catastrophes; to say nothing of the misdeeds of the nuns in question.

.   .   .   .

"When I passed through Soochow and Hangchow I saw many disgraceful advertisements that quite took my breath away with their barefaced depravity; and the people there told me that these atrocities were much practised by the denizens of the cloister, which term is simply another name for houses of ill-fame. These cloister folk do a great deal of mischief amongst the populace, wasting the substance of some, and robbing others of their good name."

The *Ming Chi Kang Mu*, or History of the Ming Dynasty, which had been begun in 1689 by a commission of fifty-eight scholars, was laid before the Emperor only in 1742 by CHANG T'ING-YÜ (1670–1756), a Minister of State and a most learned writer, joint editor of the Book of Rites, Ritual of the Chou Dynasty, the Thirteen Classics, the Twenty-four Histories, Thesaurus of Phraseology, Encyclopædia of Quotations, the Concordance to Literature, &c. This work, however, did not meet with the Imperial approval, and for it was substituted the *T'ung Chien Kang Mu San Pien*, first published in 1775. Among the chief collaborators of Chang T'ing-yü should be mentioned O-ÊRH-T'AI, the Mongol (*d.* 1745), and CHU SHIH (1666–1736), both of whom were also voluminous contributors to classical literature.

These were followed by CH'ÊN HUNG-MOU (1695–1771), who, besides being the author of brilliant State papers, was a commentator on the Classics, dealing especially with the Four Books, a writer on miscellaneous topics, and a most successful administrator. He rose to high office, and was noted for always having his room hung round with maps of the province in which he was serving, so that he might become thoroughly familiar with its geography. He was dismissed, however, from the important post of Viceroy of the Two Kuang for alleged incapacity in dealing with a plague of locusts.

YÜAN MEI (1715–1797) is beyond all question the most popular writer of modern times. At the early age of nine he was inspired with a deep love for poetry, and soon became an adept at the art. Graduating in 1739, he was shortly afterwards sent to Kiangnan, and presently became magistrate at Nanking, where he greatly distinguished himself by the vigour and justice of his administration. A serious illness kept him for some time unemployed ; and when on recovery he was sent into Shansi, he managed to quarrel with the Viceroy. At the early age of forty he retired from the official arena and led a life of lettered ease in his beautiful garden at Nanking. His letters, which have been published under the title of *Hsiao Ts'ang Shan Fang Ch'ih Tu*, are extremely witty and amusing, and at the same time are models of style. Many of the best are a trifle coarse, sufficiently so to rank them with some of the eighteenth-century literature on this side of the globe ; the salt of all loses its savour in translation. The following are specimens :—

" I have received your letter congratulating me on my present prosperity, and am very much obliged for the same.

"At the end of the letter, however, you mention that you have a tobacco-pouch for me, which shall be sent on as soon as I forward you a stanza. Surely this reminds one of the evil days of the Chous and the Chêngs, when each State took pledges from the other. It certainly is not in keeping with the teaching of the sages, viz., that friends should be the first to give. Why then do you neglect that teaching for the custom of a degraded age?

"If for a tobacco-pouch you insist upon having a stanza, for a hat or a pair of boots you would want at least a poem; while your brother might send me a cloak or a coat, and expect to get a whole epic in return! In this way, the prosperity on which you congratulate me would not count for much.

"Shun Yü-t'an of old sacrificed a bowl of rice and a perch to get a hundred waggons full of grain; he offered little and he wanted much. And have you not heard how a thousand pieces of silk were given for a single word? two beautiful girls for a stanza?—compared with which your tobacco-pouch seems small indeed. It is probably because you are a military man, accustomed to drill soldiers and to reward them with a silver medal when they hit the mark, that you have at last come to regard this as the proper treatment of an old friend.

"Did not Mencius forbid us to presume upon anything adventitious? And if friends may not presume upon their worth or position, how much less upon a tobacco-pouch? For a tobacco-pouch, pretty as it may be, is but the handiwork of a waiting-maid; while my verses, poor as they may be, are the outcome of my intellectual powers. So that to exchange the work of a waiting-maid's fingers for the work of my brain, is a great compliment to the waiting-maid, but a small one to me. Not so if you yourself had cast away spear and sword, and grasping the needle and silk, had turned me out a tobacco-pouch of your own working. Then, had you asked me even for ten stanzas, I would freely have given them. But a great general knows his own strength as well as the enemy's, and it would hardly be proper for me to lure you from men's to women's work, and place on your head a ribboned cap. How then do you venture to treat me as Ts'ao Ts'ao [on his death-bed treated his concubines], by bestowing on me an insignificant tobacco-pouch ?

"Having nothing better to do, I have amused myself with these few lines at your expense. If you take them ill, of course I shall never get the pouch. But if you can mend your evil ways, then hurry up with the tobacco-pouch and trust to your luck for the verse."

A friend had sent Yüan Mei a letter with the very un-Chinese present of a crab and a duck. Two ducks and a crab would have been more conventional, or even two crabs and a duck. And by some mistake or other, the crab arrived by itself. Hence the following banter in reply :—

"To convey a man to a crab is very pleasant for the man, but to convey a crab to a man is pleasant for his whole family. And I know that this night my two sons will often bend their arms like crabs' claws [*i.e.* in the form of the Chinese salute], wishing you an early success in life.

"In rhyme no duplicates [that is, don't rhyme again the same sound], and don't use two sentences where one will do [in composition]. Besides which, the fact that the duck has not yet turned up shows that you understand well how to 'do one thing at a time.' Not to mention that you cause an old gobbler like myself to stretch out his neck in anticipation of something else to come.

"You remember how the poet Shên beat his rival, all because of that one verse—

> *'Sigh not for the sinking moon,*
> *The jewel lamp will follow soon.'*

Well, your crab is like the sinking moon, while the duck reminds me of the jewel lamp; from which we may infer that you will meet with the same good luck as Shên.

"Again, a crab, even in the presence of the King of the Ocean, has to travel aslant; by which same token I trust that by and by your fame will travel aslant the habitable globe."

Yüan Mei's poetry is much admired and widely read. He is one of the few, very few, poets who have flourished under Manchu rule. Here are some sarcastic lines by him :—

> *"I've ever thought it passing odd*
> *How all men reverence some God,*
> *And wear their lives out for his sake*
> *And bow their heads until they ache.*
> *'Tis clear to me the Gods are made*
> *Of the same stuff as wind or shade. . . .*
> *Ah! if they came to every caller,*
> *I'd be the very loudest bawler!"*

He could be pathetic enough at times, as he showed in his elegy on a little five-year-old daughter, recalling her baby efforts with the paint-brush, and telling how she cut out clothes from paper, or sat and watched her father engaged in composition. He was also, like all Chinese poets, an ardent lover of nature, and a winter plum-tree in flower, or a gust of wind scattering dead

leaves, would set all his poetic fibres thrilling again.
It sounds like an anti-climax to add that this brilliant
essayist, letter-writer, and composer of finished verse
owes perhaps the chief part of his fame to a cookery-
book. Yet such is actually the case. Yüan Mei was the
Brillat-Savarin of China, and in the art of cooking China
stands next to France. His cookery-book is a gossipy
little work, written, as only such a scholar could write
it, in a style which at once invests the subject with
dignity and interest.

"Everything," says Yüan Mei, in his opening chapter,
"has its own original constitution, just as each man
has certain natural characteristics. If a man's natural
abilities are of a low order, Confucius and Mencius
themselves would teach him to no purpose. And if an
article of food is in itself bad, not even I-ya [the Soyer
of China] could cook a flavour into it.

"A ham is a ham; but in point of goodness two hams
will be as widely separated as sky and sea. A mackerel
is a mackerel; but in point of excellence two mackerel
will differ as much as ice and live coals. And other
things in the same way. So that the credit of a good
dinner should be divided between the cook and the
steward—forty per cent. to the steward, and sixty per
cent. to the cook.

"Cookery is like matrimony. Two things served together should match. Clear should go with clear, thick
with thick, hard with hard, and soft with soft. I have
known people mix grated lobster with birds'-nests, and
mint with chicken or pork!

"The cooks of to-day think nothing of mixing in one
soup the meat of chicken, duck, pig, and goose. But
these chickens, ducks, pigs, and geese have doubtless

souls. And these souls will most certainly file plaints in the next world on the way they have been treated in this. A good cook will use plenty of different dishes. Each article of food will be made to exhibit its own characteristics, while each made dish will be character-ised by one dominant flavour. Then the palate of the gourmand will respond without fail, and the flowers of the soul blossom forth.

" Let salt fish come first, and afterwards food of more negative flavour. Let the heavy precede the light. Let dry dishes precede those with gravy. No flavour must dominate. If a guest eats his fill of savouries, his stomach will be fatigued. Salt flavours must be relieved by bitter or hot tasting foods, in order to restore the palate. Too much wine will make the stomach dull. Sour or sweet food will be required to rouse it again into vigour.

" In winter we should eat beef and mutton. In sum-mer, dried and preserved meats. As for condiments, mustard belongs specially to summer, pepper to winter.

" Don't cut bamboo-shoots [the Chinese equivalent of asparagus] with an oniony knife. . . . A good cook fre-quently wipes his knife, frequently changes his cloth, frequently scrapes his board, and frequently washes his hands. If smoke or ashes from his pipe, perspiration-drops from his head, insects from the wall, or smuts from the saucepan get mixed up with the food, though he were a very *chef* among *chefs*, yet would men hold their noses and decline.

" Don't make your thick sauces greasy nor your clear ones tasteless. Those who want grease can eat fat pork, while a drink of water is better than something which tastes of nothing at all. . . . Don't over-salt your soups ; for salt can be added to taste, but can never be taken away.

"*Don't eat with your ears ;* by which I mean do not aim at having extraordinary out-of-the-way foods, just to astonish your guests ; for that is to eat with your ears, not with the mouth. Bean-curd, if good, is actually nicer than birds'-nest ; and better than sea-slugs, which are not first-rate, is a dish of bamboo shoots. . . .

"The chicken, the pig, the fish, and the duck, these are the four heroes of the table. Sea-slugs and birds' nests have no characteristic flavours of their own. They are but usurpers in the house. I once dined with a friend who gave us birds'-nest in bowls more like vats, holding each about four ounces of the plain-boiled article. The other guests applauded vigorously ; but I smiled and said, '*I came here to eat birds'-nest, not to take delivery of it wholesale.*'

"*Don't eat with your eyes ;* by which I mean do not cover the table with innumerable dishes and multiply courses indefinitely. For this is to eat with the eyes, and not with the mouth.

"Just as a calligraphist should not overtire his hand nor a poet his brain, so a good cook cannot possibly turn out in one day more than four or five distinct *plats*. I used to dine with a merchant friend who would put on no less than three removes [sets of eight dishes served separately], and sixteen kinds of sweets, so that by the time we had finished we had got through a total of some forty courses. My host gloried in all this, but when I got home I used to have a bowl of rice-gruel. I felt so hungry.

"To know right from wrong, a man must be sober. And only a sober man can distinguish good flavours from bad. It has been well said that words are inadequate to describe the *nuances* of taste. How much less then must a stuttering sot be able to appreciate them!

"I have often seen votaries of guess-fingers swallow choice food as though so much sawdust, their minds being preoccupied with their game. Now I say eat first and drink afterwards. By these means the result will be successful in each direction."

Yüan Mei also protests against the troublesome custom of pressing guests to eat, and against the more foolish one of piling up choice pieces on the little saucers used as plates, and even putting them into the guests' mouths, as if they were children or brides, too shy to help themselves.

There was a man in Ch'ang-an, he tells us, who was very fond of giving dinners; but the food was atrocious. One day a guest threw himself on his knees in front of this gentleman and said, "Am I not a friend of yours?"

"You are indeed," replied his host.

"Then I must ask of you a favour," said the guest, "and you must grant it before I rise from my knees."

"Well, what is it?" inquired his host in astonishment.

"Never to invite me to dinner any more!" cried the guest; at which the whole party burst into a loud roar of laughter.

"Into no department of life," says Yüan Mei, "should indifference be allowed to creep; into none less than into the domain of cookery. Cooks are but mean fellows; and if a day is passed without either rewarding or punishing them, that day is surely marked by negligence or carelessness on their part. If badly cooked food is swallowed in silence, such neglect will speedily become a habit. Still, mere rewards and punishments are of no use. If a dish is good, attention should be called to the why and the wherefore. If bad, an effort should be made to discover the cause of the failure.

"I am not much of a wine-drinker, but this makes me all the more particular. Wine is like scholarship: it ripens with age; and it is best from a fresh-opened jar. The top of the wine-jar, the bottom of the teapot, as the saying has it."

In 1783 CH'ÊN HAO-TZŬ, who lived beside the Western Lake at Hangchow, and called himself the Flower Hermit, published a gossipy little work on gardening and country pursuits, under the title of "The Mirror of Flowers." It is the type of a class often to be seen in the hands of Chinese readers. The preface was written by himself :—

"From my youth upwards I have cared for nothing save books and flowers. Twenty-eight thousand days have passed over my head, the greater part of which has been spent in poring over old records, and the remainder in enjoying myself in my garden among plants and birds."

The Chinese excel in horticulture, and the passionate love of flowers which prevails among all classes is quite a national characteristic. A Chinaman, however, has his own particular standpoint. The vulgar nosegay or the plutocratic bouquet would have no charms for him. He can see, with satisfaction, only one flower at a time. His best vases are made to hold a single spray, and large vases usually have covers perforated so as to isolate each specimen. A primrose by the river's brim would be to him a complete poem. If condemned to a sedentary life, he likes to have a flower by his side on the table. He draws enjoyment, even inspiration, from its petals. He will take a flower out for a walk, and stop every now and again to consider the loveliness of its growth. So with birds. It is a common thing on a pleasant evening to meet a Chinaman carrying his bird-cage suspended from the end of a short stick. He will stop at some pleasant corner outside the town, and listen with rapture to the bird's song. But to the preface. Our author goes on to say that in his hollow bamboo pillow he always keeps some work on his favourite subject.

"People laugh at me, and say that I am cracked on flowers and a bibliomaniac; but surely study is the proper occupation of a literary man, and as for gardening, that is simply a rest for my brain and a relaxation in my declining years. What does T'ao Ch'ien say?—

> *Riches and rank I do not love,*
> *I have no hopes of heaven above.'* . . .

Besides, it is only in hours of leisure that I devote myself to the cultivation of flowers."

Ch'ên Hao-tzŭ then runs through the four seasons, showing how each has its especial charm, contributing to the sum of those pure pleasures which are the best antidote against the ills of old age. He then proceeds to deal with times and seasons, showing what to do under each month, precisely as our own garden-books do. After that come short chapters on all the chief trees, shrubs, and plants of China, with hints how to treat them under diverse circumstances, the whole concluding with a separate section devoted to birds, animals, fishes, and insects. Among these are to be found the crane, peacock, parrot, thrush, kite, quail, mainah, swallow, deer, hare, monkey, dog, cat, squirrel, goldfish—first mentioned by Su Shih,

> *"Upon the bridge the livelong day*
> *I stand and watch the goldfish play"*—

bee, butterfly, glowworm, &c. Altogether there is much to be learnt from this Chinese White of Selborne, and the reader lays down the book feeling that the writer is not far astray when he says, "If a home has not a garden and an old tree, I see not whence the everyday joys of life are to come."

CHAO I (1727–1814) is said to have known several tens of characters when only three years old,—the age at which John Stuart Mill believed that he began Greek. It was not, however, until 1761 that he took his final degree, appearing second on the list. He was really first, but the Emperor put Wang Chieh over his head, in order to encourage men from Shensi, to which province the latter belonged. That Wang Chieh is remembered at all must be set down to the above episode, and not to the two volumes of essays which he left behind him. Chao I wrote a history of the wars of the present dynasty, a collection of notes on the current topics of his day, historical critiques, and other works. He was also a poet, contributing a large volume of verse, from which the following sample of his art is taken :—

> *"Man is indeed of heavenly birth,*
> *Though seeming earthy of the earth ;*
> *The sky is but a denser pall*
> *Of the thin air that covers all.*
> *Just as this air, so is that sky ;*
> *Why call this low, and call that high ?*

> " *The dewdrop sparkles in the cup—*
> *Note how the eager flowers spring up;*
> *Confine and crib them in a room,*
> *They fade and find an early doom.*
> *So 'tis that at our very feet*
> *The earth and the empyrean meet.*
>
> " *The babe at birth points heavenward too,*
> *Enveloped by the eternal blue;*
> *As fishes in the water bide,*
> *So heaven surrounds on every side;*
> *Yet men sin on, because they say*
> *Great God in heaven is far away.*"

The "stop short" was a great favourite with him. His level may be gauged by the following specimen, written as he was setting out to a distant post in the north :—

> " *See where, like specks of spring-cloud in the sky,*
> *On their long northern route the wild geese fly;*
> *Together o'er the River we will roam. . . .*
> *Ah! they go towards, and I away from home!*"

Here is another in a more humorous vein :—

> " *The rain had been raining the whole of the day,*
> *And I had been straining and working away. . . .*
> *What's the trouble, O cook? You've no millet in store?*
> *Well, I've written a book which will buy us some more.*"

Taken altogether, the poetry of the present dynasty, especially that of the nineteenth century, must be written down as nothing more than artificial verse, with the art not even concealed, but grossly patent to the dullest observer. A collection of extracts from about 2000 representative poets was published in 1857, but it is very dull reading, any thoughts, save the most commonplace, being few and far between. As in every similar collection, a place is assigned to poetesses, of whom FANG WEI-I would perhaps be a favourable example. She came from a good family, and was but newly married to a promising young official when the latter died, and left her a sorrowing and childless widow. Light came to her in the darkness, and disregarding the entreaties of her father and mother, she decided to become a nun, and devote the remainder of her life to the service of Buddha. These are her farewell lines :—

> "'Tis common talk how partings sadden life :
>   There are no partings for us after death.
> But let that pass ; I, now no more a wife,
>   Will face fate's issues to my latest breath.
>
> "The north wind whistles thro' the mulberry grove,
>   Daily and nightly making moan for me ;
> I look up to the shifting sky above,
>   No little prattler smiling on my knee.
>
> "Life's sweetest boon is after all to die. . . .
>   My weeping parents still are loth to yield ;
> Yet east and west the callow fledglings fly,
>   And autumn's herbage wanders far afield.
>
> "What will life bring to me an I should stay ?
>   What will death bring to me an I should go ?
> These thoughts surge through me in the light of day,
>   And make me conscious that at last I know."

One of the greatest of the scholars of the present dynasty was YÜAN YÜAN (1764–1849). He took his third degree in 1789, and at the final examination the aged Emperor Ch'ien Lung was so struck with his talents that he exclaimed, "Who would have thought that, after passing my eightieth year, I should find another such man as this one ?" He then held many high offices in succession, including the post of Governor of Chehkiang, in which he operated vigorously against the Annamese pirates and Ts'ai Chien, established the tithing system, colleges, schools, and soup-kitchens, besides devoting himself to the preservation of ancient monuments. As Viceroy of the Two Kuang, he frequently came into collision with British interests, and did his best to keep a tight hand over the barbarian merchants. He was a voluminous writer on the Classics, astronomy, archæology, &c., and various important collections were produced under his patronage. Among these may be mentioned the *Huang Ch'ing Ching Chieh*, containing upwards of 180 separate works, and the *Ch'ou Jen Chuan*, a biographical dictionary of famous mathematicians of all ages, including Euclid, Newton, and Ricci, the Jesuit Father. He also published a Topography of Kuangtung, specimens of the compositions of more than 5000 poets of Kiangsi, and a large collection of inscriptions on bells and vases. He also edited the Catalogue of the Imperial Library, the large encyclopædia known as the *T'ai P'ing Yü Lan*, and other important works.

Two religious works, associated with the Taoism of modern days, which have long been popular throughout China, may fitly be mentioned here. They are not to be bought in shops, but can always be obtained at temples, where large numbers are placed by philanthropists for distribution gratis. The first is the *Kan Ying P'ien*, or Book of Rewards and Punishments, attributed by the foolish to Lao Tzŭ himself. Its real date is quite unknown ; moderate writers place it in the Sung dynasty, but even that seems far too early. Although nominally of Taoist origin, this work is usually edited in a very pronounced Buddhist setting, the fact being that Taoism

and Buddhism are now so mixed up that it is impossible
to draw any sharp line of demarcation between the two.
As Chu Hsi says, "Buddhism stole the best features
of Taoism, and Taoism stole the worst features of Buddhism; it is as though the one stole a jewel from the
other, and the loser recouped the loss with a stone."
Prefixed to the *Kan Ying P'ien* will be found Buddhist
formulæ for cleansing the mouth and body before
beginning to read the text, and appeals to Maitrêya
Buddha and Avalôkitêsvara. Married women and girls
are advised not to frequent temples to be a spectacle for
men. "If you must worship Buddha, worship the two
living Buddhas (parents) you have at home; and if you
must burn incense, burn it at the family altar." We are
further told that there is no time at which this book may
not be read; no place in which it may not be read; and
no person by whom it may not be read with profit. We
are advised to study it when fasting, and not necessarily
to shout it aloud, so as to be heard of men, but rather to
ponder over it in the heart. The text consists of a com-
mination said to have been uttered by Lao Tzŭ, and
directed against evil-doers of all kinds. In the opening
paragraphs attention is drawn to various spiritual beings
who note down the good deeds and crimes of men,
and lengthen or shorten their lives accordingly. Then
follows a long list of wicked acts which will inevitably
bring retribution in their train. These include the ordinary offences recognised by moral codes all over the
world, every form of injustice and oppression, falsehood,
and theft, together with not a few others of a more
venial character to Western minds. Among the latter
are birds'-nesting, stepping across food or human beings,
cooking with dirty firewood, spitting at shooting stars

and pointing at the rainbow, or even at the sun, moon, and stars. In all these cases, periods will be cut off from the life of the offender, and if his life is exhausted while any guilt still remains unexpiated, the punishment due will be carried on to the account of his descendants.

The second of the two works under consideration is the *Yü Li Ch'ao Chuan*, a description of the Ten Courts of Purgatory in the nether world, through some or all of which every erring soul must pass before being allowed to be born again into this world under another form, or to be permanently transferred to the eternal bliss reserved for the righteous alone.

In the Fifth Court, for instance, the sinners are hurried away by bull-headed, horse-faced demons to a famous terrace, where their physical punishments are aggravated by a view of their old homes :—

"This terrace is curved in front like a bow; it looks east, west, and south. It is eighty-one *li* from one extreme to the other. The back part is like the string of a bow; it is enclosed by a wall of sharp swords. It is 490 feet high; its sides are knife-blades; and the whole is in sixty-three storeys. No good shade comes to this terrace; neither do those whose balance of good and evil is exact. Wicked souls alone behold their homes close by, and can see and hear what is going on. They hear old and young talking together; they see their last wishes disregarded and their instructions disobeyed. Everything seems to have undergone a change. The property they scraped together with so much trouble is dissipated and gone. The husband thinks of taking another wife; the widow meditates second nuptials. Strangers are in possession of the old estate; there is nothing to divide amongst the children. Debts long since paid are brought again for settlement, and the survivors are called upon to acknowledge claims upon the departed. Debts owed are lost for want of evidence, with endless recriminations, abuse, and general confusion, all of which falls upon the three families of the deceased. They in their anger speak ill of him that is gone. He sees his children become corrupt and his friends fall away. Some, perhaps, for the sake of bygone times, may stroke the coffin and let fall a tear, departing quickly with a cold smile. Worse than that, the wife sees her husband tortured in the yamên; the husband sees his wife victim to some horrible disease, lands gone, houses destroyed by flood or fire, and everything in unutterable confusion—the reward of former sins."

The Sixth Court "is a vast, noisy Gehenna, many leagues in extent, and around it are sixteen wards.

"In the first, the souls are made to kneel for long periods on iron shot. In the second, they are placed up to their necks in filth. In the third, they are pounded till the blood runs out. In the fourth, their mouths are opened with iron pincers and filled full of needles. In the fifth, they are bitten by rats. In the sixth, they are enclosed in a net of thorns and nipped by locusts. In the seventh, they are crushed to a jelly. In the eighth, their skin is lacerated and they are beaten on the raw. In the ninth, their mouths are filled with fire. In the tenth, they are licked by flames. In the eleventh, they are subjected to noisome smells. In the twelfth, they are butted by oxen and trampled on by horses. In the thirteenth, their hearts are scratched. In the fourteenth, their heads are rubbed till their skulls come off. In the fifteenth, they are chopped in two at the waist. In the sixteenth, their skin is taken off and rolled up into spills.

"Those discontented ones who rail against heaven and revile earth, who are always finding fault either with the wind, thunder, heat, cold, fine weather, or rain; those who let their tears fall towards the north; who steal the gold from the inside or scrape the gilding from the outside of images; those who take holy names in vain, who show no respect for written paper, who throw down dirt and rubbish near pagodas or temples, who use dirty cook-houses and stoves for preparing the sacrificial meats, who do not abstain from eating beef and dog-flesh; those who have in their possession blasphemous or obscene books and do not destroy them, who obliterate or tear books which teach man to be good, who carve on common articles of household use the symbol of the origin of all things, the Sun and Moon and Seven Stars, the Royal Mother and the God of Longevity on the same article, or representations of any of the Immortals; those who embroider the Svastika on fancy-work, or mark characters on silk, satin, or cloth, on banners, beds, chairs, tables, or any kind of utensil; those who secretly wear clothes adorned with the dragon and the phœnix only to be trampled under foot, who buy up grain and hold until the price is exorbitantly high—all these shall be thrust into the great and noisy Gehenna, there to be examined as to their misdeeds and passed accordingly into one of the sixteen wards, whence, at the expiration of their time, they will be sent for further questioning on to the Seventh Court."

The Tenth Court deals with the final stage of transmigration previous to rebirth in the world. It appears that in primeval ages men could remember their former lives on earth even after having passed through Purgatory, and that wicked persons often took advantage of such knowledge. To remedy this, a Terrace of Oblivion was built, and all shades are now sent thither, and are forced to drink the cup of forgetfulness before they can be born again.

"Whether they swallow much or little it matters not; but sometimes there are perverse devils who altogether refuse to drink. Then beneath their feet sharp blades start up, and a copper tube is forced down their throats, by which means they are compelled to swallow some. When they have drunk, they are raised by the attendants and escorted back by the same path. They are next pushed on to the Bitter Bamboo floating bridge, with torrents of rushing red water on either side. Half-way across they perceive written in large characters on a red cliff on the opposite side the following lines :—

> "*To be a man is easy, but to act up to one's responsibilities as such
>   is hard;*
> *Yet to be a man once again is perhaps harder still.*

> "*For those who would be born again in some happy state there is no
>   great difficulty;*
> *It is only necessary to keep mouth and heart in harmony.*"

"When the shades have read these words, they try to jump on shore, but are beaten back into the water by two huge devils. One has on a black official hat and embroidered clothes; in his hand he holds a paper pencil, and over his shoulder he carries a sharp sword. Instruments of torture hang at his waist; fiercely he glares out of his large round eyes and laughs a horrid laugh. His name is Short-Life. The other has a dirty face smeared with blood; he has on a white coat, an abacus in his hand, and a rice-sack over his shoulder. Around his neck hangs a string of paper money; his brow contracts hideously and he utters long sighs. His name is They-have-their-Reward, and his duty is to push the shades into the red water. The wicked and foolish rejoice at the prospect of being born once more as human beings, but the better shades weep and mourn that in life they did not lay up a store of virtuous acts, and thus pass away from the state of mortals for ever. Yet they all rush on to birth like an infatuated or drunken crowd, and again, in their new childhood, hanker after forbidden flavours. Then, regardless of consequences, they begin to destroy life, and thus forfeit all claims to the mercy and compassion of God. They take no thought as to the end that must overtake them ; and, finally, they bring themselves once more to the same horrid plight."

CHAPTER IV

WALL LITERATURE—JOURNALISM—WIT AND HUMOUR—PROVERBS AND MAXIMS

THE death of Yüan Yüan in 1849 brings us down to the period when China began to find herself for the first time face to face with the foreigner. The opening of five ports in 1842 to comparatively unrestricted trade, followed by more ports and right of residence in Peking from 1860, created points of contact and brought about foreign complications to which the governors of China had hitherto been unused. A Chinese Horace might well complain that the audacious brood of England have by wicked fraud introduced journalism into the Empire, and that evils worse than consumption and fevers have followed in its train.

From time immemorial wall-literature has been a feature in the life of a Chinese city surpassing in extent and variety that of any other nation, and often playing a part fraught with much danger to the community at large. Generally speaking, the literature of the walls covers pretty much the same ground as an ordinary English newspaper, from the "agony" column downwards. For, mixed up with notices of lost property, consisting sometimes of human beings, and advertisements of all kinds of articles of trade, such as one would naturally look for in the handbill literature of any city, there are to be found announcements of new and startling remedies for various diseases or of infallible pills for the cure of depraved opium-smokers, long lists of the names of subscribers to some coming festival or to the pious restoration of a local temple, sermons without end directed against the abuse of written paper, and now and then against female infanticide, or Cumming-like warnings of an approaching millennium, at which the wicked will receive the reward of their crimes according to the horrible arrangements of the Buddhist-Taoist purgatory. Occasionally an objectionable person will be advised through an anonymous placard to desist from a course which is pointed out as offensive, and similarly, but more rarely, the action of an official will be sometimes severely criticised or condemned. Official proclamations on public business can hardly be classed as wall literature, except perhaps when, as is not uncommon, they are written in doggerel verse, with a view to appealing more directly to the illiterate reader. The following proclamation establishing a registry office for boats at Tientsin will give an idea of these queer documents, the only parallel to which in the West might be found in the famous lines issued by the Board of Trade for the use of sea-captains:—

> "*Green to green, and red to red,*
> *Perfect safety, go ahead,*" &c.

The object of this registry office was ostensibly to save the poor boatman from being unfairly dealt with when impressed at nominal wages for Government service, but really to enable the officials to know exactly where to lay their hands on boats when required:—

" *A busy town is Tientsin,*
A land and water thoroughfare;
Traders, as thick as clouds, flock in;
Masts rise in forests everywhere.

" *The official's chair, the runner's cap,*
Flit past like falling rain or snow,
And, musing on the boatman's hap,
His doubtful shares of weal and woe,

" *I note the vagabonds who live*
On squeezes from his hard-earned due;
And, boatmen, for your sakes I give
A public register to you.

" *Go straightway there, your names inscribe*
And on the books a record raise;
None then dare claim the wicked bribe,
Or waste your time in long delays.

" *The services your country claims*
Shall be performed in turn by all
The muster of the boatmen's names
Be published on the Yamên wall.

" *Once your official business done,*
Work for yourselves as best you can;
Let out your boats to any one;
I'll give a pass to every man.

" *And lest your lot be hard to bear*
Official pay shall ample be;
Let all who notice aught unfair
Report the case at once to me.

" *The culprit shall be well deterred*
In future, if his guilt is clear;
For times are hard, as I have heard,
And food and clothing getting dear.

" *Thus, in compassion for your woe,*
The scales of Justice in my hand,
I save you from the Yamên foe,
The barrack-soldiers' threat'ning band.

" *No longer will they dare to play*
 Their shameful tricks, of late revealed;
 The office only sends away
 Boats—and on orders duly sealed.

" *One rule will thus be made for all,*
 And things may not go much amiss;
 Ye boatmen, 'tis on you I call
 To show your gratitude for this.

" *But lest there be who ignorance plead,*
 I issue this in hope to awe
 Such fools as think they will succeed
 By trying to evade the law.

" *For if I catch them, no light fate*
 Awaits them that unlucky day;
 So from this proclamation's date
 Let all in fear and dread obey."

It is scarcely necessary to add that wall literature has often been directed against foreigners, and especially against missionaries. The penalties, however, for posting anonymous placards are very severe, and of late years the same end has been more effectually attained by the circulation of abusive fly-sheets, often pictorial and always disgusting.

Journalism has proved to be a terrible thorn in the official side. It was first introduced into China under the ægis of an Englishman who was the nominal editor of the *Shên Pao* or *Shanghai News*, still a very influential newspaper. For a long time the authorities fought to get rid of this objectionable daily, which now and again told some awkward truths, and contained many ably written articles by first-class native scholars. Eventually an official organ was started in opposition, and other papers have since appeared. An illustrated Chinese weekly made a good beginning in Shanghai, but unfortunately it soon drifted into superstition, intolerance, and vulgarity.

Attempts have been made to provide the Chinese with translations of noted European works, and among those which have been produced may be mentioned "The Pilgrim's Progress," with illustrations, the various characters being in Chinese dress; Mr. Herbert Spencer's "Education," the very first sentence in which is painfully misrendered; the "Adventures of Baron Munchausen," and others. In every case save one these efforts have been rejected by the Chinese on the ground of inferior style. The exception was a translation of Æsop's Fables, published in 1840 by Robert Thom as rendered into Chinese by an eminent native scholar. This work attracted much attention among the people generally; so much so, that the officials took alarm and made strenuous efforts to suppress it. Recent years have witnessed the publication in Chinese of "Vathek," in reference to which a literate of standing offered the following criticism :— "The style in which this work is written is not so bad, but the subject-matter is of no account." The fact is, that to satisfy the taste of the educated Chinese reader the very first requisite is style. As has been seen in the case of the *Liao Chai*, the Chinese will read almost anything, provided it is set in a faultless frame. They will not look at anything emanating from foreign sources in which this greatest desideratum has been neglected.

The present age has seen the birth of no great original writer in any department of literature, nor the production of any great original work worthy to be smeared with cedar-oil for the delectation of posterity. It is customary after the death, sometimes during the life, of any leading statesman to publish a collection of his memorials to the throne, with possibly a few essays and some poems. Such have a brief *succès d'estime*, and are then used by binders for thickening the folded leaves of some masterpiece of antiquity. Successful candidates for the final degree usually print their winning essays, and sometimes their poems, chiefly for distribution among friends. Several diaries of Ministers to foreign countries and similar books have appeared in recent years, recording the astonishment of the writers at the extraordinary social customs which prevail among the barbarians. But nowadays a Chinaman who wishes to read a book does not sit down and write one. He is too much oppressed by the vast dimensions of his existing literature, and by the hopelessness of rivalling, and still more by the hopelessness of surpassing, those immortals who have gone before.

It would be obviously unfair to describe the Chinese people as wanting in humour simply because they are tickled by jests which leave us comparatively unmoved. Few of our own most amusing stories will stand conversion into Chinese terms. The following are specimens of classical humour, being such as might be introduced into any serious biographical notice of the individuals concerned.

Ch'un-yü K'un (4th cent. B.C.) was the wit already mentioned, who tried to entangle Mencius in his talk. On one occasion, when the Ch'u State was about to attack the Chi State, he was ordered by the Prince of Ch'i, who was his father-in-law, to proceed to the Chao State and ask that an army might be sent to their assistance; to which end the Prince supplied him with 100 lbs. of silver and ten chariots as offerings to the ruler of Chao. At this Ch'un-yü laughed so immoderately that he snapped the lash of his cap ; and when the Prince asked him what was the joke, he said, "As I was coming along this morning, I saw a husbandman sacrificing a pig's foot and a single cup of wine ; after which he prayed, saying, 'O God, make my upper terraces fill baskets and my lower terraces fill carts ; make my fields bloom with crops and my barns burst with grain !' And I could not help laughing at a man who offered so little and wanted so much." The Prince took the hint, and obtained the assistance he required.

T'ao Ku (A.D. 902–970) was an eminent official whose name is popularly known in connection with the following repartee. Having ordered a newly-purchased waiting-maid to get some snow and make tea in honour of the Feast of Lanterns, he asked her, somewhat pompously, "Was that the custom in your former home ?" "Oh, no," the girl replied ; "they were a rough lot. They just put up a gold-splashed awning, and had a little music and some old wine."

Li Chia-ming (10th cent. A.D.) was a wit at the Court of the last ruler of the T'ang dynasty. On one occasion the latter drew attention to some gathering clouds which appeared about to bring rain. "They may come," said Li Chia-ming, "but they will not venture to enter the city." "Why not ?" asked the Prince. "Because," replied the wit, "the octroi is so high." Orders were thereupon issued that the duties should be reduced by one-half. On another occasion the Prince was fishing with some of his courtiers, all of whom managed to catch something, whereas he himself, to his great chagrin, had not a single bite. Thereupon Li Chia-ming took a pen and wrote the following lines :—

"'Tis rapture in the warm spring days to drop the tempting fly
In the green pool where deep and still the darkling waters lie;
And if the fishes dare not touch the bait your Highness flings,
They know that only dragons are a fitting sport for kings."

Liu Chi (11th cent. A.D.) was a youth who had gained some notoriety by his fondness for strange phraseology, which was much reprobated by the great Ou-yang Hsiu. When the latter was Grand Examiner, one of the candidates sent in a doggerel triplet as follows :—

> *" The universe is in labour,*
> *All things are produced,*
> *And among them the Sage."*

"This must be Liu Chi," cried Ou-yang, and ran a red-ink pen through the composition, adding these two lines :—

> *" The undergraduate jokes,*
> *The examiner ploughs."*

Later on, about the year 1060, Ou-yang was very much struck by the essay of a certain candidate, and placed him first on the list. When the names were read out, he found that the first man was Liu Chi, who had changed his name to Liu Yün.

Chang Hsüan-tsu was a wit of the Han dynasty. When he was only eight years old, some one laughed at him for having lost several teeth, and said, "What are those dog-holes in your mouth for ?" "They are there," replied Chang, "to let puppies like you run in and out."

Collections of wit and humour of the Joe Miller type are often to be seen in the hands of Chinese readers, and may be bought at any bookstall. Like many novels of the cheap and worthless class, not to be mentioned with the masterpieces of fiction described in this volume, these collections are largely unfit for translation. All literature in China is pure. Novels and stories are not classed as literature ; the authors have no desire to attach their names to such works, and the consequence is a great falling off from what may be regarded as the national standard. Even the *Hung Lou Mêng* contains episodes which mar to a considerable extent the beauty of the whole. One excuse is that it is a novel of real life, and to omit, therefore, the ordinary frailties of mortals would be to produce an incomplete and inadequate picture.

The following are a few specimens of humorous anecdotes taken from the *Hsiao Lin Kuang Chi*, a modern work in four small volumes, in which the stories are classified under twelve heads, such as Arts, Women, Priests :—

A bridegroom noticing deep wrinkles on the face of his bride, asked her how old she was, to which she replied, "About forty-five or forty-six." "Your age is stated on the marriage contract," he rejoined, "as thirty-eight ; but I am sure you are older than that, and you may as well tell me the truth." "I am really fifty-four," answered the bride. The bridegroom, however, was not satisfied, and determined to set a trap for her. Accordingly he said, "Oh, by the by, I must just go and cover up the salt jar, or the rats will eat every scrap of it." "Well, I never !" cried the bride, taken off her guard. "Here I've lived sixty-eight years, and I never before heard of rats stealing salt."

A woman who was entertaining a paramour during the absence of her husband, was startled by hearing the latter knock at the house-door. She hurriedly bundled the man into a rice-sack, which she concealed in a corner of the room; but when her husband came in he caught sight of it, and asked in a stern voice, "What have you got in that sack?" His wife was too terrified to answer; and after an awkward pause a voice from the sack was heard to say, "Only rice."

A scoundrel who had a deep grudge against a wealthy man, sought out a famous magician and asked for his help. "I can send demon soldiers and secretly cut him off," said the magician. "Yes, but his sons and grandsons would inherit," replied the other; "that won't do." "I can draw down fire from heaven," said the magician, "and burn his house and valuables." "Even then," answered the man, "his landed property would remain; so that won't do." "Oh," cried the magician, "if your hate is so deep as all that, I have something precious here which, if you can persuade him to avail himself of it, will bring him and his to utter smash." He thereupon gave to his delighted client a tightly closed package, which, on being opened, was seen to contain a pen. "What spiritual power is there in this?" asked the man. "Ah!" sighed the magician, "you evidently do not know how many have been brought to ruin by the use of this little thing."

A doctor who had mismanaged a case was seized by the family and tied up. In the night he managed to free himself, and escaped by swimming across a river. When he got home, he found his son, who had just begun to study medicine, and said to him, "Don't be in a hurry with your books; the first and most important thing is to learn to swim."

The King of Purgatory sent his lictors to earth to bring back some skilful physician. "You must look for one," said the King, "at whose door there are no aggrieved spirits of disembodied patients." The lictors went off, but at the house of every doctor they visited there were crowds of wailing ghosts hanging about. At last they found a doctor at whose door there was only a single shade, and cried out, "This man is evidently the skilful one we are in search of." On inquiry, however, they discovered that he had only started practice the day before.

A general was hard pressed in battle and on the point of giving way, when suddenly a spirit soldier came to his rescue and enabled him to win a great victory. Prostrating himself on the ground, he asked the spirit's name. "I am the God of the Target," replied the spirit. "And how have I merited your godship's kind assistance?" inquired the general. "I am grateful to you," answered the spirit, "because in your days of practice you never once hit me."

A portrait-painter, who was doing very little business, was advised by a friend to paint a picture of himself and his wife, and to hang it out in the street as an advertisement. This he did, and shortly afterwards his father-in-law came along. Gazing at the picture for some time, the latter at length asked, "Who is that woman?" "Why, that is your daughter," replied the artist. "Whatever is she doing," again inquired her father, "sitting there with that stranger?"

A man who had been condemned to wear the *cangue*, or wooden collar, was seen by some of his friends. "What have you been doing," they asked, "to deserve this?" "Oh, nothing," he replied; "I only picked up an old piece of rope." "And are you to be punished thus severely," they said, "for merely picking up an end of rope?" "Well," answered the man, "the fact is that there was a bullock tied to the other end."

A man asked a friend to stay and have tea. Unfortunately there was no tea in the house, so a servant was sent to borrow some. Before the latter had returned the water was already boiling, and it became necessary to pour in more cold water. This happened several times, and at length the boiler was overflowing but no tea had come. Then the man's wife said to her husband, "As we don't seem likely to get any tea, you had better offer your friend a bath!"

A monkey, brought after death before the King of Purgatory, begged to be reborn on earth as a man. "In that case," said the King, "all the hairs must be plucked out of your body," and he ordered the attendant demons to pull them out forthwith. At the very first hair, however, the monkey screeched out, and said he could not bear the pain. "You brute!" roared the King, "how are you to become a man if you cannot even part with a single hair?"

A braggart chess-player played three games with a stranger and lost them all. Next day a friend asked him how he had come off. "Oh," said he, "I didn't win the first game, and my opponent didn't lose the second. As for the third, I wanted to draw it, but he wouldn't agree."

The barest sketch of Chinese literature would hardly be complete without some allusion to its proverbs and maxims. These are not only to be found largely scattered throughout every branch of writing, classical and popular, but may also be studied in collections, generally under a metrical form. Thus the *Ming Hsien Chi*, to take one example, which can be purchased anywhere for about a penny, consists of thirty pages of proverbs and the like, arranged in antithetical couplets of five, six, and seven characters to each line. Children are made to learn these by heart, and ordinary grown-up Chinamen may be almost said to think in proverbs. There can be no doubt that to the foreigner a large store of proverbs, committed to memory and judiciously introduced, are a great aid to successful conversation. These are a few taken from an inexhaustible supply, omitting to a great extent such as find a ready equivalent in English :—

Deal with the faults of others as gently as with your own.

By many words wit is exhausted.

If you bow at all, bow low.

If you take an ox, you must give a horse.

A man thinks he knows, but a woman knows better.

Words whispered on earth sound like thunder in heaven.

If fortune smiles—who doesn't ? If fortune doesn't—who does ?

Moneyed men are always listened to.

Nature is better than a middling doctor.

Stay at home and reverence your parents ; why travel afar to worship the gods ?

A bottle-nosed man may be a teetotaller, but no one will think so.

It is easier to catch a tiger than to ask a favour.

With money you can move the gods ; without it, you can't move a man.

Bend your head if the eaves are low.

Oblige, and you will be obliged.

Don't put two saddles on one horse.

Armies are maintained for years, to be used on a single day.

In misfortune, gold is dull; in happiness, iron is bright.

More trees are upright than men.

If you fear that people will know, don't do it.

Long visits bring short compliments.

If you are upright and without guile, what god need you pray to for pardon?

Some study shows the need for more.

One kind word will keep you warm for three winters.

The highest towers begin from the ground.

No needle is sharp at both ends.

Straight trees are felled first.

No image-maker worships the gods. He knows what stuff they are made of.

Half an orange tastes as sweet as a whole one.

We love our own compositions, but other men's wives.

Free sitters at the play always grumble most.

It is not the wine which makes a man drunk; it is the man himself.

Better a dog in peace than a man in war.

Every one gives a shove to the tumbling wall.

Sweep the snow from your own doorstep.

He who rides a tiger cannot dismount.

Politeness before force.

One dog barks at something, and the rest bark at him.

You can't clap hands with one palm.

Draw your bow, but don't shoot.

One more good man on earth is better than an extra angel in heaven.

Gold is tested by fire; man, by gold.

Those who have not tasted the bitterest of life's bitters can never appreciate the sweetest of life's sweets.

Money makes a blind man see.

Man is God upon a small scale. God is man upon a large scale.

A near neighbour is better than a distant relation.

Without error there could be no such thing as truth.

BIBLIOGRAPHICAL NOTE

WHAT foreign students have achieved in the department of Chinese literature from the sixteenth century down to quite recent times is well exhibited in the three large volumes which form the *Bibliotheca Sinica*, or *Dictionnaire Bibliographique des Ouvrages rélatifs à l'Empire chinois*, by Henri Cordier : Paris, Ernest Leroux, 1878 ; with Supplément, 1895. This work is carried out with a fulness and accuracy which leave nothing to be desired, and is essential to all systematic workers in the Chinese field.

By far the most important of all books mentioned in the above collection is a complete translation of the Confucian Canon by the late Dr. James Legge of Aberdeen, under the general title of *The Chinese Classics*. The publication of this work, which forms the greatest existing monument of Anglo-Chinese scholarship, extended from 1861 to 1885.

The *Cursus Literaturæ Sinicæ*, by P. Zottoli, S.J., Shanghai, 1879–1882, is an extensive series of translations into Latin from all branches of Chinese literature, and is designed especially for the use of Roman Catholic missionaries (*neo-missionariis accommodatus*).

Another very important work, now rapidly approaching completion, is a translation by Professor E. Chavannes, Collège de France, of the famous history described in Book II. chap. iii., under the title of *Les Mémoires Historiques de Se-ma Ts'ien*, the first volume of which is dated Paris, 1895.

Notes on Chinese Literature, by A. Wylie, Shanghai, 1867, contains descriptive notices of about 2000 separate Chinese works, arranged under Classics, History, Philosophy, and Belles Lettres, as in the Imperial Catalogue (see p. 387). Considering the date at which it was written, this book is entitled to rank among the highest efforts of the kind. It is still of the utmost value to the student, though in need of careful revision.

The following Catalogues of Chinese libraries in Europe have been published in recent years :—

Catalogue of Chinese Printed Books, Manuscripts, and Drawings in the Library of the British Museum. By R. K. Douglas, 1877.

Catalogue of the Chinese Translation of the Buddhist Tripitaka. By Bunyio Nanjio, 1883.

Catalogue of the Chinese Books and Manuscripts in the Library of Lord Crawford, Haigh Hall, Wigan. By J. P. Edmond, 1895.

Catalogue of the Chinese and Manchu Books in the Library of the University of Cambridge. By H. A. Giles, 1898.

Catalogue des Livres Chinois, Coréens, Japonais, etc., in the Bibliothèque Nationale. By Maurice Courant, Paris, 1900. (Fasc. i. pp. vii., 148, has already appeared.)

The chief periodicals especially devoted to studies in Chinese literature are as follows :—

The Chinese Repository, published monthly at Canton from May 1832 to December 1851.

The Journal of the North-China Branch of the Royal Asiatic Society, published annually at Shanghai from 1858 to 1884, and since that date issued in fascicules at irregular intervals during each year.

The China Review, published every two months at Hong-Kong from June 1872 to the present date.

There is also the *Chinese Recorder*, which has existed since 1868, and is now published every two months at Shanghai. This is, strictly speaking, a missionary journal, but it often contains valuable papers on Chinese literature and cognate subjects.

Variétés Sinologiques is the title of a series of monographs on various Chinese topics, written and published at irregular intervals by the Jesuit Fathers at Shanghai since 1892, and distinguished by the erudition and accuracy of all its contributors.

INDEX

Other TUT BOOKS available:

BACHELOR'S HAWAII *by Boye de Mente*

BACHELOR'S JAPAN *by Boye de Mente*

BACHELOR'S MEXICO *by Boye de Mente*

A BOOK OF NEW ENGLAND LEGENDS AND FOLK LORE *by Samuel Adams Drake*

THE BUDDHA TREE *by Fumio Niwa; translated by Kenneth Strong*

CALABASHES AND KINGS: An Introduction to Hawaii *by Stanley D. Porteus*

CHINA COLLECTING IN AMERICA *by Alice Morse Earle*

CHINESE COOKING MADE EASY *by Rosy Tseng*

CHOI OI!: The Lighter Side of Vietnam *by Tony Zidek*

THE COUNTERFEITER and Other Stories *by Yasushi Inoue; translated by Leon Picon*

CURIOUS PUNISHMENTS OF BYGONE DAYS *by Alice Morse Earle*

CUSTOMS AND FASHIONS IN OLD NEW ENGLAND *by Alice Morse Earle*